The Lion and the Giraffe

Also by Jack Couffer

NON FICTION

Song of Wild Laughter
The Lions of Living Free
Bat Bomb, World War II's Other Secret Weapon
The Cats of Lamu

FICTION

Swim, Rat, Swim
Nights with Sasquatch (as John Cotter)
The Concrete Wilderness

JUVENILE

Galápagos Summer (with Mike Couffer)
African Summer (with Mike Couffer)
Canyon Summer (with Mike Couffer)
Salt Marsh Summer (with Mike Couffer)

The Lion and the Giraffe

A Naturalist's Life In the Movie Business

by Jack Couffer

BearManor Media
2010

The Lion and the Giraffe:
A Naturalist's Life In the Movie Business

Photos by the author unless otherwise noted.

For information, address:

BearManor Media
P. O. Box 71426
Albany, GA 31708

bearmanormedia.com

Cover photo by Wolfgang Shuschitzki

Typesetting and layout by John Teehan

Published in the USA by BearManor Media

ISBN—1-59393-538-2

Table of Contents

Our African neighbors called her *Mama Simba* (Lion Lady); my nickname was *Bwana Twiga* (Mister Giraffe).

Prologue

I've traveled far and wide, and I've often used the term *journeyman* to describe myself. I didn't mean it as a cute play on words, but in the true dictionary sense: "*any sound, experienced, craftsman. A worker who has learned his trade.*" Following that definition has been the aim of my working life. I've had no aspirations to fame or greatness, and when one or another of my projects has come off with success and critical acclaim it has always rather surprised me, as if I didn't deserve the cheers.

The movie books that line library shelves are often about deceit, fraud, the misuse of power, and the eccentric personalities of the players in the business. Thus perhaps it's an odd conceit to think that anyone might be interested in the professional life of a simple journeyman filmmaker. The foul plays, infidelities, double crosses, and stabs-in-the-backs of stars, directors, and top producers are the deeds of personalities people want to read about. Still, I feel justified in taking the plunge and reminiscing about fifty juicy years in the entertainment industry with all the headaches, heartaches, laughs and joys this business has given me.

Thanks are due to all of the folks I have written about. To Wolfgang Shuschitzky, Mike Couffer, Elliot Marks, Hubert Wells, and Bill Bacon for their photographs, Mik and Cici Lennartson and 360 degree for the cover design and digital service, and to Ben Ohmart for his care in publishing. For the help I have had in writing this story I am indebted to Hank Searls and Allan Duffin, and most greatfully to Lilly Golden for the final edit and pulling it all together. Portions of these writings have appeared in my books *Song of Wild Laughter*, *The Lions of Living Free,* and in *Natural History* magazine.

To those folks whose words I have quoted, I apologize if their memories differ from mine. The dialogue is not meant to be accurate to the letter, but I've repeated conversations and recounted events as I remember them.

I dedicate this ramble through a lifetime to the exceptional women who have enriched my life—Mom, Joan, Sieuwke, and Jean. How lucky I have been.

1

Meeting Sieuwke

Producer Paul Radin and I were in Africa to make the sequel to *Born Free*, called *Living Free,* which I'd been hired to direct.

Living Free would depict the next stage in the lives of a game warden named George Adamson who, with his wife, Joy, had raised Elsa, an orphaned cub lioness and taught her how to live in the wild. Five years had passed since the original film had appeared in theaters.

Now Paul and I were making a frenzied whirl in a clapped-out stage coach—or was that only the way it felt? It had four wheels, an engine, and a little plaque on the front that said LAND ROVER, so maybe it really was a car.

At last I saw what I was looking for. "Whoa!" I shouted, and Phil Leakey, youngest son of the famed archeologists and our guide to Kenya, reined the coach to a stop in a cloud of dust.

Nestled in a depression of the Great Rift Valley, Lake Naivasha was surrounded by shady groves of yellow-barked acacia. Dense stands of the water grass called papyrus lined the shores, each ten-foot-tall stem topped by a feathery pom-pom.

Within the wide expanse of the greater lake, the rim of an old volcano rose in a gentle crescent. Beyond the rift escarpment to the east stood the Aberdare Range. There, on the summits above a belt of broad-leafed forest, the slopes changed to open moorlands with dark stands of giant heath. To the west, the wall of the Mau Escarpment rose steeply to forested plateaus.

This sublime bowl of foliage and sparkling water, teeming with game, blessed by the benefit of sheltering mountains, was the perfect spot to set up our filming base. I was singing "Big Rock Candy Mountain" as we pulled into the parking lot of a small hotel.

> *Oh, the buzzin' of the bees in the cigarette trees near the soda water fountain.*
> *At the lemonade springs where the bluebird sings in the Big Rock Candy Mountains....*

The cozy Marina Hotel on the lakeshore was the perfect headquarters for a film crew. There was a shady area where we could build housing for our lions. Nearby were many scenic locations—and all of this less than fifty miles from Nairobi, the biggest city in Kenya and base of logistical support.

It wasn't far to our next stop. Back in the Land Rover, we turned off the highway onto a shady lane. A mile along the road a white pole barrier stopped us.

A man with the limbs of a long-legged spider came toward us, his spindly frame stepping over the potholes in the road. Then a long narrow face craned down and peered through the window. A hole in his lower lip was plugged with a white ivory button, and one ear with a big hole in the lobe held a yellow film cannister in which he kept his snuff.

Phil leaned out of the driver's seat, said something in Kiswahili, and Spiderman lifted the barrier for us. We drove on under the arching limbs of flat-topped trees, racing our dust cloud as we sped toward the house hidden in the hills ahead.

I rode next to Phil. Paul leaned forward with his elbows on the back of my seat. We'd been talking about the woman I was soon to meet. I'd learned that she was Dutch, had spent three years in a Japanese concentration camp during World War II, and that she'd been living in Africa for ten years. Like so many from small European countries she was fluent in half a dozen languages. She was also a Marchesa, the Italian equivalent of a countess. That appetizing bit of information evoked my curiosity. Paul's next statement hooked me like a catfish grabbing a worm.

"These lions she raises," Paul said, "story is, they sleep with her."

Phil slowed our vehicle to maneuver through a washout, then put the pedal to the metal before the dust caught up with us again. "She's rum for all sorts of animals," he said. "Aside from lion cubs, she's brought up the odd leopard, zebra, antelope, ostrich—even a cape buffalo."

"Why?" I asked.

"Biggish farm," said Phil. "Wild game all over the place. An impala fawn gets itself tangled in fence wire, then a herdsman finds it dying out in the bush and brings it in. What's she going to do, let it croak?"

The woman under discussion had worked for Paul when he'd produced the film *Born Free*, but I knew little more about her than that. Sieuwke's pair of lions had produced three cubs only a few weeks before the filming of *Born Free* began. The coincidence of Sieuwke owning a family of lions with three cubs just when Paul needed them couldn't have been more serendipitous, and she'd been happy to help. Now Paul had proposed that we ask her to help us with *Living Free.*

I glanced at the notepad propped on the dashboard of the Land Rover. "Curious name," I said.

"Marchesa Sieuwke Bisleti van der Laan," Paul said. "Dutch parents—that's the Sieuwke and the van der Laan. Married to an Italian Marchese—that's the Marchesa and the Bisleti. She was born in Java, went to school in Amsterdam, lives in Kenya, has a Dutch name and an Italian passport. Totally international."

"Does give one the impression that she's been around," added Leakey.

"And ever a surprise," said Paul. "Comes on soft as feathers. Two minutes later she's belting a snarling lion on the arse with a *kiboko*."

"*Kiboko*?" I interjected.

"Hippo hide whip," said Paul. "The local persuader. Tough as a meter of spring steel. It's the buzz that she's never without one—equally useful on grouchy lions and pushy Romeos."

"Sounds like just the person we need," I said. "Like another hole in the head."

"I wouldn't get your hopes up too high," Paul smiled, "but somebody's got to take care of our lion cubs."

* * * * *

The Bisleti farm, called Marula, was fifty-five thousand acres of grazing land, one of the last great ranches in the Rift Valley highlands of Kenya. Its southern border lay at the base of an extinct volcano, Mount Longonot. I could just make out its perfect crater cone, dim in the blue haze ten miles away. The western boundary of the ranch was at the edge of Lake Naivasha somewhere in the papyrus swamp ahead, and the north line lay in the golden hills on the other side of Maasai Gorge.

The track into the farm from the main highway was overhung with jacaranda trees dripping flowers, a cerulean tunnel through the blue sky. Then the house appeared through the trees. It was a low ramble of white stucco and red tile that crowned a ledge of lichened stone. We wound up an incline and stopped in the shade of a huge acacia tree.

Then the lions began to roar. My God, but they roared! So close, so frightening, so moving, so magnificent. We looked up to see a fenced enclosure at the edge of a rock outcrop above the house where a huge male lion and his mate stared down at us. At that moment I realized why someone would want to keep lions—if only to experience that roar.

They continued to roar their welcome or their warning, whatever it was, but nobody came out to greet us. We were not expected. Because the old hand-cranked telephones of the time weren't working we had taken our chances and driven from Nairobi unannounced.

Then a smiling black man in a starched white jacket came from the house and said something in Swahili to Phil. Phil translated: The *bwana*—the Marchesa's husband—was on a safari with clients. The Marchesa had taken her animals for a walk and would be back soon.

He pointed in the direction where we could meet her. We got out of the Land Rover and strolled up a nearby path.

Because I was from America, where we don't encounter peerage every day, I didn't quite know how a person should address a titled female aristocrat. Mistress? Madame? Your Ladyship? In spite of my New World reverse snobbishness toward classes, I did hold some feelings of awe about European aristocracy. Above all, I wanted to do things right.

While I was considering my options, out of the bush two lions came charging toward us. I now had concerns more urgent than how to say hello to the Marchesa.

It was too late to run. Climbing a tree, if one wasn't fast enough, could get one's backside severely mauled, and and I'd had enough experience filming other large carnivores—cougars, wolves, and bears—that I knew showing any hint of fear wasn't the best deterrent either. So I stood my ground, setting an example for Paul and Phil, and braced for whatever might happen.

The lions were followed by a couple of dogs—a big mixed-breed type and a German shepherd.

It was a tense moment. The young lions skidded to a stop at our feet in a puff of dust. They rubbed their shoulders against my thighs and knees, pleading to be stroked. They were pussycats. It was the cursed dogs that we were worried about.

The dogs circled us, growling and rumbling, stiff-legged, hair on end—but stopped short of attacking. While one lion happily rubbed his ears against my right leg, the German shepherd sniffed menacingly at my left. He seemed to be telling me that if I made one suspicious move, calf and thigh would be chewed into minced meat. Dogs speak a universal language, understandable to humans of any race, tongue, political persuasion, or religious affiliation. This dog was very clear, saying just one word: "Beware!"

I stared down the trail from where they'd come, hoping that their keeper would make a quick appearance.

The rumble in the big German shepherd's throat continued as he sniffed my shoes. I put aside, as best I could, all thought of danger and awaited the arrival of his mistress.

After a few moments she appeared in front of us. She was dressed in khaki safari trousers, short desert boots, and a tailored tan shirt with a burgundy silk scarf knotted around her throat. She wore a wide silver Tuareg bracelet and small silver buttons in her ears. Her attire was so natural and fitting to the African bush as to be almost a cliché.

Tanned from a life lived outdoors, she was beautiful and athletic-looking. She was small—not at all the large-boned type one would expect of a woman who had mastery over lions. Her hair was tied back from a face untouched by makeup. I looked in vain for the lady's legendary *kiboko* whip.

When she saw her old friends Paul and Phil, the Marchesa smiled, showing teeth as white as pearls. She made a quick, not unkind, command to her dogs in a language I didn't understand (I learned later that it was Dutch), and I had the uncomfortable sense that rather than scolding, she was praising them for being such good guard dogs. Whatever she said, they responded like obedient children and relaxed. We did the same.

The shepherd poked his cold nose into my hand, asking to be forgiven. When I didn't respond right away he nudged my palm insistently. I obliged and stroked his ears.

Sieuwke greeted Phil warmly, reserving a kiss for Paul whom she knew better. She shook my hand and invited us into the house. Already

I'd forgotten that she was The Marchesa. Meeting her in the flesh she became instantly human, albeit no less interesting—simply an attractive and intriguing woman named Sieuwke.

* * * * *

We followed Sieuwke and her pack back to her home and entered a cozy room with windows facing the sunset. A huge fireplace behind us crackled with aromatic logs, a comfort at any season when chilly darkness falls over the Rift Valley highlands.

Paul laid out our reason for being here. The new movie would follow the three cubs which audiences had seen as newborns at the end of *Born Free.* Sieuwke's pair of lions and their cubs had played those roles at the fadeout of that film. Our new story was about the cubs growing up.

We would import trios of young lions from America to play the parts of the maturing cubs at different stages of growth. For the youngest set of three, Paul told Sieuwke that we would soon be receiving newborn cubs from Ethiopia. It was these baby lions that we hoped Sieuwke would care for.

As we joked about the irony of bringing lions to Africa, Sieuwke glanced my way and caught me staring at her. She pulled her shirt down over her bosom, closing a gap in the buttons. With a twinge of embarrassment I wondered if she thought I'd been peeking. (Of course I had been.)

Paul spoke of the professional animal trainers who would be coming from California with the older cubs.

"But I don't know anything about training," Sieuwke said. "I'm only a mum to orphaned babies. Actually, I'm probably a better mother than many lionesses," she laughed.

"Fiercer, I'm sure," said Paul.

I didn't try to fool myself about Sieuwke. The moment I saw her with those dogs and lions I was intrigued.

Shortly before I'd left California for Kenya, an old friend who had once taken a safari to the continent called me.

"I hear you're off to Africa," he said.

"That's right. Leaving next week."

"Well, I'm afraid we've lost you," he said.

"What's that mean?"

"Once you've been to Africa," Joe said, "you'll never come back."

My friend knew me too well. His prophetic words might have been spoken as a joke, but they would prove to be dead-on.

My meeting with Sieuwke was the beginning of a relationship that was to last for many years—but that's getting way ahead of my story which began thirty years before in California.

2

Mentor Jim

I had a mother who loved all birds and animals and encouraged my yen to raise and befriend as many as possible. My father put up with us even to the extent of allowing a pet skunk named Aroma to live under the dining room hutch. My uncle, Tom Craig, was a botanist and well-known painter of the so-called California School and also an amateur *Lepodopterologist.* Another uncle with whom I bonded early was Lowell Sumner. From the age when my parents put me on a train with a delivery tag pinned to my collar I spent summers at his ranch in the mountains west of Palo Alto, California. He was known as "The Maverick Biologist" in the U.S. National Park Service, and along with writing books on wildlife he had made the initial biological survey and was instrumental in establishing the Arctic National Wildlife Refuge (ANWR). Through these close family connections I had a strong introduction to natural history as a child.

When I was in high school, I took a weekend trip to the Mojave Desert with my friend Jim Dannaldson to help him shoot a school lecture film—my first taste of what would become my life's passion.

I was fourteen. Jim was my elder by fifteen years and made his living working reptiles and insects for films. The iguanas that wore fake tall dorsal fins, passed for giant dinosaurs, and were the menace to Carole Landis and Victor Mature in the movie *One Million Years B.C.* were Jim's creations.

Jim also collected reptiles for zoos and venom extraction laboratories. As a sideline along with our desert filming trip, he planned to fill an order for sidewinder rattlesnakes. I came along to help Jim tote his camera and tripod. The good vibes of that experience must have stuck in my head for many years until they finally surfaced and I acted upon them.

Jim's technique for collecting sidewinders was to drive through the desert after sunset when cold-blooded snakes are attracted to the daytime heat retained by the black road's surface. On cool nights, snakes like to lie on the pavement soaking up the warmth—the reason one sees so many squashed reptiles on the road.

That evening, after a day of filming lizards and tortoises, Jim drove until he saw a sidewinder. Then he stopped, picked it up with a hooked pole, dropped it into a box, and we went looking for another. He'd bagged a dozen by midnight and we started home. I crawled onto the back seat and went to sleep.

I awoke when the car bounced and banged and stopped at a crazy angle. Jim had fallen asleep and driven into a ditch. I was fine; no injuries. Jim had hit his head; he was dazed and groggy, but not seriously hurt.

In a few minutes a Highway Patrolman came along. He put me into his patrol car, where I quickly nodded off again. A tow truck came. I was aware of a whining winch and voices as they got Jim's car back on its wheels. The Ford suffered only a few dents and we could have driven on home, but the cop said that Jim had damaged State property—a "Caution" sign had been knocked down—and an accident report was necessary. Due to the late hour, the patrolman told us that if we took beds in a local motel Jim could file the required paper in the morning.

We found the same patrolman at the office the next day. After Jim had filled out the report and we were taking our leave, the officer said: "That was really awesome last night. You stuffing those rattlesnakes into the box with your bare hands."

Jim had no recollection of the incident. In his right mind he'd never pick up a sidewinder by hand, yet the cop swore he'd strolled around casually plucking up deadly snakes as if they were mere pieces of rope.

3

The Niche

I was eighteen in the year 1943 and the country was at war. As a high school senior, I spent every afternoon at the Los Angeles County Museum of Natural History where I was a student assistant in the mammalogy laboratory. My mentor was Jack von Bloeker, a leading specialist in *chiroptera*—bats.

I was hard at work writing a label for a new specimen when a cheerful man visited. He pulled a sheaf of papers from his tattered briefcase and laid them on the desk. Letterheads stood out boldly: THE WAR DEPARTMENT. There was even a page with the White House seal, signed by our President, Franklin Delano Roosevelt.

The letters bore a large red ink stamp on the border—TOP SECRET. And that's as deep a look as our visitor let us take.

The President's letter might have made a far different impression had we been allowed to read the text, something I didn't do until fifty years later while researching the FDR archives for a book on the subject. Roosevelt's message was addressed to Colonel Wm. J. Donovan, U.S. Government, Coordinator of Information. (General "Wild Bill" Donovan would become the first head of the Office of Strategic Services (OSS) which later became the CIA.)

There were only three short sentences: "This man is <u>not</u> a nut. It sounds like a perfectly wild idea but is worth looking into. You might reply for me to Dr. Adams' letter. FDR."

Dr. Lytle S. Adams, put before us an idea that sounded utterly crazy. His plan was to collect a million bats and induce them to hibernate. In that state of suspended animation they wouldn't need to be fed; they could be stored in climate-controlled conditions and handled more-or-less as living machines—and then at the moment of demand they could be thawed out, ready to go to work.

The job…?

Develop a potent incendiary bomb the size and weight of a baby bat (which ride on their mummy's tummies in flight), build-in a time-controlled ignition device, attach the mini-incendiary to a torpid bat, pack 500 "armed" bats into a bomb shell that has climate control, a parachute, and an altimeter device that deploys the parachute and opens the shell as the unit descends, put 2000 of these shells into a dozen B-24 bombers, and drop a million incendiary bats at dawn over Japan.

When a million fires from these widely dispersed incendiaries broke out at the same time in the attics and hidden places where the bats had gone to roost, the conflagration would be impossible to control. Whole cities would be devastated, factories destroyed, and, because burning houses could be vacated more easily than bombed ones, all at minimal loss of life.

One must view Doc's concept, which would be deadly to the bats, in the mind-set of the time. There were few people in the United States during World War II who were not personally involved in the war effort. Nearly every family had a father, husband, son, daughter, wife, or mother who was contributing, many with their lives. Everyone was making a sacrifice. The death of a million bats of a common species was a small price to pay in comparison to the thousands of human lives being taken.

An emergency Government office, The National Defense Research Committee (NDRC), had already assigned an official name to the scheme. They called it, *The Adams Plan*.

Von Bloeker's reaction to this bizarre idea was like any other thinking person's first response—it was insane.

But he also had a scientist's take on it. "Yes, the idea seems utterly gaga," he said. "But looking at it from the biological standpoint, it does make some sense."

As a result of Adams' visit and his urgent request, within a month, von Bloeker and I were drafted, attended boot camp, and assigned through the direction of General "Hap" Arnold, commander of the U.S. Army Air Force, to this mad—if credible—project.

After a year and a half of experiments and testing, the project proved to be not so crazy after all. Bat bombs worked—better than the conventional incendiaries currently in use over Europe and Japan—but there was already a far more deadly secret weapon nearing the end of its development program: the A-bomb.

As a result, the bat bomb project was hung up in the attic along with the bats, and I spent the remainder of my wartime duty in the Air-Sea Rescue Service as a crewman on a high-speed boat.

A few years later, I was twenty-four and a commercial fisherman and boat bum living in Newport Beach, California, an aimless ex-G.I. with no prospects.

Balboa Pavilion was already regaining its pre-war status as a popular tourist center. The big bands were playing again at the dance hall by the pier. I went one Saturday night to hear Glenn Miller. I heard his standard when I walked in the door, *In the Mood.* The place was swinging. I wasn't a dancer, but I loved the music.

I watched from the sidelines for awhile, and my eye kept locking onto the same tall blonde girl who danced with a kind of wild joy. There was something about her.

When the break came, I found myself shuffling over and saying something really clever like, "I don't dance, but how about having a drink with me?"

A few weeks later, after several dates, the young lady and I were "going steady," as the term for a relationship went in the '40s. Her name was Joan. Soon we married. I sold my interest in the fishing boats *Jubilee* and *Santa Cruz,* and bought a salty thirty-eight foot schooner, the *Kuuipo,* (Sweetheart in Hawaiian) that would be our home afloat—and a way to keep my dream of ocean cruising alive.

I'd always had an urge toward a career in natural history. I enrolled at the University of Southern California with biology as my intended major. The G.I. Bill paid my tuition and a small living allowance.

As it happened, USC was my school of choice for all the wrong reasons. I could have selected one of the best biology departments in the country. Because I was California-born, U.C. Berkeley was the obvious place. But USC, if not the best, was the closest to home.

Soon I learned that biology at USC wasn't the plunge into the world of natural history I imagined it would be. My classmates were studying biology for a different reason than I. They were all pre-med students, not naturalists. They had no interest in natural history. I had none in human physiology. I was a fish out of water.

I also realized that at my age I was already an elderly duffer among my classmates, most of whom were just out of high school. I had six years of age and experience on them and a wife who had a good job as an executive secretary, whereas my pink-cheeked classmates were frivolously dating. Still, in spite of my image as a mossback among fry, I managed to make a few friends.

During a required course in English composition I found myself sitting at a desk next to another elderly student of twenty-four. His name was Conrad Hall, and when I learned that he had been born in Tahiti, destination of all those South Sea island cruises I'd dreamed of, I knew I had to get to know him better. Conrad's father was James Norman Hall, author of *Mutiny on the Bounty*, *Men Against the Sea*, and other favorites stacked across my shelf of ocean-oriented books.

It seemed natural for Conrad to step into his father's shoes. Indeed, he was pursuing a major in journalism. But like me, Conrad had become unsure about which educational road he should travel. One day he told me, "I've been auditing a class over in the Department of Cinema Studies. It's pretty interesting. Why don't you come along and have a listen?"

A university course in movies? And a degree that went with it? At the time, it was a whole new concept in education and not a tinkle in my mind for a future.

The Cinema Department occupied a cluster of low wooden buildings at the eastern edge of the USC campus. Set in a copse of trees and shrubs, with the look of an old farm, Cinema had no resemblance to the other modern campus structures, many of which had copied their architecture from old Europe. Rumor had it that the buildings were originally a stable.

The staff consisted of a handful of full-time instructors and a wider cadre of working directors, writers, editors, cameramen, and producers who taught classes one or two nights a week after spending the day in Hollywood.

The department head, a Yugoslavian immigrant named Slavko Vorkapich, was a visionary advocate of film as an art form. He was known in Hollywood as a master at creating the montage—a visual method of compressing a story point into several symbolic shots, precursor to the best of today's TV commercials. Vorkapich had worked at RKO, Paramount, and MGM, where he created some of his most famous montage sequences. The earthquake in the film *San Francisco* was a Vorkapich creation. He'd also supervised montages for *Boys Town*, *David Copperfield*, *A Tale of Two Cities*, the Frank Capra features *Mr. Smith Goes to Washington* and *Meet John Doe*, and many more. But the Vorkapich films that impressed me most were two black-and-white productions which he used to illustrate the visual principles espoused in his lectures. *Fingal's Cave* and *Forest Murmurs* were filmic poems without words that artfully visualized the symphonic music to which they were shot and edited.

In the fall of 1949 I joined Conrad at one of Vorkapich's lectures. After only one session I was hooked. With his engaging personality and style, Vorky was the teacher all teachers should aspire to be, so loving of the art of film that his enthusiasm was contagious. Vorky's forté was in the theory and principles of the visual side of the art. Sixty years later, I still remember his first lecture. The subject dealt with dots in motion, and Vorky demonstrated how a single moving dot on a static screen would automatically catch the eye and lead it to wherever the filmmaker wanted it to go. Vorky had the knack of analyzing the effect of "a dot in motion" (the title of his lecture) in a way that made this simple device an important cinematic principle. Equipped with a whole notebook full of similar visual lessons, many of which had as much to do with editing as photography, Vorky encouraged his students to take a fresh look at filmmaking.

The USC Cinema Department at the time was underfunded and equipment was scarce. We were lucky to get 100 feet of black-and-white 16mm film with which to fulfill an assignment, and there was always a waiting list to check out a camera. Conrad and I joined ranks with another cinema student, Marvin Weinstein, and we became known around the department as The Three Musketeers. Only seniors and graduate students were chosen as crew on the university-produced documentaries on which we all hoped to work. As beginners, we'd be stuck for the next couple of years with shooting and editing the three-minute class exercises assigned by the staff.

That wasn't enough for The Three Musketeers. When the summer break came around, we decided to put the lessons we'd learned into practice and make a film that would include as many Vorkapichian principles as possible.

From this first production of our careers we established an ethic that we've followed ever since: to have as much fun as possible while doing the work.

Joan and I were living aboard *Kuuipo* at the time. During the previous school break I'd rigged trolling poles, put a couple of ice chests on deck that would hold a half a ton of albacore, and we'd spent the summer replenishing our bank account as commercial tuna fisherfolk. We were sailing out of San Clemente Island—an occasional U.S. Navy gunnery range—up anchor at four a.m. to be on the banks at dawn, and back to anchor at Pyramid Cove every evening after dark. Sometimes the Navy would kick out the fishing fleet for firing practice, so we would move to the other side of the island where we anchored close under the sheer bluffs of the north shore.

On those nights, pebbles kicked up from the explosions of naval artillery on the other side of the hill clattered down on our decks and cabin top.

At the end of one day's fishing, I was asleep below deck and Joan was at the helm as we sailed briskly in to anchor accompanied by a dozen diesel-powered trollers. I was awakened by a racket of slatting sails and shuddering spars. I poked my nose out of the companionway to see the gray hull of a Navy destroyer looming close abeam and towering above us. A row of sailors were leaning on the rail goggling down at the rather unusual sight of this blonde chick, apparently all alone at the helm of a salty fishing schooner under full sail.

Nobody seemed to notice that the huge destroyer idling along close beside us had blocked off all our wind—and that the schooner had been made completely powerless.

The captain aimed his electric megaphone down at Joan from the bridge. "You are entering an official Navy gunnery zone," he thundered. "Firing is to commence at twenty-two hundred hours. You are ordered to vacate the area immediately."

Joan brushed the hair out of her eyes and stood up at the helm. "Well," she shouted back, "get that tub underway and out of our wind, skipper. It's pretty damned hard to move a sailboat without some air. How about you get some sea smarts?"

The sailors got a snicker out of that, and I was proud of my salty spouse as she jibed the schooner single-handed and put knots between us and the U.S. Navy.

* * * * *

Meanwhile the Three Musketeers made preparations for their first production. We'd call our film *Sea Theme* and shoot it aboard the *Kuuipo* off Catalina Island. The picturesque clipper-bowed schooner with her taut sails and white hull was a picture-perfect subject. Joan and I would be the cast, not a role with which either of us were comfortable, but Joan was photogenic and leggy and I could get by as a non-speaking actor as long as I was only called upon to do what I did naturally—in this case, sail a boat. Joan's and my weaknesses as performers weren't important anyway, as the star of the film would be our beautiful old-fashioned schooner in her different moods. Joan and I performed various functions as needed—skipper, cook, cameraman, and cast.

The plot was simple: dawn comes and the anchor is pulled. Sails are raised, a few everyday sailing situations occur. Dolphins cavort under the bow, sails slat on a becalmed sea, a breeze comes, canvas fills, we encounter rough seas and reef the sails. The sun sets and the schooner glides into a lovely cove, douses sails in the twilight, and drops anchor as the moon comes up.

Conrad had met the young manager of a hole-in-the-wall camera shop in the city of Westwood, home to the campus of UCLA. Bob Gottschalk, who a few years later would invent the Panavision anamorphic lens and create one of the most profitable motion picture equipment houses in the world, gave us a good price on a used Bolex camera and enough outdated but still useable black-and-white film for a half-hour movie. I canceled a couple of weekend yacht charters on my calendar, and the week after school was out, The Three Musketeers and one wife set sail for Catalina Island.

Except for my moments in front of the camera, Conrad, Marv, and I shared the cameraman's job. We shot it all silent, not only for technical and economic reasons, but also because in the style of Vorkapich's musical-visual poems, the only sound in our film would be symphonic music.

We spent more time, more passion, and had more arguments in editing our footage than we did in shooting. A rented editing table with rewinds, a Moviola, film bins and racks, were jammed into the tiny West Hollywood apartment Conrad was sharing with a visiting Tahitian friend, Chief Charlie Mauu. Charlie had been brought to Hollywood by MGM to complete scenes shot in Tahiti for a South Seas feature. With his black wavy hair, great physique, talent with a ukelele, his repertoire of Tahitian songs (including everyone's favorite, *Tamure*), plus his islander's charm and Hollywood connections (however impermanent), Charlie was a hit with starlets. Our editing sessions were often interrupted by pretty girls whose faces we recognized from the big screen as they winged in and out of Charley's bedroom nest.

Sea Theme was finished when fall semester classes began. The day had come to show our summer's work to our mentor, and we faced his judgement with hope and fear. To our delight, Vorky was complimentary and arranged for a campus screening at the university's huge Bovard Auditorium. The Cinema Department put up posters on campus bulletin boards. The entire student body was invited, and we had a full house. They applauded. It was a wonderful gesture of approval that encouraged us to submit our opus to the first-ever student film competition—since then an annual event—of the American Society of Cinematographers, Hollywood's distinguished association of cameramen. The gold-plated award that we won, as treasured to us as an Oscar, had our names engraved on it.

Our next break came in the form of a phone call from producer Jack Voglin, who bought the rights to *Sea Theme* and made deals to show it on television. The sale more than paid our costs. Then Voglin thrilled us even more when he asked if we had any other ideas for TV. We proposed a documentary series, *All in a Day's Work*, which would explore unusual occupations. Voglin financed a pilot episode. So while we were still in film school we had become TV entrepreneurs and thought we had the world by the tail.

We edited *Dory Fishermen*, the title of our pilot, while a parade of lovely young women continued to squeeze between our Moviola and editing bins, bound for our Tahitian roomie's bed.

And then we met with our first Hollywood intrigue.

I don't remember the chap's name—maybe it was Louie; Louie will do—and I don't recall how he got Conrad's phone number. It had something to do with a friend of Con's cousin, or maybe it was a friend of his uncle's "cousin." It being "all in the family," so to speak, however remote the connection, Louie knew he could trust us to keep our mouths shut if things didn't work out.

We had no idea of his mission when Louie called to set up an appointment. I do recall the night he knocked on the door to discuss "a business deal". Traffic outside on Larabee Street was humming. We were all standing around the table in Conrad's living room. Louie introduced himself as a shrimp fisherman working out of Guaymas, Mexico—or so he said. We shook hands. He had the rough paws of a shrimp fisherman all right. He slithered to the window, cracked open the drapes, looked outside, up and down the street, watched for awhile, then overlapped the blinds. We waited in uncertain silence while he checked to make sure no crack in the curtain was open to admit prying eyes.

He looked in all the rooms, checking for eavesdroppers or hidden bugs. Mauu was out. Louie locked the doors, rattled them to be sure.

So far there had been no words beyond introductions. Marv, Con, and I stood fidgeting at the table wondering what was going on. Louie sat down. We sat down. He wore an open Hawaiian shirt and a sports jacket with leather patches on the elbows. His face was as wrinkled as old sharkskin. From an inside pocket he produced a purple velvet sack and dangled it in front of us theatrically. We looked at each other, then back at the dangling sack. It made a metallic sound and looked like it was full of money.

"This here is what this here meeting's all about," Louie said.

With a flourish he upended the sack and a double handful of bright gold coins tumbled onto the table. We hadn't the slightest doubt they were real. "I've got another quarter of a ton of this stuff," he said.

We stared at the mountain of wealth with wonder.

"Everybody thinks how great it would be to find a treasure, huh?" Louie said. "Yeah, then what do you do with it? Country where you find it makes big claims on your horde."

"Everybody thinks you stole it," he told us. "You can't tell anybody where it came from. They wouldn't believe it. So how do you get rid of it? How do you change the gold into money without getting shot or goin' to the pokey?"

He looked around the table and continued, "That's a big problem, boys. Oh, there's plenty of guys who'll pay for it. Pay plenty. And there's plenty more who'll slit your throat for it."

But say you sell it, Louie said, and still have your hide intact. Then what do you do with the cash? Bury it in the garden? If you put the money in the bank where you can use it, then you need to have a way to account for your sudden wealth.

"So I tell you what," he said. "You've got to have a legitimate business that makes a lot of profit. Then you can float in the cash you got for the gold and nobody's the wiser. Get it?"

We all sat looking at the gold and shuddering as if it was a bomb with a short fuse.

"No," Conrad said at last. "I don't get it."

"You make a movie, right? The movie makes a lot of money, right? Or it doesn't make a cent but it doesn't matter. Get it? Because the movie's only a cover. It *coulda* made a lota money. It didn't, but it don't matter, don'tcha see?"

We were definitely uneasy about this shrimp fisherman and what he'd caught in his net. There's something about a big pile of illegal gold sitting on the table in front of you that just doesn't bring on the emotions you might imagine it would bring. What it brings is something more like fear. Or sheer terror.

Louie left us with the proposition that he would finance the making of a feature movie to be shot in Mexico. We'd be paid, and it didn't seem to matter what the show was about, whether it was good or bad, a box office success or not. He seemed to have ways of making all contingencies irrelevant as long as the movie got completed.

After Louie had checked the street through a crack in the curtain and disappeared into the night, the Musketeers held a serious meeting. The next morning Conrad called Louie and told him thanks, but we didn't have a script ready to go into production just now.

A couple of months later, Marv opened a copy of *Time* magazine and saw an article about an unusual smuggling bust. A Cadillac car was being shipped to Europe, and the customs inspector noticed a discrepancy between the published and actual weight of a Cadillac of this particular year and model. It weighed half a ton more than it should. And what did they find in the gas tank? A thousand pounds of gold coins.

It had to be Louie. He'd said a quarter of a ton. We only wondered where that extra five hundred pounds of gold had come from.

* * * * *

During my time in the Army and later as a fisherman and boat bum, through a series of coincidental meetings, I'd been given every opportunity to acquire an interest in the movie business. While working on the bat bomb research, one of my closest buddies had been the project's executive officer. He was actor Tim Holt, already a well-known player in westerns and star of the early wartime hit *Hitler's Children*. Although Tim later co-starred in one of my all-time favorite films, *The Treasure of the Sierra Madre*, we never talked movies during our months together in the service.

During the time I crewed on an Air Force air-sea rescue boat, our usual mooring while on patrol was at Isthmus Cove on Catalina Island. Commercial fishing boats hung out around the island in the later months of the war, and a few yachts whose owners had some clout were allowed to leave mainland harbors and make the weekends at Catalina.

Humphrey Bogart and Lauren Bacall were frequent guests aboard sixty-five foot crash boat P-625 at Isthmus Cove. Bogie owned a little motor cruiser named *Sluggy* which was anything but the pretentious big yacht one might expect of a famous Hollywood star. I was told that the boat's name was inspired by his wife's mean right arm. Rumor was that they'd had a few tiffs where punches were thrown, but on that score I had no personal confirmation.

Bogie and Bacall were always sweethearts when they joined us aboard P-625 for dinner and late-night poker games. Their weekend outings aboard *Sluggy* were probably secret lover's trysts as their extramarital courtship hadn't yet made headlines in the gossip columns, but they knew we'd never tell.

Lauren was fascinated when I showed her some Native American artifacts I'd found on the island, and she wanted to see where they had come from. We took a picnic lunch and a spade, hiked to a midden where the greasy soil had been blackened by ancient cooking fires and was richly peppered with the abalone shells and cockles of Indian feasts, and spent a few hours turning the earth. We came upon a human skeleton which we carefully reburied.

Then I turned up a stone arrowhead and handed it to Lauren. She spit on it and rubbed the dirt off on her trousers. The artistic chirt arrowhead had a gemlike look and feel, for whoever had flaked it had been an expert. Lauren treasured the find, and I was smitten with her charm. I hadn't met many famous people, but here was one who was just as real as the girl next door.

Lucky Bogie, I thought.

If someone had told me then how many film people I was to meet in my life, and how predatory some of them could be, I'd have appreciated her even more.

* * * * *

I made several friends among the teaching staff at USC who held daytime jobs in the Hollywood industry and taught evening classes. Andrew Marton and László Benedek (whose classic *The Wild One* with Marlon Brando would soon be a hit) both taught directing. They were buddies—if one was away on location the other took his place. Marton had just completed directing *King Solomon's Mines* in Africa, and he used clips from the film to illustrate various points in his lectures.

Stirling Silliphant was a junior writer with a studio contract who taught screenwriting one night a week. He said candidly that his motivations for teaching weren't only that he got a kick out of jawboning with young talent, but also that the exercises he required them to write were a good source of ideas. I had the notion that if he came up against a difficult situation in a piece he was working on, he'd turn his problem into a class assignment, then incorporate the best student solution into his script. In any event, the method was inspiring to his students and he must have learned a lot from us, as he went on to write such classics as *In The Heat of the Night*, *The Poseidon Adventure,* and *Charley.* Another Hollywood professional who gave his time to the university and influenced the Muskateers was cinematographer Ralph Woolsey who taught camera and lighting technique.

Aside from the inspiration we all got from Vorky, the professor with whom I bonded most closely and who became a lifelong friend was Irving Lerner, who taught a class in documentary film. When he screened his own offbeat Pete Seeger classic *To Hear Your Banjo Play*, I knew this was someone from whom I could learn a lot. The documentary *Tchaikovsky* was also a Lerner classic, and he had worked with those greats of the Depression-period documentaries who made *The Plow That Broke the Plains, Night Mail*, and *The River*—all of which were part of our classroom studies.

During the time I studied at USC, Irving was teaching part-time while working with a producer named Philip Yordan, who was giving Lerner (whose primary niche was as a film editor) his first break at directing a feature film. Yordan was widely regarded as the writer of a well-known Broadway play-turned-film called *Anna Lucasta.* He was also known as one who hired unknown new talent to ghostwrite his material and rewarded them with peanuts and no credit.

Irving was directing a black-and-white feature for Yordan called *Man Crazy,* starring Neville Brand. On this picture Irving gave Con, Marv, and me our first break in feature films. Because of tight union control at the time, any movie made without the seal of the International

Alliance of Theatrical Stage Employees (IATSE), certifying that it had been made by union employees, didn't stand a chance of being shown in theaters. If it was, someone had paid off a union mogul to get the seal. Nearly all theaters employed IATSE projectionists, who wouldn't turn on the lamp on a movie without the seal.

Faced with this situation, Con and I, as budding cinematographers, had a limited field of opportunity. Hollywood cameramen belonged to a closed-shop union tightly guarded by its hardnosed business agent, Herbert Aller, and membership was pretty much limited to the sons of cameramen. Without that hereditary connection one's chances of getting into Local 659 were zilch.

But there was a way to get around the closed shop, if only on the edges. Productions often bought stock footage—shots made for previous movies and sold through film libraries to be reused in new features. This hole in the system gave us a devious way to break into the business.

We went over the *Man Crazy* script and picked out shots that didn't have the principal actors in them—car run-bys, people entering or exiting buildings ("comin's and goin's," as Irving called them), scenics, establishing shots of locations, long shots where doubles could replace the actors. Conrad or I, with an assistant and a double or two when the shot called for them, made shots which could pass as stock footage. Then the production bought the film from us at a fraction of the cost of hiring a full crew. We had no compunction about union-busting because of the union's discrimination in not allowing us to join. Shooting these scenes and calling them stock shots gave us experience, a few bucks in the bank, and saved the production money—a happy compromise all the way around—except for the fact that Herb Aller would have had a heart attack had he known.

* * * * *

With Irving Lerner's help in getting us a roundabout entry into Hollywood by shooting phony stock footage, along with the *Dory Fishermen* shoot on tap, we Musketeers incorporated a company which we called Canyon Films. Ivan Tors, a successful producer for Universal (*Flipper, Sea Hunt, Daktari*) became our biggest customer for stock footage. On some films with lots of car chases or sequences of shadowy walk-throughs, we shot as many as ten pages of a 110-page script. If we'd been paid half of what a legitimate production would have spent on a full crew to shoot that material, we'd have been rich. But of course we weren't. That was whole the point in hiring us.

Then came a fortuitous meeting with a Hollywood great. Cameraman Floyd Crosby had become a good friend of Conrad's father while he was in Tahiti working as a camera assistant for Robert Flaherty on the feature *White Shadows in the South Seas.* Crosby renewed the friendship when he returned to Tahiti in 1930 to shoot *Tabu*, for which Floyd received the fourth-ever Academy Award for cinematography.

When Floyd found out that his friend's son was studying to be a cameraman, Crosby invited Conrad out to the set where he was shooting *High Noon.* Con brought along his partners. Not only was this visit—which we parlayed into several return sessions—an education in technique, it gave us insight into the way things were done in Hollywood.

Floyd was the consummate gentleman. From the way he introduced us to people on the set one might have thought we were royalty. "Permit me to introduce my good friends...." He always used these words in this rather stilted and formal manner of introduction, not at all typical of his everyday speech. Gary Cooper, Fred Zinnemann, Katy Jurado, Lloyd Bridges—we met all of the cast and crew, prefaced by Floyd's prim and stuffy words. Zinnemann was interested in us as university film students—a new breed coming into the business—and invited us to hang out all day behind the camera where between takes he chatted with us about everything in the world, even including what we wanted to hear most—directing.

Conrad and I became good friends with Floyd—although in my case he at first seemed more interested in my seafaring skills than my aspirations with a camera. Floyd had loved sailing in the South Seas and wanted to keep the experience alive with a business venture. He asked me to find a boat he could buy and use for inter-island trading. It seemed to me like a hairy dive into venture capitalism, but after several weeks I located the perfect vessel. Floyd, Con, and I went to San Pedro to inspect her. Crosby stood at the helm of this big schooner, quickly realized the impracticality of his impulse to become a South Seas Island entrepreneur, and the idea flew out the porthole like a scared seagull.

Later, when Conrad and I visited Floyd at his Carpinteria home, we were driven out of the house by the bang and clatter of drums emanating from his teenage son's bedroom. We had no idea that what we were hearing was a budding talent which this noisy kid would one day parlay into a great career—the rock group Crosby, Stills and Nash.

It became our habit, whenever we were faced with a difficult question in cinematography, to call Floyd to get the answer. Some of our problems—often phoned in a panic of doubt from the set—must have seemed pretty basic to Crosby, but he was always kind and took our questions seriously.

These were the times when we took any assignment we could get. On one scary job, a documentary for the National Safety Council, Marv, Conrad, and I took shifts riding with a highway patrol officer whose assignment was to get us to accident scenes before the ambulance arrived. The footage was to be used in a fright film—gruesome wreckage and maimed bodies—as a required lesson for traffic violators to shock them into improving their driving habits. After a month of filming terrible car accidents I learned that an automobile can be a moving coffin. I also found out that if you ever do have a car accident, the first person you want to see is a highway patrolman. The calm way a trained officer takes command of a chaotic accident scene won my admiration.

Some of the scenes we witnessed were so emotional that it was difficult to film them. We avoided following in the footsteps of our predecessors, who, on another film of this ilk, had used open-flamed magnesium flares to light a night accident and the open flare ignited spilled gasoline and turned a minor collision into a ghastly inferno.

We also regularly shot for a TV series called *You Asked For It*, a series that ran in various versions for over thirty years. The idea of the show was to fulfill the mailed-in requests of viewers to see on TV the wild—and usually dangerous—stunts or silly things they had heard about. The request letters were obviously rigged by the production company to suggest topics (eating live worms, flying a plane with wings verticle through a narrow gap, kissing rattlesnakes, anything strange, disgusting, or perilous) according to the subjects available to be filmed.

We'd already decided to quit when we realized that as often as not, we as cameramen were taking chances equal in danger to the risky stunts being performed for the lens. The day we quit for good was after we'd filmed a man dropping to the ground—without a parachute—from a low-flying plane. We realized that he'd done this trick as an act of desperation. He wasn't a stuntman whose specialty was jumping from airplanes without a parachute. He'd never done it before. But he needed the money so badly he'd do anything. If he'd killed himself—which seemed the most likely prospect—wouldn't we have been morally implicated?

We were happy that he came out of it with little more than scrapes and bruises, but it was the last show of the series that we chose to shoot.

We accepted an assignment shooting an NAACP Convention documentary. It took place at the Shrine Auditorium in Los Angeles. We hadn't realized what we'd taken on until we checked the place out the day before the shoot. How could we possibly illuminate that cavernous space? How to light all those black faces on a dark stage? "Quick! Get Floyd Crosby on the phone." Floyd's solution was as simple as Bill Clinton's familiar wise words: "It's the economy, stupid!"

"Get some light colored drapes," Floyd said.

Ever the gentleman, Floyd had been kind enough to drop the word "stupid," but we felt the punch in his tone. Floyd's tip was all we needed to succeed in filming the meeting.

We shot a documentary on Los Angeles smog. One of our USC instructors had taken a contract from an association of petroleum producers, so the message we were to give was pretty clear even before we received copies of the research we were supposed to document. It was a good lesson for us in how through the medium of film, which is so easily distorted by the moviemaker's bias, you can tell convincingly whichever side of the story you want to sell. Viewers of this whitewash, shot in the days before smog controls, were convinced that backyard incinerators, not hundreds of thousands of cars belching exhausts, were the sole cause of smog in the L.A. basin.

The Three Musketeers often took individual jobs and put the proceeds into the communal kitty that was Canyon Films. I was hired by a New York documentary producer and cameraman named Larry Madison, of MPO Productions, to assist on a short industrial shoot in L.A. During one lunch break he told me about the series of duck hunting documentaries he was making for Remington Arms, and I spent the rest of my employment with Larry Madison distracting him from the job at hand with irrelevant conversation about nature films.

When he showed me his movies, I knew I had to get an assignment from MPO. Larry's footage was the first I'd seen that had been shot during those brief intervals of dawn when the ducks and geese fly in to prairie potholes. The film featured wonderful soft light, foggy pink skies, mist on still water with the decoys out, the honking of the hunter's lure and the birds' eerie replies. It was magic to me.

Larry shot from a duck hunter's point of view—birds winging in through the blur of foreground reeds, the sharp silhouettes of flocks out beyond the fuzzy out-of-focus shapes of stark foreground limbs, ducks appearing out of the low sun's flare. It's run-of-the-mill stuff today, but Larry was filming this in a time when such things were thought by most cameramen to be unacceptable technical flaws.

Larry gave me a job shooting a film on Canada geese. I spent a wonderful spring in a skiff powered only by oars, alone on the Snake River, camping on islets and gravel bars, drifting through the Washington State wilderness. Throughout the project I tried to emulate Larry's style which caught so well the atmosphere in which I was living. This was the kind of filming I knew I had been made for.

Then I heard a rumor that Walt Disney Studios was gearing up to make a feature about desert wildlife.

4

My Boss Walt

In 1951 I was busy shooting faux stock footage of cars pulling up in front of hotels and actors doubling for the stars getting in and out of the vehicles. I was earning enough money to buy groceries and I was learning a few tricks of the trade, but I wasn't having a lot of fun doing it. At the same time, a husband-and-wife camera team had convinced Walt Disney to finance a couple of three-reel documentaries they wanted to shoot in Alaska. Their *Seal Island* won an Oscar in 1949, but with its companion *Alaskan Sled Dog* yielded only modest box office success. Walt was about to give up on their idea of a nature series, but he gave them one more chance.

Their next effort was a featurette they called *Beaver Valley*. In today's marketplace the title would probably mean it was a sex film, but Al and Elma Milotte's movie was a wildlife documentary. It was hugely popular and cleaned up at the box office.

Walt was hardly a wildlife enthusiast, but he saw the potential of the genre: send out a naturalist-cameraman with some film, a tent, and a pocketful of change, and you could make a movie the public would pay as much to see as a conventional multimillion-dollar feature shot by a hundred people on a union crew.

Shortly after the Milottes' groundbreaking success, another young man showed up at the Disney gate with a roll of film under his arm. Paul Kenworthy was more interested in his technical achievement—building a beam-splitter that turned an ordinary 16mm Kodak Ciné Special movie camera into a reflex model—than he was in the content of his demo footage. His new optical system allowed him to see exactly what he was filming through the lens rather than through an attached viewfinder. The subject he chose to illustrate the versatility of his new optical system—close-up studies of insects—came at just the time Disney was looking for a subject to premiere as the studio's first *True Life Adventure* feature-length documentary.

The topic Paul happened to focus on was an exciting sequence of a fierce desert wasp fighting a huge hairy tarantula. It was exciting material—life and death, the screen filled with action—and it set a style and told a story which proved that even a couple of bugs, if filmed in an imaginative way, could engage a wide audience.

At about this time, I got wind of what was going on at Disney Studios. I made an appointment with a producer there named Ben Sharpsteen, who was in charge of developing the new nature series.

When I met Mr. Sharpsteen, I was full of myself. Hey, these blokes need me more than I need them—a guy with a bent as a biologist who has just graduated from university with a cinema degree. With that rare combination, I was just the person they were looking for, probably to head up the natural history unit or at least to be a lead cameraman on the series.

The demeanor I projected when I headed into the job interview was that of a swell-head. Fortunately, Ben was a kind and generous man. He listened without laughing, then broke the news: "Do you know how many applications we get every week from people with your qualifications? Every biologist, naturalist, zoologist, and nature freak in the world thinks he or she should be shooting for Disney."

He told me that the best advice he could offer was that I go out and shoot some film. "When you've got something you want to show me, I'll happily look at it. As our next film will be called *The Living Desert,* I suggest you try something that would fit into that theme."

I slunk out of Walt Disney Studios with my ego around my ankles, but I was already thinking about the many trips I'd taken to the desert as a teenager on museum collecting trips. I was at home in the desert. It was a wild place where you could move for a hundred miles without meeting a fence or a road. And we still owned the old Bolex camera with which we'd shot *Sea Theme.*

Canyon Films had rented an office and a small combination cutting room and studio on Highland Avenue in Hollywood. I went into the arid hills a mile away and dug up half a dozen chunks of compacted earth that held the nesting burrows of trapdoor spiders, the most accessible and dramatic performers I could think of for a natural history film.

I placed the clods in a row on our editing table and began a monthlong exercise in "training" my nocturnal spiders. Having constructed a web-hinged dirt door about the size of a nickel, a hungry trapdoor spider crouches just beneath the camouflaged portal of her burrow. Her sensitive hairs tell her of vibrations made by any insect that treads within a six-inch radius. Somehow the spider is able to detect the direction and distance of an approaching arthropod and might even be able to determine the species. If a distasteful creature wanders close, she seems to know and seldom opens her door to let it in.

But when something as tasty as a fat sowbug gets close enough that the spider can grab it while still keeping a foot in the door—a trapdoor spider never goes completely outside to take her prey—she pounces with astounding speed and accuracy.

Of the six nests on the table, only four of the occupants readily took the sowbugs I presented and thus became potential actors. In the first month of conditioning, my cast of hopefuls learned to accept the food I offered in near darkness. Now it was necessary to induce them to comport themselves in unnatural conditions—under the glare of the bright lights that I'd need to film them.

I took the two clods that hadn't made the cut back to the hills and replanted those washouts where I'd found them.

In addition to training my novice actors, I had technological difficulties to deal with. Lacking Paul Kenworthy's inventiveness, I had no beam-splitter to give my camera reflex viewing while shooting—a definite disadvantage for this kind of macro photography. (Macro is a step up from micro in the order of photographing small things.) I settled on a less than state-of-the-art solution and put together a primitive diagonal rackover (a device to compensate for the difference in position between the viewfinder and the lens) for the Bolex. Because the spider's movements happened so quickly, I had to shoot in slow motion, which required more light for exposure than usual. Since light produces heat, I worried that I'd fry my actors. I solved this technical problem by aiming the lights through jars of cold water to cool the rays.

In my office-studio I set up lamps-through-water bottles to create a dramatically spooky backlight and began conditioning my remaining spiders for the next phase of their acting careers.

Unhappily they didn't like opening their doors in bright light. Every night I turned on the lights and coaxed a sowbug to run a few laps around the holes where I knew hungry spiders were waiting. But nobody bit. I thought that given time, hunger would make the spiders reconsider. But days went by and not a single door opened to receive my proffered sowbugs. It seemed that this might be the end of my effort to impress Ben Sharpsteen. I began thinking of other things that I could film.

Then, after three weeks of dieting, a couple of spiders decided to break their fast and grab a meal. Their doors opened for less than a second—all the time it took to throw back the portal on its hinge, lunge out and enfold a sowbug steak in hairy arms, pull it inside, and close the door.

Five weeks went by. Of my original six aspiring actors, only two of the spiders became stars—a far better percentage of success than New York Actor's Studio director, Lee Strasberg, could dare to hope for. Two more washouts went back to the hills. I filmed my remaining stars with a variety of prey and under different lighting setups. The spiders became so dependable and I grew to know them so well that it was a cheerless day when I finally decided that I'd shot all I needed and took my pets back where I'd found them.

The biggest natural history lesson for me was the surprising individuality of these primitive animals, who showed differences of character and behavior far more profound than I expected.

I put together my demo reel and called Ben Sharpsteen at Disney. He didn't seem to remember me, but when I humbly reminded him of the guy who'd swaggered in like a hot dog he chuckled, obviously surprised to hear from me again, and said he'd set up a screening room.

The black spiders, with their shiny bright eyes, popping up from hidden doors in the earth to grab any unsuspecting prey that happened to be ambling by, were devilish beings. This was the classic fright shot, the "sting" like that unexpected dead body in the closet that you can count on to bring a startled scream from an audience.

Sharpsteen ran my reel once and picked up the phone. I didn't know who he was talking to, but he seemed to be enthusiastic and I knew it was a good sign. Presently half a dozen men drifted into the projection room. Later I'd get to know them all—Stormy Palmer, the editor on the *True Life Adventures* series, Winston Hibler, Jim Algar, Harry Tytle, Roy Disney, Jr.—all to become old hands as *True Life Adventures* producers. Jack Spears and Dwight Hauser, writers, and Erwin Verity, the series production manager, also joined the group.

Sharpsteen ran my reel again. As the five minutes of film ran in the background, the audience talked about various completely disassociated and irrelevant topics—golf games, restaurants—gabbing away about things in general as if I wasn't in the room. Once in awhile someone would comment on the film that was unspooling. "Good subject, good action, okay lighting." Then back to mundane matters: "What'dja do last night?" Typical projection room yakkety-yak, the last thing anyone with a vested interest in the film that's being shown wants to hear.

There followed a discussion about the love life of someone I didn't know. Then Hibler said, "Spooky as hell."

I wasn't sure whether he was talking about someone's wife or girlfriend or my spiders. Hibler looked at the editor in the room.

"Stormy, can you build this into a suspense sequence, maybe set up a sympathetic character whom the audience knows is heading toward this hidden monster and sure doom?"

Then, without pausing, Hibler queried one of his writers: "What do you think, Spears?"

"Like what kind of sympathetic?" someone said from the darkness.

"Victim sympathetic," Hibler said. "Whoever's gonna get et.... the bug victim."

"What the hell kind of a bug is sympathetic?" snorted Jack Spears.

"Cricket," Algar said. "Everybody loves Jiminy Cricket."

Hib turned to me. "Do these spiders ever grab crickets?"

Before I could answer, Spears grouched that the show wasn't an animated cartoon. "Did you ever see a real cricket in macro photography? Eyes like a jar full of light bulbs, bloody black hairs sticking out all over—it's a fuckin' monster. Nobody's gonna think sympathetic."

"You got any other ideas for a desert sequence?" Hibler asked me as the reel ended and the lights came up. "Sorry. What was your name?"

"Couffer," I said. Then, thinking fast, I told them about the bat flights I'd seen during the war in Texas, where millions of bats poured out of a hole and made a snakelike column in the sky a mile long.

"So what's the story?" Hib said. "Any conflict, or just bats flying around?"

"Hawks and owls dive through the stream and grab bats out of the air. It's exciting action—very cinematic," I said, hoping to impress by using the Vorkapich word.

"Might be interesting," said Hib. "Maybe we should give it a try."

And so the conversation went, ending up with me following Erwin Verity, the production manager, to his office to hear the terms with which they were acquiring footage from other would-be naturalist-cameramen.

In retrospect, it's hard to believe the lousy deal that Verity offered—and which I accepted and thought was swell. But put into perspective, I've never grumbled. I was the new kid on the block and Disney offered a summer teaching something I wanted to learn—and I could have a wonderful time doing it. Maybe come the fall, under the penurious terms offered, I'd even break even.

The deal was this: Disney would loan me the latest in technology—one of the newly-invented 16mm Arri S reflex cameras. Verity seemed to feel that this bonus alone was such a wonderful break for an aspiring nature photographer that I'd be crazy if I didn't jump at the chance. Disney would also reward me by paying living expenses and travel costs to go down to Texas and film the bat flight. They'd also supply the raw film.

As Erwin Verity saw it, Disney was going way out on a limb on the slim chance that I'd produce something useful. If I did shoot something they could use in *The Living Desert,* they'd pay me thirty dollars per foot for the selected footage. Any exposed film they didn't choose I could keep for myself.

Charged with the excitement of this fantastic opportunity, I told Erwin about the armadillos and coyotes and coati-mundis that I could also shoot for the film. He allowed that as long as I was down there anyway and was tying up this splendid new Arri S camera—which he implied could be put to better use in the hands of another cameraman on another sequence—he'd provide enough raw stock that I could do some work with these subjects too.

I convinced Verity that I'd need help, and he threw in expenses for Conrad and Marv. I was proud of my arbitrating skills. Hadn't I ended up with more than the original offer? I even fantasized that after this—my first real studio negotiation—I was on the road to becoming a genuine Hollywood player.

We had a wonderful time camping in the bush near Bandera, the dude ranch capital of Texas. In addition to the spectacular sight of massed clouds of bats exiting in weaving lines out of the cave, with hawks and falcons diving into the columns and snatching bats in flight, we also filmed them by using bright photo lights inside during their daytime rest.

The ceilings were covered by a five-bat-deep blanket of squirming bodies. The surface pulsed like a waving sea. The result of that episode—the awakening of five million unexpecting bats when the lights suddenly came on—produced a rain of falling bat pee. The deluge splashing onto hot photo lamps caused the bulbs to explode. The loud popping further agitated the bats and turned on their other bodily excretions. We, our camera, lights, and equipment were slippery and soiled when we dragged ourselves out of the cave for a reappraisal.

After buying raincoats, hats, and making "roofs" for the lights, we had better luck the next time.

The Texas shoot went well, and Disney bought enough film that we almost made expenses. But the greatest profits came with all the other advantages that little assignment would lead to. *The Living Desert* won a feature-length documentary Academy Award for Walt Disney. The success of the project was one of a series of nature films which won Academy Awards in the years 1949, '50, '51, and '55. My five-minute demo of trapdoor spider footage (which was never bought or used) resulted in a series of Disney contracts that kept me busy filming natural history shows for the next ten years. Eventually they even paid me enough to buy my own camera.

* * * * *

Walt Disney is a name recognized by more people in the world than Abe Lincoln, and the black and white mouse with big ears may be the most widely known trademark figure on earth. With this famous credential on my résumé, the Disney name has gotten me into more places, out of more scrapes, and won me more favors than I deserved. But only once did I exceed propriety in the use of my employer's name—and that offense was excusable in the name of charity.

I was in Oregon shooting a film about salmon. Dwight Hauser was a *True Life Adventures* writer obsessed with a story he saw as his breakthrough to becoming a producer. He pushed the Disney story department to purchase a book called *Salar the Salmon,* which he thought he could shape into a popular entry for the new *The Wonderful World of Disney* TV series. Unfortunately for Dwight, what he didn't realize was that no matter how much fascinating natural history you cram into a subject, for a successful entry into the Disney series the featured animal had to have a charming personality and character. Those cuddly Disneyesque characteristics of audience identification expressed by kittens and chipmunks just don't transfer to a cold-blooded fish.

I was employed as a one-man-band to shoot this film that would never make it out of the cutting room.

One day, as I was walking down a forest path with my camera and tripod over my shoulder, a gray-haired lady accompanied by a black and white border collie came around a bend in the trail ahead. She stopped abruptly and stared at me with what I assumed was a look of fear. I thought my sudden appearance in this lonely part of the woods had startled her.

She quickly overcame whatever had caused her abrupt reaction and hurried toward me. Her look had not been one of fear; rather, it was awe.

"Oh, Mister Disney," she said. "I heard you were in the neighborhood making another of your wonderful nature films. I can't tell you how much pleasure you've brought to me and my family."

As she began digging into her bag I tried to correct the mistaken identity. [2]I'm sorry, lady, but I'm not…."

"I've been a fan of yours for as long as I can remember," she interrupted, pulling out pen and paper and thrusting them at me. "Oh, please, Mister Disney, if could I have your autograph I'll treasure it forever."

I tried to resume my denial but she wouldn't hear of it. Then I began to reconsider. What was the point in disappointing this nice old lady? Why embarrass her? I took the pen and paper.

She continued with her praise. "How do you do those things? How in the world did you get yourself way down in a tiny hole to film those adorable gophers? And such a large man…."

I smiled modestly, pen poised. "What's your name?" I said.

"Martha Johnstone," she said. "Oh, how wonderful. You're going to personalize it. Would you include my granddaughter? Her name is Lily Marston. She adored your wonderful work in *Beaver Valley*. She's such a nature freak."

To Lily Marston, I wrote. *From another nature freak. Your friend, Walt Disney.*

Sorry, Lilly, wherever you are. Your treasured autograph is a fake.

* * * * *

Disney's business strategy for the *True Life Adventures* series was brainstormed by studio production manager Erwin Verity. We shot the films away from Hollywood on 16mm film, which at the time was considered an amateur format. Thus our operations, always in remote locations, were slipped through the cracks insofar as the unions were concerned. Verity arranged for each of the wildlife filmmakers, who at the peak of the series' success numbered some half-dozen naturalist-cameramen like myself, to set up independent companies. In this way we became subcontractors without guild affiliations.

I called my corporation Grey Owl Pictures, not in recognition of the night-flying bird, but in homage to an early naturalist filmmaker. An Englishman who called himself Grey Owl and passed himself off as a Native American had shot a movie about beavers in the Canadian woods. He returned to London in buckskins and long braids and was celebrated as a real Indian wildlife filmmaker—another charlatan like so many others of us in this business.

At the peak of production, the Disney *True Life Adventures* shows—and later the spinoff wildlife segments of the TV series, a continuum that remained on the air longer than any other in history—employed five full-time producer-directors ensconced at the studio. They sat in the same offices they'd previously occupied as animation directors whose job wasn't done on a set but in a room on the third floor of the animation building. Ben Sharpsteen had directed *Snow White* and produced *Fantasia* from his office cluttered with storyboards, just as Jim Algar somehow "directed" *The Living Desert* without ever embarking for the arid wastelands.

At the beginning it probably seemed like a reasonable changeover, but as the series exploded in popularity the situation must have become clear to these men, who were truly producing the shows but calling themselves directors.

I made or helped to make twenty of these shows, each of which took several months (a couple nearly a year) to shoot. I shot everywhere from the Arctic to the Antarctic and points in between, but I never saw a Disney "director" on the set. I worked with wolverines, grizzly and black bears in Canada, with wolves and cougars in Arizona and Alberta, and penguins in Antarctica. Like the other field producers (a meaningless title invented by Erwin Verity) I directed my shows—and the Disney producers took director's credit and collected the residuals and guild benefits.

Yet, despite my gripes about the greedy strategies of a few former associates, my years at Walt Disney Studios were among the best, and I'm indebted even to the folks who hit below the belt. It was a part of my apprenticeship, and I benefited by some of the greatest adventures of my life. Thanks, guys, from my heart—fondest memories.

At the time *The Living Desert* was filmed "ecology" was a new word to the general public. In retrospect, I realize that the Disney *True Life Adventures* series was an important catalyst in the ecological movement. Up until that time nature documentaries were educational films interesting to people already interested in nature. The Disney nature movies and TV shows sparkled with entertainment and changed the public perception of wildlife in many ways. Most importantly to the producers, it made a ton of money. No, the Disney series was not made with an altruistic motive, but the films succeeded in creating a fresh awareness of the beauties in nature and opened a window into the lives of wild animals in an engaging way that no other media had done before. I've always been proud to have been a part of that generally unrecognized accomplishment.

* * * * *

During those years I had a strange relationship with the boss. When I made a rare visit to the studio from the field, I occasionally met Walt in the hallway or elevator of the animation building, where his office and those of the producers I worked with were located. Walt and his brother Roy and their wives had visited me while I was on location in British Columbia shooting a feature called *Nikki, Wild Dog of the North* at the time they were on a Banff vacation. Maybe by looking me up on the set they could write off the trip as a business expense, but at the same time Walt did have a genuine interest in what I was doing.

Thereafter, whenever we met at the studio, Walt would engage me in cheerful conversation. The thing that struck me as most remarkable was that Walt always knew exactly what I was doing. He knew the project I was working on or had just finished or was about to begin, and he always had some comment to make appropriate to that particular show.

When one considers the dozens of films and TV shows in production at the Disney studio at that time, and how many hundreds of people were involved in making them, isn't it extraordinary that Walt was so in touch with everything that was going on? Is it possible that he knew all of those people and their projects as well as he knew mine? I can only assume that was the case.

Walt's brother Roy, on the other hand, who was the business manager of the company, was less in touch. When we met on similar occasions, Roy always recognized my face, but he wasn't sure from when or where. His recall was strong enough that he'd engage me in some small talk, and then—and this same scenario must have happened half a dozen times—just as the elevator arrived at his floor and the door opened, Roy held out his hand for me to shake and said, "Good to see you. What was your name again?"

Wisteria Cottage (Cheese)

At the beginning of every film project, one expects the finished movie to be moving or funny or exciting depending upon the genre, and one always has at least modest expectations that it will be successful—or why do it?

And of course one also hopes that the shooting will be fun—or why do it?

I've endured awful misery in getting films made but the movies turned out to be wonderful, and I've had about as many joyful months of filming that yielded absolutely rotten movies. The process is nobody's idea of the way it should be. There are no rules, no guarantees that a happy production will produce a wonderful movie. Contrary to expectations, all the fun or torment in which one participates during the making of a film hasn't the slightest connection with the success or failure of the end product.

Of course the dream is to have a marvelous time making a wonderful movie that will make stars of its actors and piles of dollars for its producer. It happens, but you never know at the beginning if this is going to be "the one."

Not long after we had finished our Disney assignment filming bats in Texas, Irving Lerner brought Con and Marv and me together with a first-time producer named Robert Gurney. Gurney wanted Irving to direct *Wisteria Cottage,* an intriguing script about a young homicidal maniac who terrorizes a mother and her daughter when he moves into the tool shed of their remote South Carolina beach cottage. An important aspect of the story was that the boy had recognized his problem and had tried unsuccessfully to get psychiatric help. As the production was to be totally financed by Bob's father, he had to do it cheaply. That's where we came in.

Irving asked The Three Musketeers if we could do the whole thing—camera, lighting, grip, set decoration, the lot. Of course we said, "Sure."

Gurney found a New York sound man with a self-invented contraption which he strapped to his body like a one-man-band. He hung a Nagra tape recorder around his neck with its meters and knobs on his chest, and carried the microphone pole with its butt stuck into a fisherman's pole socket in his crotch. This way he had one hand for the mike boom and one hand for the knobs.

Because the murderer in the script was an artist, and an important story device was the visualization of his mental deterioration through the changes in his paintings, we needed a painter. Lerner prevailed on his artist friend Irving Block to join the crew.

A week later, we all flew to Myrtle Beach, South Carolina, for one of the most wonderful summers of my life.

It all had to do with relationships.

* * * * *

Except for Lerner and the Muskateers we were all strangers to one an other when we first gathered. There wasn't money in the budget for wives' travel or accomodation, thus they stayed home. Joan and I had moved off the boat to an apartment in Hollywood and she had a good job as an executive secretary, which she couldn't leave.

In spite of our original divergence, the cast and crew of *Wisteria Cottage*, which eventually was released as Edge of Fury, were a perfect amalgam of personalities and bonded quickly. We enjoyed each other, the experience, the work, and the location. Of course my remembrances might be tinted with rainbow colors because of the relationship that grew between me and the ingénue in the cast.

Jean Allison was 23, the first real actress I'd ever met. I was 27, and smitten from day one—first with her charm and beauty, then with her intelligence and ability, and later with her passion. She had grown up in Catholic schools and as a girl thought she wanted to be a nun. In high school she'd been a jock and participated in sports: swimming, diving, fencing, basketball, skiing, ice skating, equestrian, field hockey, and tennis. Later, in college, through an interest in psychodrama, she found theater. Something changed in her religiosity and she became agnostic.

Jean and I began to feel a mutual attraction early during the ten-week shoot. At the motel café where we all stayed, we moved tables end-to-end each evening so the whole cast and crew could sit together for dinner.

Soon Jean and I were always sitting side-by-side at the dinner table.

The proprietress thought we were all crazy when we played silly games such as "spoon hanging." Irving Block—Blocky—held the spoon-hanging record in this game of willpower. The premise was that if you concentrated hard enough you could literally will an inanimate object such as a spoon to hang by the concavity of its dished shape from your protruding nose as if it was suspended there on a hook. Not only your nose works as a hanging place but also your chin, cheeks—and, in Blocky's record-breaking case, your forehead. Spoon-hanging sites abound on just about any place on the human body if one's concentration is adhesive enough. Surely Blocky's record—five spoons all hanging simultaneously from the face—can never be broken. It was a truly magnetic feat.

Every evening ended up as a festivity, not always as silly as spoon hanging, but alive with interesting conversation and laughter.

One warm afternoon when for some reason neither of us were needed on the set, I noticed that Jean wasn't around. I'd seen her strolling away toward the dunes and I walked up that way and began following her footprints in the sand.

When I came upon her taking a sun bath in a steep basin in the dunes she was surprised, but unembarrassed of her nudity. I sat down and we chatted in a normal way under what semed to me to be a most abnormal situation. Jean's unselfconsciousness wasn't provocative, it was simply natural. When we felt it was time to return to the set she slipped back into her clothes and we walked back together. It was my first exposure to a woman who was imbued with an innate self-confidence that revealed itself in such a total lack of modesty. It made a deep impression.

At the end of a day's shooting we often took long walks along the beach, through the dunes, and deep into the cypress swamps where turtles and alligators watched from the dark still waters. Jean was a New York girl who took to the nature I showed her with a strong appetite.

Somehow, I connected Jean with the Nat King Cole rendition of the song *Nature Boy* that had wide popularity and was recorded by many artists a few years before and after our meeting. The song relates a reverie of "a strange enchanted boy who wandered very far over land and sea..."

only to learn that "the greatest thing...was just to love and be loved in return."

The lyrics were off the mark in the respect that although Jean had been a tom-boy in her youth, she was all girl now. But in spite of that difference, I couldn't get the romantic notion out of my head. Jean was *Nature Girl* to me.

At the end of the South Carolina shoot, Bob Gurney flew to New York City to arrange for a last week of filming there. He asked Jean and me if we'd like to drive his car back for him. That trip—which we turned into an outing that took a few days longer than the express bus—was the most generous bonus Gurney could possibly have given us.

Jean had an apartment near where I was staying in Greenwich Village. From Jean I learned to love Manhattan, so different from anything I'd known before.

Of course we were living in sin as both of us were married, but it was sin of a kind we could easily suffer. If there is such a thing as innocent wickedness, this was it. Our romance was only a wild wonderful fling, a youthful affair of the heart about which neither of us has ever felt the slightest guilt or regret. She was the wildest, most adventurous, most wonderful woman I'd ever known.

At the time, our relationship had seemed transitory. Jean stayed in New York and I returned to Los Angeles. But those joyous weeks together had made a lasting impression and we stayed loosely in touch—a postard now and then, a phone call if one or the other of us was travelling though the other's turf. Months and years went by without connection of any kind, but then occasionally a chance contact came and went.

Unfortunately for all of us, *Wisteria Cottage* wasn't that rare project that was both fun to make and a marvelous film. Irving had to leave at the end of shooting to fulfill a commitment to help edit *Spartacus.* Whatever life *Wisteria Cottage* had, it died with Irving's exit—in the editing room.

Although we ended up referring to the film fatuously as *Wisteria Cottage Cheese,* it was one of the most enjoyable filming experiences I've ever had. It was the people who made it so—all of them—but most of all, Jean Allison.

The film was eventually released in 1958, six years after it was filmed, as *Edge of Fury*, but to me it shall always be *Wisteria Cottage*—or *Wisteria Cottage Cheese.*

6 World's End

Toward the end of our shoot in South Carolina the phone rang in my motel room. It was Disney Studios, Erwin Verity on the line. How he found me was anyone's guess. But Erwin's detective methods interested me a lot less than what he had to say. He asked me if I was interested in an assignment to shoot film in the Galápagos Islands.

The little I knew about these desolate specks of land in the far Pacific was that they epitomized one of man's oldest dreams, a world where humans and animals lived side by side without fear or animosity. This idyllic relationship is the subject of myths and legends the world over, but the wild animals we usually know are shy, secret and afraid, forever hiding from human eyes.

There has never been a native human culture occupying the remote Galápagos. No tribe of primitive aborigines ever taught the island's many species the fear of prey, and the population of colonizing humans in the archipelago was small and localized. The animals had yet to learn the ways of man.

In 1952 the Galápagos Islands were one of the most remote and unvisited places on earth, and there was only one way to get there—aboard your own boat. Verity knew about my experience as a seaman, and I still owned the schooner. That's what put the buzz in his ear.

Visiting yachtsmen and ship's crews on natural history expeditions had shot film in the Galápagos before. But what they'd brought back was of home movie quality. Conrad and I were to be the first real filmmakers to visit the archipelago and professionally photograph the wildlife.

Erwin's offer hit me with great joy. A long cruise into those wild waters would be the adventure of a lifetime. Although Conrad had recently gotten married, he didn't hesitate to say he'd join me. Six months away from his new wife, Virginia (it turned out to be closer to a year) was the price one had to pay to be in our chosen profession.

Joan wasn't keen on the prospect of my taking off again. She said that no marriage could survive our long and frequent separations. But both of us were feeling doubts about our wedlock. It seemed that our common interests had dwindled, and my passion for travel and adventure was not one of hers. I wondered if our separations didn't serve us in a different way. Was it the time apart that threatened our marriage? Or was that what kept it together?

Thinking more deeply about Verity's plan, I decided against sailing my schooner to the islands. Skippering a yacht in strange waters is a full-time job. Managing the *Kuuipo* in the islands would take my time away from filming. I wasn't happy with the idea of playing this dual role.

When I got the job with its prospect of sailing across 1000 miles of empty ocean, I enrolled in a class in celestial navigation to enable finding our exact whereabouts by observing the sun and stars—my skills heretofore had consisted of piloting by running time, landmarks, and compass bearings. I knew the old sailor's ditty: You can't get lost in the Pacific. Just sail due east or due west until a large continent heaves into sight. But that axiom was a bit vague even for us.

Eventually we hired a 28-foot ketch, *Highlander,* which was easily stowed on the deck of a freighter. The ketch was smaller than my schooner by a third. We shipped *Highlander* with her owner, Doug MacIntire, to the Panama Canal Zone where Conrad and I joined him by plane and helped to re-step the masts and stow provisions. Our skipper had built his boat with his own hands and managed her ably. As salty as they came, Doug knew everything about the sea except how to swim in it. With three aboard and provisions for four months, the waterline was deep below the blue striping as we began our voyage from Panama.

With a war surplus plastic lifeboat sextant and a book full of numbers, we sailed with a shrug into the west. I knew that by taking a look through the sextant at the precise time when the sun was at its highest—dead noon—and noting the markings on the instrument's index, then properly relating them to the numbers in the book, I could fix our position accurately north and south. But it surprised me when on dawn of the third day, that beacon of rock called Malpelo, a welcome fragment of basalt that jutted from the deep sea at the outer edge of the Gulf of

Panama, materialized in the morning gloom. It stood dead abeam and only three miles away, exactly where it should have been.

Some ten dawns later, a dim grey shape on the horizon that gradually resolved itself into land proved to be the island of San Cristóbal, our first landfall in the Enchanted Islands.

Depending upon the whereabouts of the fish, big oceangoing tuna clippers operated frequently between their base in San Diego, California, and the Galápagos. Verity made arrangements with the skippers to carry raw film stock and supplies to us and bring back exposed film. But the climate during the year of our trip was unusual; the tuna hung close to the coast of Peru and few clippers came our way. After four months we were able to ship only one lot of exposed film on the lone San Diego tuna boat that briefly prospected the Galápagos grounds.

We made our base at Academy Bay, where a few hardy colonists had established a small settlement. Two families from a failed Norwegian attempt at colonization farmed small plots hacked out of the bushy highlands. From them we were able to buy fresh fruit and vegetables, which were brought down the mountain on a donkey's back. In addition to the Norwegians, one New Zealander, a yachting couple from the United States who put down roots, a few Equadorian families, and three German brothers with their wives and children made up the community on Santa Cruz Island.

The Angermeyer brothers—Heinz, the eldest, was 26, Hans, Gus, Carl, and Fritz, the youngest at age 17—had set sail toward their imagined paradise from Hamburg in 1935. With surprising foresight, their cabinetmaker father had seen the way his country was headed and told his sons that they had to leave Germany. Using his life savings, Herr Angermeyer, who stayed behind, bought the schooner that took his sons only as far as the coast of England where their ship was wrecked. Heinz, the only one with a wife, who was pregnant, realized that the trip would be too rigorous and returned to Hamburg where the whole family was killed in a bombing raid. The others took the cash they got from salvage and made their way to Guayaquile in Ecuador, where they bought plows and scythes for the farm they expected to clear in the tropical paradise.

Unfortunately the magazine account they'd read about the Enchanted Islands was fiction. The writer had never been there.

The Angermeyer boys arrived in Ecuador in time to catch the once-yearly voyage of the ship that supplied a small Navy garrison on one of the archipelago's larger islands. One port of call was at Ecuador's version of Devil's Island, a penal colony where the ship dropped off a few condemned felons who were restrained only by their isolation. There was no wire or bars even for the most incorrigible murderers. The ship's other duty was to cruise on through the islands watching for signal fires from possible shipwrecked mariners.

The Navy captain told the brothers about the only place he'd seen where he thought they might be able to settle: a green spot along the shore that might indicate fresh water. Aside from that, the desiccated rocks were a habitat only of lizards, tortoises, and cactus.

He put them ashore at what was to become the port of Academy Bay. That's where we met Carl, Fritz, and Gus (Hans had sickened shortly after their arrival and sailed to Ecuador where he died). The Angermeyers, who became our best friends, taught us how to live off the land and sea in this most inhospitable-looking place of lava, cactus, and volcanos. The farming tools they'd brought with them were useless along the dessicated shores and being children of the sea, the brothers had no desire to live near the few colonists who chose to farm in the damp highlands. They made their living by catching and drying fish which they sent to Guayaquile whenever an opportunity came their way.

You couldn't find three more dissimilar personalities than the brothers Angermeyer. Gus—the elder, the leader, the thinker—was known as "The King of the Galápagos." Carl—the flamboyant raconteur, handsome and gregarious—always wore a Robin Hood hat with a long feather stuck in the band. He sported this jaunty chapeau almost as symbol of his adventuresome nature. Fritz—competent in all things requiring the use of his hands—was shy, very shy.

On a visit to the archipelago by the Royal British Yacht *Brittania*, Carl met Prince Philip, the Duke of Edinburgh. The Prince was so impressed with this handsome character and his knowledge of the islands that he invited Carl to join the ship as its guide. Carl was delighted, but he didn't own so much as one dress shirt, much less a tie, and he came aboard with only the clothes on his back. Dinners aboard the Royal Yacht were formal affairs, and Prince Philip dug into his ample wardrobe and appropriately outfitted Carl to join the captain's table. There, amid the Sterling silver and linen napkins, they all dined every night and Carl amused them with his endless repertoire of island lore—of romance, pirates, treasure, wildlife and history.

One evening as they came to anchor in a remote and otherwise deserted cove, Carl nodded to a small fishing boat that shared the anchorage. "My brother, Fritz, is over there," Carl said.

"Really?" the Prince said. "Your brother? Way out here in that tiny boat? How extraordinary."

The Prince picked up binoculars and focused them on Fritz's little sloop. "He seems to be all alone," said the Prince. "Doesn't he have a crew?"

"He always fishes alone," Carl said.

"That must be very lonely," said the Prince.

Prince Philip paged the Captain and told him to send an invitation across to Carl's brother.

The gigboat of the *Brittania,* all spit and polish and gleaming brass, was let down on her davits forthwith. The Yacht's chief steward, resplendent in starched uniform, dusted off his epaulets and stepped aboard, and with gold stripes shinning in the evening sun, the gigboat sped away. In a few moments the launch from the Royal Yacht drew alongside Fritz's boat, which was decorated with smelly strings of drying salted grouper.

"Ahoy!" spoke the chief steward to the empty-looking boat.

Fritz stuck his head out of the companionway hatch. "Aye?" he said.

"Good day to you," said the chief steward.

"Good day," said Fritz.

The chief steward spoke in the patrician manner that suited his station: "I have the pleasure to pass an invitation from His Highness Prince Philip. His Highness would be honored by your presence at dinner aboard the Royal Yacht *Brittania.*"

Fritz looked puzzled. He paused, thinking. When he replied at last, his tone out-cooled even this most genteel master of the cool: "Oh, I think not."

Then Fritz turned back to the seclusion of his cabin and closed the hatch.

* * * * *

We sailed out many times from Academy Bay to the other islands, and then returned to our base for replenishing food and spirit with the Angermeyers. Each island was different from its neighbors; each island was inhabited by different kinds of wildlife to film. These remarkable brothers not only taught us how to survive in the wilderness—they showed us how to have fun doing it. Stalking wild goats and catching the chosen one by hand was an Angermeyer skill we mastered. And catching sea turtles for their delicious meat and rendering the fat for butter was another Angermeyer-taught skill. (Yes, in those early days of prolific wildlife we killed a few sea turtles—something I wouldn't dream of doing today). While Conrad and I were having the time of our lives, our skipper, Doug, was stuck on the boat most of the time. But that's where he wanted to be. Somewhat like Fritz, MacIntyre was most comfortable aboard his boat with the hatches closed.

While Con and I were ashore in some exotic spot, excited by filming beautiful things, Doug was aboard his boat, puttering around doing little chores and bored stiff. At the end of each day's shooting, when we rowed back to our home afloat, Doug's first question was always the same: "How much film did you shoot?"

If our reply was, "Only fifty feet, but it was great," he grew a long face.

If our reply was, "Five hundred feet, but it was no good," he beamed. Doug couldn't wait for the day when we ran out of film and could all go home.

As so often happened in my business of shooting films in far-off places, one of my greatest rewards was in the people I met. In the Galápagos I was visiting a world of rugged individualists, real-life characters out of adventure novels. One of the most interesting was "Sandy" Sanderson, beachcomber of the Enchanted Islands. He lived in a shack built of driftwood at Academy Bay and had been there some five years when I met him.

Sandy's résumé—if he had one—would have shown that he'd fought with one of the high-morale military outfits similar to today's Commandos or Special Forces in the North African campaign of World War II. The group was called Popski's Private Army, and the men were highly trained in covert, hand-to-hand, sneak-behind-enemy lines, attack-outposts, kill-sentries, kinds of missions. Sandy was a New Zealander by birth and passport, but he was truly a citizen of the world.

He'd ended up in England after the war, where he met a young couple who owned a yacht and had a treasure map. He signed on, and they set sail for Cocos Island off the coast of Costa Rica in the Eastern Pacific, which they believed to be the unnamed treasure island shown on the map.

Two months later, having crossed the Atlantic, sailed through the Caribbean, through the Panama Canal, and up the Central American coast, they arrived at desolate, seldom-visited Cocos. During their first night there, the wind blew strong, the anchor dragged, and they found themselves on the rocks.

Sandy and his shipmates salvaged what they could from the stricken yacht and used the pieces to make a crude camp on the beach. A couple of days later, a San Diego tuna boat chugged in and dropped anchor. They made contact; the tuna boat was sailing home for San Diego and offered to "rescue" them. The boat-owner couple, having lost everything, were fed up and gratefully accepted the offer.

Sandy had a different idea. "We've come this far," he said, "been here only two days and along comes a rescue boat. I'll stick around awhile, see what I can find. If nothing looks like treasure, I'll just catch the next boat, thank you very much."

So Sandy, alone under the tropical sun, set out to explore rugged Cocos. He found old holes where previous treasure hunters had dug, but no sign of gold or silver. He ate seabirds, fish, and wild fruit from the big-leafed trees. Fresh water was plentiful. One of his discoveries, made as the months went by, was that the arrival of a boat so soon after their shipwreck had been a fluke. A year passed before he saw the next vessel—the schooner *Chance*, out of California.

To Sandy, the yacht's name seemed full of promise. The *Chance* was sailing to the Galápagos and offered Sandy passage. He'd seen all he wanted of Cocos and was sick of his diet of seagulls and limpets. He jumped at the opportunity.

They put him ashore at Academy Bay. There, studying a chart of the islands and comparing it to the treasure map, he thought he saw a wonderful similarity. The island of Española seemed to fit the topography and outline of the treasure map to a T. There was even a crack in the lava, marked on the chart in exactly the place such a feature was indicated on the treasure map—the place with the black "X" that showed the placement of the casks of gold. But Espaniola was fifty miles away across wide channels with unknown currents. Only one person in the Galápagos had a boat capable of making such a trip: Carl Angermeyer, with his homebuilt sloop the *Indefatigable.* (Indefatigable is the English name of the island of Santa Cruz where the Angermeyers settled.) He'd sawed the timber for frames and planks out of trees, even made the nails from heavy copper wire salvaged at an abandoned World War II radar station.

Sandy told Carl about his conviction that the treasure lay on Española and that he knew the spot where the riches lay buried. He offered to split the treasure if Carl would take him there. But Sandy had shown himself to be an unusually mercurial character. Perhaps he was a bit punch-drunk or suffering from combat fatigue, as this ailment common to veterans of hand-to-hand combat is sometimes called. In any case, he was subject to wild mood swings and was always ready for a fist fight if things didn't agree with him.

Carl thought that traveling with Sandy would be a risky trip with an unpredictable conclusion. Not because of the hazards of the sea or that they might not find the treasure—but what if they did?

So Sandy waited. He knew that someday he'd get his chance to land on Española and examine the place where he believed the treasure was hidden.

Five years went by before another candidate dropped anchor in Academy Bay—us, in the twenty-eight-foot ketch *Highlander*.

We already knew something of the lore of Galápagos treasure before Sandy decided that we were the ones he wanted as partners and made his pitch. We declined his offer. We were too wary of him.

For the brothers, nothing could be more up their alley than pirate treasure, and they knew all the stories. Carl had sailed with us to Buccaneer Bay on the island of San Salvador. It had been a favorite spot for old-time pirates to careen their ships. Buccaneer Bay was a calm, protected cove with a wide sandy beach. The pirate crews camped on the beach for the few days and nights it took to scrape off the barnacles from one side, slap on a fresh coat of shark oil, then lay the boat over on the other side with the next high tide and clean that.

We anchored in the cove, spent a day carefully walking the upper beach, picking up artifacts from pirate and whaling days. Pieces of old clay pipes and lead musket balls were common in the sand. Potsherds, chunks of old glass, and bent brass nails were scattered here and there. Conrad found a beautiful brass spoon of ancient design, and my prize was a pair of bronze navigational dividers that after soaking in oil for a few days still worked perfectly. (The dividers are now in the collections department of UNESCO's Darwin Research Center at Academy Bay.) In the bush beyond the edge of sand we found stone-walled corrals where live tortoises had been held until loading into ship's holds. Lacking refrigeration, tortoises could survive for months without food providing a ship with an always available source of fresh meat.

We hiked up to the fertile summit of San Salvador where the pirates had left members of their crew and captured slaves to maintain a farming base to which they could return and resupply. Gnarled citrus and avocado trees, progeny from trees planted by pirates, were still growing and bearing fruit where the buccaneers planted them. Feral pigs, cattle, burros, and goats, descendants from the original stock that were brought to the farms by pirates still thrived until they were recently eradicated because of the damage they caused to the native ecology.

There was no question that the oral history of this place was true. And there is a lode of literature detailing various pirates and their ships who sailed to the Galåpagos for refuge after looting South American seaports or merchant ships.

We would soon dig more deeply into treasure lore.

* * * * *

After a month-long filming trip to Tower Island, nesting home to thousands of boobies and frigatebirds, we returned to Academy Bay to reprovision. The nesting season of the waved albatross on Española, a must in our itinerary, was about to begin, and we set a time a couple of weeks away to depart for Sandy's treasure island.

Before we left for Española we hired Sandy's chum and *puro* drinking buddy, (*puro*, made of distilled guava juice, is the local grog) Eduardo, to guide us to the peaks of the island of Santa Cruz. Here we hoped to find giant tortoises.

The high country where we were headed was watered for several months of the year by the mists called *garua* and were thus far richer in foliage than the lower slopes of cactus and stone. The summits, covered with grassy meadows and fields of shoulder-high ferns, were home to herds of the wild cattle originally introduced by the buccaneers. There was a single hunter on the island who killed one wild bovine per week, every Tuesday, and brought the bloody slabs of beef, black with flies and mud, down to the community of colonists who lived at Academy Bay.

As often as possible we tried to make Tuesday our day to be in port so we could buy a chunk of beef. It was dirty, unrefrigerated, and invariably tough, but it was fresh. With the outer layer cut away and tossed to the crabs, we relished the change from our everyday diet of goat meat and fish.

With our kit packed onto two burros we set off up a rocky trail. It was to be a four-day trip, camping among the peaks. Eduardo told us he wanted to get back as soon as possible because there was a small war going on between Ecuador and Peru over their disputed international boundary. He planned to take passage to the mainland on the annual trip of the Ecuadorian Navy ship so he could get in on the shooting. Eduardo hadn't the slightest interest in the politics of the situation—his only motive was to be given the legal chance to shoot at other people.

An item of deeper interest than his bent for murder we learned from Eduardo while he was nipping at a jug of *puro*. He told us that he'd seen Sandy's treasure map, and he wasn't loathe to describe its dearest details. He spoke of the deep slot in the lava which was marked with the black "X" and described exactly where the portentous crack lay relative to other geographical features drawn on the map. By the time we came down off the mountain, we had the whole layout engraved in our heads exactly as it had been etched on paper back in jolly old England a century ago.

When we returned to the boat and Sandy learned that our next port of call was to be the island of Española, he immediately appeared on the shore opposite our anchorage and gave a shout.

Doug fetched him in the skiff, and we hunkered down in the cabin and listened to his pitch. Sandy was dead-sure about the identity of the treasure island—there was no doubt that Española was the one.

He made us the same proposal he'd made to Carl five years before: Take me with you to Española and we'll share the wealth. We turned him down for the same reason. We recalled the bloody stories he'd told us of his escapades with a knife as a member of Popski's Private Army. Just what if he did find it? Which of our throats would he slit first?

We sent Sandy home to his shack that night with a bellyful of disappointment.

Our intended day of departure was Tuesday, three days away. On Sunday, Carl Angermeyer hailed us from the beach. It seemed that Sandy had gotten word that his drinking pal, Eduardo, had wagged his tongue during our outing to the top of the island. Now, packing a few tots of *puro* under his belt, along with a dirk the length of a machete, Sandy was plotting to stop the *Highlander* from setting sail to his island to claim his treasure. Carl suggested that we get as much open sea between us and Sandy as we could, as quickly as possible.

This we did immediately with no regrets.

* * * * *

We had been in the islands now for five months. Two months earlier, we'd had our first rendezvous with a San Diego tuna clipper, the *Paramount.* We received supplies sent by the studio—canned foods, mail, packages of film stock—and sent off our first shipment of exposed footage.

Although treasure hunting was on our agenda, it came second to the job at hand. We had arrived at Española when the nesting season of the waved albatross was in full swing. The waved albatross was perhaps the most beautiful species of this most attractive variety of ocean wanderers, and the entire world population nested within a few hundred square meters on a single hilltop. We had been there only two days and had hardly begun our work when we saw the red flag flying from the mast of the *Highlander*—something urgent required our immediate return. It was the first time this emergency signal had been hoisted, and we hurried to pack up our camera gear, hike back to the skiff, and row out to the little yacht.

We found Doug at the radio, trying to answer a mayday broadcast from a tuna clipper, the M.V. *Queen Mary,* that had run aground on an island at the other end of the archipelago. Their distress call had received no reply, and it was obvious that they couldn't clearly pick up the signal from our small transmitter. But they did seem to know that Doug was trying to call them. Each time he went on the air they came right back, giving their position and asking for help. They could hear our weak signal breaking through the airwaves but couldn't make out the words.

We didn't hesitate. The location of the emergency at Albemarle Point was over a hundred miles away, but the weather was fair with a favorable breeze. We had our gear stowed, the anchor aboard, and were underway within half an hour.

We sailed all night, trying periodically to contact the M.V. *Queen Mary* on the radio. When we transmitted, she always came right back with, "*Queen Mary* to ship calling," then repeated her predicament and coordinates.

Then at dawn, a most curious effect of the ether took over. A tuna clipper off Peru, a thousand miles away, picked up both of our signals and told the stricken ship that rescuers were on the way. Then even that remote contact was lost. But we knew the stranded vessel was aware that we were coming.

This responsibility both encouraged and worried us. It wouldn't be possible to assist in salvaging the ship. There was no way our little ketch could pull a huge tuna clipper off the rocks. If it became necessary for them to abandon ship, an option that by the urgent tone of their transmissions we judged to seem quite likely, our only way to help would be to take them all aboard the *Highlander.*

We tried to imagine what we might do with the fifteen-man crew of a big tuna clipper.

Weeks before, we'd sailed past this formidable headland and knew too well the forbidding northern shore of Isabella Island. If we had to take the crew aboard *Highlander* we'd be overloaded, in danger of being swamped ourselves. We prayed for calm seas when we arrived.

We'd been sailing all night and most of the following morning and were about halfway to our destination by noon when we were surprised to see a large boat appear on the horizon—the first we'd seen in weeks. Soon we could make out the shape of a tuna clipper steaming across our bow, a craft that could take over our rescue mission with far more capability than we could give. Obviously, as they were heading directly away from the emergency, they were unaware of the problem so close at hand. They could be there in a fraction of the time it would take for us—and do a hundred times more when they got there.

Doug was on the radio again, able to make immediate contact at this close range, and a surprising message boomed back on the speaker. "M.V. *Queen Mary* back to the *Highlander.* Yeah, we see you down there to the southeast."

Doug told them that we were headed for Albemarle Point to rescue them, and what the hell were they doing down here when they should be stuck on the rocks fifty miles away?

With those words, the big shape on the horizon turned abruptly and headed toward us. In a few minutes we pulled alongside, passed lines, drifted together in the middle of the Pacific, and climbed aboard to a warm welcome we hardly expected.

The crew couldn't believe this little yacht was the one intending to rescue them. They'd managed to kedge the *Queen Mary* off the rocks on the high tide and were headed to Panama for repairs. There was some damage to her wooden hull; all pumps were going and water was streaming out over her decks and through her scuppers, but she was in no danger of sinking.

As I stepped aboard the *Queen* I saw a familiar face. The navigator—the poor bloke who'd plotted the course that put the *Queen Mary* on the rocks at Albemarle Point—was the same one who'd taught the refresher course in celestial navigation I'd taken to sharpen my skills before setting out on our cruise. I had no idea what the crew thought of him now, but that they hadn't keel-hauled him yet was a good sign.

We were toasted by the crew of the *Queen* and offered anything we wanted from her ample stores. Gallons of ice cream which we couldn't possibly consume and would melt in an hour were loaded aboard the *Highlander*, along with bread, canned hams, and all the cases of beer we could stow (for which Doug found nooks and crannies that Con and I hadn't known existed).

Then the skipper said, "Anything else we can do for you?"

"All that sharp lava rock," I said. "It's torn up my last pair of shoes."

"What size?" the skipper asked.

"Twelve," I said.

"Same as mine," the skipper said as he took off his shoes and handed them to me.

We drifted together for a couple of hours. Then the *Queen* pulled out for Panama and we headed back toward where we'd come from some twenty-four hours ago, well repaid in more than the material things we'd been given—in friendship and camaraderie and with feelings of self-worth beyond all measure.

* * * * *

After we arrived back at Española and dropped anchor, we continued filming where we'd left off.

A week later, with *waved albatross* crossed off our list, the next thing we looked for was the crack in the lava marked "X" on the treasure map.

And there it was, deep and dark, exactly as Eduardo had said it would be.

We explored that twisting hole in the ground—every corner, crack, niche, and hollow. It was a hundred yards long, at places forty feet deep, with side-going cracks, wedged boulders blocking one possible route—all of the subterranean impediments to spelunking that make the sport so intriguing to the few whose motive had less to do with greed than ours—it took awhile.

Only a few inches of sand lay in the bottom of the crack. There was no place to dig and hide a treasure. We found nothing unnatural to give a clue that something had once been here and had been taken away: no bronze shoe buckle, lost doubloon, skull, saber, or gem. Only black lava, a bit of sand, and darkness. It was the home of foot-long centipedes the diameter of my thumb, nothing more.

We knew that Sandy's long sought-after wish would someday be realized and he would reach this holy place. Wouldn't it be sad if after all those years of hope, our friend's great quest would end as disappointingly as our spur-of-the-moment and rather frivolous search had? Wouldn't it be more satisfying to Sandy if he found at least one clue?

We thought it would, and so in a dark corner of the cave we chipped a mysterious glyptographic image. It was meaningless and impossible to decipher, but it was a sign that someone had been there and left a message. However equivocal it might be, it was something on which Sandy could ponder and hold onto a goal still to yearn for. He would assign a meaning to our sign, and it was no unkind joke we played—we did Sandy a favor.

* * * * *

All of my expectations about meeting animals that had no fear of man were realized in the Galápagos. Groups of owls came to our campfires and stood on the sand at the edge of the fireglow watching us with curiosity. Mockingbirds landed on our hats. Sea lions were unafraid. On the beach a person could touch them, and when in the water the young sea lions and seals seemed curious and playful with us and our underwater camera. Hawks nearly the size of eagles could be approached to touching distance. Finches pecked at our shoelaces. Still today, 174 years since Charles Darwin had written of the surprising tameness of the islands' wildlife, the same conclusion he noted remains true: "We may infer from the tameness of the wildlife what havoc the introduction of any new beast of prey must cause in a country, before the instincts of the aborigines become adopted to the stranger's craft or power."

Then when we had been in the islands for six months, Doug got word that his girlfriend had grown tired of waiting and was dating one of his rivals. MacIntyre wanted to throw in the towel and sail straight back to California.

At this time, with our film supply nearly exhausted and our food stores gone—we had been living on goat meat and fish for weeks—we met up with a tuna clipper and I got through to Erwin Verity via phone patch from the radio room. Doug was eagerly hoping for the order to set sail for home. But it didn't happen. Everyone at the studio loved the film we had sent in and wanted more. Verity asked us to extend our stay beyond the six months of our contract.

Conrad and I quickly talked it over and agreed to stay—but our pay was a paltry $500 each per week. I told Erwin that we'd like a raise.

The radio went silent for a long time. I thought we'd lost contact. Then Verity came back. Even through the crackle in the system a distinct change of tone sounded through the airwaves. Suddenly our material wasn't so good after all. This was wrong, that could have been better, one whole roll—surely the best we'd shot—was lightstruck and useless. I relayed the message to my mates.

"Tell him to stuff it," said Doug. "If the film's no good, what's the use anyway? Let's up anchor and go home."

I told Verity that Con and I would stay on if we got the pay raise but Doug wanted to leave. Verity was ready for that one. We had always assumed that Verity's spies were limited to the filming end of the business; apparently that wasn't so—his ears were everywhere. It seemed he knew more about Doug's love life than our skipper did.

Grudgingly, he agreed to give us the raise, and we ended up staying in the islands for nearly a year.

Verity had already chartered a forty-foot ketch to bring us film and food and become our new home afloat. Doug could leave when she arrived.

A month later, when *Tropic Bird* sailed into Academy Bay, she carried a scorching letter from Verity. We'd put a gun to his head with our demand; we'd unfairly put him on the spot. From the tone of that letter, I figured my career with Walt Disney Studios was over.

Doug was ready to get going. He'd already hired a deck hand, and we'd barely transferred our gear from one boat to the other when Doug was off. No freighter from Panama to California this time—he made a beeline for home.

After sailing to the Galápagos, cruising through those lonely and dangerous islands for six months, Doug then sailed all the way back to California, where he found his girlfriend still loved him after all. It was a sad irony that one night shortly after he'd arrived home, while the *High-*

lander lay peacefully on her mooring in Newport Harbor, Doug fell overboard and drowned. His inability to swim—and a crate of empty beer bottles on the boat—were the only clues.

* * * * *

Our life became easier when we moved aboard the *Tropic Bird.* She arrived with a crew of three, bringing us to five aboard. Pat Miner, the skipper's wife, performed miracles in the galley. We had made our own music aboard the *Highlander* and ashore at the port of Academy Bay where the Angermeyer brothers and their wives and children played accordion, harmonica, and guitars. I wasn't a musician, but I surprised myself by making music with a pair of spoons. I was the rhythm section.

Now we had our skipper's collection of tapes and 78-rpm records from which to choose. Still, all the technology of the *Tropic Bird* never equalled the pleasures of our homemade music, pounded out under the stars on Carl Angermeyer's stone terrace to an audience of bright-eyed iguanas.

* * * * *

It was dusk when we felt our way into the shallow bay that was to be our last anchorage in the Galápagos and put down our ground tackle. The rattle of chain in the hawse startled three herons on the rocks, and they flapped slowly away across the water. Stretched around us in a jagged curve was a black and green shore of lava and mangroves. On the point that arced out to form the cove, white beaches lay between black lava outcroppings and the surf broke over the reefs that gave the place its name, *Espinosa*—spiny, dangerous. We had come here to film the herds of giant marine iguanas that crowded the rocks so densely that they occupied every available inch of space.

For us, Espinosa was not an unfriendly anchorage.

Conrad and I set out, rowing our little eight-foot skiff through a white-walled corridor of breakers toward the mouth of a pass. At the end of the surf-rimmed channel lay a calm pool edged by a wall of low mangroves.

Swells, like moving foothills sweeping up to mountains, rolled in from the sea and rose high on the seaward side of the reef. They swept over the rocks, climbing toward us as we rowed, white tops hissing in the bright sunshine. Paralleling the combers, we pulled into the center of a narrow valley between surging hills. A wave rolled in, foaming, tumbling forward as it gathered itself behind. It seemed certain to overwhelm us, but it didn't break. Then it lost its breath and flattened out, lifted us on its smooth crest, rose again and hurled itself into a crash and smother of foam at our other side. Spray blew back against our faces in a cool mist.

As each wave swept in from the sea it looked larger than the one just past. Each time we wondered: will this one break across our channel? If a wave broke across the outside reef and came on rolling white, we, along with our camera gear, would be overwhelmed, flung into the churning sea and and battered against the jutting rocks to our lee. But each wave spared us, and we rowed giddily with drunken immunity down our path between the wild combers.

Beyond the reefs we entered a still pool. Ahead lay a wall of leaves and twisted mangrove trunks. We drifted, carried by the backwash. I leaned over and peered into the water. A school of spotted rays the size of throw rugs slid past us. They dipped away in unison like a formation of motorless aircraft and were gone.

Three sleeping turtles, looking like overturned wheelbarrows, floated on the pond. We bumped into one as the current carried us past. It raised its head in panic and awkwardly tilted its shell to dive. Once below the surface, the turtle gracefully glided to the bottom and looked up as we went by.

At first we noticed one fin, then many. On our right two fins cut the water side by side. All around us now, in pairs, in threes, in fives, the fins knifed through the still surface. The sharks seemed to materialize from nowhere. Many were longer than our skiff. They simply appeared, coming to the surface from where they had been lying in the ooze.

Our boat seemed to attract them. They swam to us and rubbed their backs along its bottom. Perhaps the sharks were merely curious, but we didn't drag our feet.

We pulled to the wall of mangroves and with machetes cut a channel through the tangle. Above the high-tide line, using a tarp stretched between mangroves and the shattered part from a wrecked tuna clipper's launch, we built a rude shelter. It was a secret place, hidden all around by leaves and the dank roots of the grove.

At night we slept aboard the ketch, rowing back to the boat in our skiff, leaving our cameras in the makeshift shelter so they wouldn't be endangered by the many runs to and from the boat and shore. Every morning we rowed into the cellar coolness of our canal through the mangroves, pulling ourselves around corners, ducking low limbs, leaves brushing our faces as we glided toward our mooring place. From there it was only a short walk down the trail we had cut out of the foliage. The slanting limbs all angled one way, so when looking down the path it seemed that one must walk bent over. A dozen big iguanas lay in our path. We nearly stepped on them before they crunched away through the dry leaves. Then we arrived at the rocky point where we would spend the morning filming penguins, flightless cormorants, herds of marine lizards, sea lions, crabs, the whole menagerie.

Then we returned to our camp for lunch. I waded out with a machete and cut an armload of mangrove roots encrusted with oysters which we pried open and ate raw.

On this trip, in each other's faces on a tiny yacht for nearly a year, as stressful a living condition as can be imagined—literally, "rub-adub-dub, three men in a tub"—Conrad and I cemented a bond that remained deep and strong until Con's death in 2003.

Here in this camp was the summation of my purpose; here was everything for which I had come to the Galápagos. Built of broken boards and flotsam from the sea, our camp was beautiful. Its secrecy, the crooked trail, the land hermit crabs that shuttled past rattling in their shells, the mockingbird that sat like a tamed companion on my toe, the sharks gliding in patrol out in the bay, the snorting of the lizards on the point, the frigate birds wheeling across the sky—these were for me everything in the world.

Through the spaces between the mangrove limbs I could see the white coral sand, brilliant in the sun, the black lava, and the green water of the shoals and the blue of deep water beyond. I saw the clouds roll over the peaks of Isabella Island across the canal, the lines of creaming breakers, the ketch at anchor out in the bay. I watched a hawk that circled low, calling; the heron that stood, watching—all the satisfaction of a good camp.

We sat sweating in the shade, filming and swatting flies.

7

Running Target

Our Galápagos footage was featured in the October 1954 opening segment of a new ABC television series called *The Wonderful World of Disney* and sequences in *True Life Adventures* featurettes called *Islands of the Sea* and *Secrets of Life*. Erwin Verity seemed to have forgotten what he thought of as my stab in the back, as the subject of our demand for a raise in pay was never mentioned again.

Conrad decided that he wanted to hang closer to the Hollywood mainstream, whereas I was happy in my niche as a wildlife filmmaker. I took a couple of other Disney assignments and Con did some more "stock footage" shows while pushing different buttons trying to break into the cameraman's union.

Meanwhile, the great adventure of filming in the Galápagos did little for us in the way of career advancement. We decided that the answer to crashing Hollywood would be to produce our own feature film. Other independents were doing it, why not Canyon Films? Youthful naivete propelled us to the edge of our capabilities, beyond anything we could imagine.

When we had considered sailing on our own in a small boat to remote islands far out in the Pacific, we eased our apprehensions by telling ourselves, "It's easy to sail one whole day from dawn 'til dark without getting into trouble, right? Well, all the way to the Galápagos is just sailing one day after another. *No problema.*"

Now we talked ourselves into the impossible dream that producing a feature film with little experience and empty pockets was much the same thing—just jump the hurdles as they came day by day.

The first roadblock was obvious even to us. It was unlikely that any studio or distributor would finance the first movie of three greenhorns from film school. The fact that we'd shot some footage for Disney didn't help: in the crazy way of Tinseltown, our experience was viewed by the old guard as a stigma. We'd shot our film in the amateur format—16mm wasn't up to Hollywood standards. Sure, Disney had used 16mm in the successful feature, *The Living Desert,* but that had been a specialized kind of movie that nobody else was interested in producing.

Then Marv read a short story called *My Brother Down There* in the annual Martha Foley collection *Best Short Stories of 1954*. We all agreed that this story should become our first movie. *My Brother Down There* was about a modern-day posse, six characters of diverse personality and motive chasing down three escaped convicts in the Colorado Rockies. The grabber was that one of the men on the lam was a better woodsman, a more likeable person, and probably more caring as a human being, than any of those in the posse hunting him.

First we needed to option the story. The writer, Steve Frazee, was accomplished in the western genre and had recently sold his novel *Many Rivers to Cross* to MGM, where it had been made into a big movie starring Robert Taylor, Eleanor Parker, Victor McLaglen, and James Arness. We knew that Frazee's price would be far more than we could afford, but we got in touch with him anyway. To our surprise he seemed intrigued by the chutzpa of three kids trying to break into the business and he went along with us. Beyond the small option payment we offered him, the only condition Steve put on the deal was that we shoot the movie near his home in Salida, Colorado, because he thought it might make for an amusing summer to have a movie company in his backyard.

In 1955, Ben Maddow, an established screenwriter (*The Asphalt Jungle, Intruder in the Dust, The Unforgiven)* was deeply (and unjustly) engraved on the Hollywood blacklist and so we could afford him to polish our draft of the screenplay. Ben apparently didn't resent this act of shameless exploitation, since he became one of my best friends.

When we sent the script off to Frazee for his comments. He mentioned in passing that because of our option, he'd just had to turn down a bid on the story from MGM. We had no idea what the big studio had offered but were sure it was many times more than we'd agreed to pay. The fact that the author didn't make a big deal out of this hard knock was one more thing that endeared me to Steve Frazee.

A young production manager with a couple of pictures behind him came aboard to help us with a schedule and budget. Bobby Justman (later the production manager on the *Star Trek* TV series) figured that if the partners of Canyon Films took no pay, the movie could be made for $150,000. In these days of profligate budgets, that doesn't seem like much for a 35mm color feature with a cast of nine main players, horses, and a remote location. But back then it looked to us like a king's ransom. Where was Louie with his ton of gold now when we needed him? Probably sitting it out in Leavenworth.

We went to Conrad's father's movie agent for advice. Ben Benjamin was in charge of the literary department at Famous Artists Agency, but he also had some high-powered acting clients—Burt Lancaster, Lee Remick, and Jacqueline Bisset were a part of his stable, as the expression goes—and he seemed to know everyone in the business. Ben was one of the most highly regarded agents in town, honest and gentlemanly. Nobody ever said an unkind word about him. He gave us some tips and said that if we actually got the movie made and it was as good as our script, he'd try to help sell it. But he confirmed our suspicion that no studio would be interested in financing us. He couldn't help us over our first hurdle.

It was a frustrating time. We had a good script but no money with which to take the next step.

In the meantime, to keep the homefires burning we took a job from a producer of educational films. The project involved editing some footage on lettuce farming. We wondered what kind of schools would place that subject in their curriculum? But the producer sold enough copies that he came back a few months later and asked us to edit his new title, *Celery Farmers.* We figured that his lettuce farming clientele must extend to celery and hoped his new film was a winner.

Finding no joy at conventional movie financing offices, we realized that there was only one way to get our feature into production: raise the dollars from private sources. That meant asking friends and family for help. My dad came in for $5000; for a railroad freight agent that was a lot of money. A cousin found $2000, another cousin (I had a lot of cousins) bought in for $500—and that's the way it went. Conrad's brother-in-law, Nick Rutgers, was at loose ends and thought it might be fun to spend the summer with a movie crew in Colorado. If Nick hadn't had a rich and generous mother we never would have made our debut feature. But he did, and she unselfishly footed the biggest share of our budget.

With money in the bank, Con, Marv, and I drew straws for the three main jobs. Conrad got the one he wanted: cameraman. Marv got the one he wanted: director. My good luck failed and I pulled the short straw: producer.

* * * * *

A few months prior to our brainstorm to make our own feature, the three members of Canyon Films had been involved in a project of another kind. We'd been attending meetings with a group of like-minded cinema graduates and film technicians who were working underground, crewing on the rare non-union films being made in this highly unionized industry.

We couldn't get into the cameraman's union because of its closed-shop policy. Covertly making nature films under Disney's thumb was one thing; shooting real Hollywood features was quite another. So we decided to form our own union.

All over America the branch unions, from the giant Teamsters and Auto Workers to the small Makeup Artists and Dog Trainers, were affiliated with one of the two largest union alliances in the country the American Federation of Labor and the Congress of Industrial Organizations—AFL and CIO. (At the time they were competitive organizations; nowadays they are amalgamated.) All Hollywood crafts, including the camera local, were associated with the AFL.

The CIO had some contracts with television but no foothold in the motion picture industry. We wondered if they'd be interested in supporting a core group of film technicians who wanted to establish a competitive motion picture union. We made a few phone calls and wrote a couple of letters to CIO headquarters. They replied with more than mere interest. They were eager to get into this lucrative industry, and a professional organizer was assigned to help us get started. We called our group the Film Craftsmen's Guild—later changed to the Association of Film Craftsmen—and we actually got a CIO charter. Today the group is called NABET—National Association of Broadcast Employees and Technicians—and it's a properly functioning union, now mainly in the television business, with hundreds of active members.

At the time we created the union, our selling point to encourage producers to hire us rather than AFL film technicians was that our members would work in multiple functions. Producers had been complaining for years that AFL film crews were so stuck in their roles that they wouldn't lift a finger to help out in any other specialty than the craft to which they belonged. No producer liked to see his drivers, whom he was paying for a full day's work, drive to the location in the morning and then sit around all day playing dominoes until it was time to drive home. Employers felt that it shouldn't be beneath a driver's ethic to stir his butt during the day and help out when equipment was being moved or when an electrician needed a hand pulling a cable. But that wasn't the way it worked. Drivers drove, and only drove; grips handled reflectors and wouldn't touch a light stand.

In the FCG, we did it differently—no featherbedding. We doubled in brass and as a result a producer only needed to hire half the crew. Trouble was, during those years of strong union controls AFL projectionist members of the cameraman's union could simply call in sick if the film they were to screen didn't display the seal that proved it had been made by an AFL union crew. So who was going to screen a CIO feature movie, if one ever got made?

* * * * *

As we prepared to produce our own feature film, we saw the conflict looming long before it hit us. As founders of the Film Craftsmen's Guild, our buddies naturally expected us to employ them on the first FCG Hollywood feature. And of course that idealistic concept had been our original aim.

On the other hand, we'd just raised $150,000 from our friends and families. Was it fair to them to put all of that money into jeopardy on the chance that we would make a decent film and then couldn't get it into theaters? We were caught in an ethical dilemma that had only one resolution.

As the newly-chosen producer of our film-to-be, it fell into my lap to inform my friends and brothers in the FCG that they wouldn't be employed on our film, and that we would be making it with an IATSE (AFL) crew, the despised "other side" " in this war of rival unions. To say that our former "brothers" were disappointed would be a gross understatement.

With that unpleasant chore behind us, and in the doing having acquired the status of pariahs—for we received in effect dishonorable discharges from the union we had so conscientiously helped to found—we moved on. It was a disturbing lesson in how yesterday's conscience can be reshaped by today's reality.

We had given up our principles and sacrificed our souls, but it didn't get us any closer to using our chosen cameraman. Conrad wasn't an IATSE union member. That became our next battle.

Congress had just passed a law called The Taft-Hartley Act. The factor in this law that was relevant to us was that no employer could be barred by a union from hiring any qualified person he wanted to hire. If a union required employers holding a union contract to hire only union members, and the employer wanted to hire some nonunion person, then the union was required to take that person into the fold. But it was a blind alley. What reasonable producer would face off with the powerful labor alliance over the hiring of one film crew member? Even with the law behind him, he'd be confronting the inevitable wrath of a vengeful union.

As the producer—the hiring body—it was my duty to be one of the first, if not the first, film producer to use the Taft-Hartley Act to force the issue. It was my job to face the formidable Herbert Aller, the hard-nosed business manager of the IATSE cameraman's local, and tell him that I intended to hire Conrad Hall—a non-member—for my picture. If he didn't like it he could damned well just let Con join his exclusive club.

On the afternoon of my meeting in Herb Aller's inner sanctum, Aller sat at his desk. Looming over him was his even more formidable interference: union secretary, organizer, enforcer, and ex-football great Doyle Nave, who stood 6'6" and weighed in at 250 pounds—all muscle and brawn.

They had an idea of what was coming as I had to let my mission be known in order to arrange the audience. But when I stated my case, Herb Aller's cheeks turned pink and his eyes blazed red. Herb's first words came out with the ferocity of one who was used to having young men bow and scrape for the favor of admission into his fiefdom. He wasn't used to people who took a defiant stance. He'd never, but never, had a young man speak to him in this office before with any voice of authority.

"You fuckin' punk...." He began. "You think you can come in here and shove that Taft-Hartley crap up my ass?"

Doyle Nave, a cooler mind, interceded, "Look," he said, "maybe we should all sit down and talk about this. I'm sure we can work something out."

Aller was gasping for breath. I thought he might pass out as I told him that our production company had signed the IATSE union basic agreement. Therefore, Conrad, our chosen cameraman, was required to become a IATSE member. According to the new federal law, I was entitled to make the demand that the union accept Conrad, and Aller was obligated to accept.

At the end of the day, Aller agreed to conciliatory terms, and though they were hardly ideal, they broke the ice for a whole new way of doing business.

One: Aller would let Conrad join the union but in the lowest rank—as a film loader.

Two: We had to hire a "legitimate" director of photography from the union ranks. Conrad would be allowed to assist or offer suggestions on location in whatever way the two could work it out between themselves. (Director of Photography Lester Shore got the job. He let Con adopt the highbrow-sounding but meaningless screen credit of "Cinematographic Consultant.")

Three: After the film was completed, Conrad could remain a union member but he'd have to go through an apprenticeship and up the ladder like everyone else. There was just no way Herb Aller was going to let a new kid start at the top rung.

Four: Aller's last condition was the ringer. When Con and I had returned from our long sojourn in the Galápagos, we both wore beards. I'd shaved mine off; Con decided that he liked the look of his. In fact, the neatly-trimmed article on his chin gave him a distinguished aura. But Herb Aller didn't like it at all.

"You can tell your friend that he's got to shave off that high-falutin beard," Aller said. "He looks more like a D.P. (Director of Photography) than a bottom-of-the-heap film loader. He can't strut around on one of my sets lookin' like what he ain't."

That was the deal that got Conrad Hall into Local 659, the Hollywood cameraman's union. He moved up the ranks in record time. His beard stayed shaved off only until it grew back in. He became the youngest-ever director of photography. During his long career he would be nominated for ten Academy Awards, and he won three—for *Butch Cassidy and the Sundance Kid, American Beauty,* and *Road to Perdition,* which he won posthumously. He also received another 21 wins and 19 nominations for other awards.

* * * * *

We had a lot of ideas about casting *My Brother Down There,* which had by then been retitled *Summer Game* and would later be released as *Running Target.* Common sense told us that with the kind of money we could offer we could forget about stars. Still, with an exception or two, we did assemble a wonderful cast. Our first choice for the sympathetic young sheriff who'd lead this party of legal manhunters into the mountains was James Whitmore, already well-established as a character actor and thus beyond our means. But we tried for him anyway. He read the script and said he liked it. But when we met at his agent's office I had the feeling that Whitmore didn't fancy putting himself into the hands of such inexperienced filmmakers. He said he didn't think he was right for the part—the nice way of saying "no"—and suggested Arthur Franz, who had just appeared in *The Sniper,* his first leading role. Franz had portrayed the sniper of the title, a homicidal killer—so the sympathetic part we offered would be a nice turnaround for him. Arthur took it.

We'd seen black-haired Doris Dowling, with her hard cheekbones and sultry eyes, in *Bitter Rice.* When an agent suggested her for the role of the tough but libidinous female posse member, we agreed.

There were four more members of the posse to be cast. For the sharpshooting manhunter who carried a magnificent sporting rifle with a telescope sight we cast a well-known character heavy named Murvyn Vye. Nick Rutgers, whose mother had put up most of the money for the budget, would play the convict who set the tone of the movie by getting picked off with a long rifle shot in the opening sequence. Nick's debut acting performance consisted of throwing up his arms, rolling down a long grassy hill, and lying dead at the bottom, and he did it splendidly.

Three other convicts—two baddies and a goody—completed our cast.

We rented a cottage motel in Salida, Colorado, and the forty-five members of the cast and crew moved in on the first Sunday of July, 1956. On Monday, we started filming in the colorful ruins of an abandoned mine on a secluded hillside an hour's jeep ride into the mountains.

The first shot was in the can shortly after the sun hit the ridges at nine A.M. At nine-fifteen a Caterpillar tractor about a half a mile across the canyon fired up its engine. Sound mixer Jack Solomon took off his earphones and announced, "That's it! Kill the tractor or we're out of business."

From our side of the canyon we could nearly hit the tractor driver on the head with a well-thrown stone. But to get from our location to the tractor's was half an hour's drive down to the mouth of the canyon and then another half an hour back up the other side.

Bobby Justman piled into a Jeep and tore out. The rest of us turned our attention to some silent scenes that could just as well have been shot with a second unit.

An hour later, the clatter of steel against stone and the bellows of exhaust echoing through the canyon came to a stop. We looked across to see the Jeep parked beside the tractor. Bobby stood on the ground talking up to the man in the driver's seat. Negotiations were underway. But soon the tractor started up again and resumed shoving boulders off the ledge. Big rocks bounded down the hillside and crashed into the bottom of the canyon.

Then Bobby was again running alongside the tractor, waving his arms and shouting. Once more the tractor paused, engine thrumming; more discussion took place. At last the engine coughed and stopped and a wonderful silence fell on the wilderness.

"Buying" the tractor for the day was our first dip into the "contingencies" line item in our budget, but it was far from the most expensive element of the first day's shoot.

That evening, back at the motel, The Three Musketeers and Bobby Justman held a production meeting. We didn't know whether Murvyn Vye was just getting into his role as a tough guy or if he was always as ill-tempered as he'd been all day. He'd argued every directing point with Marv, stalked around in a funk, fought with other members of the cast, and told me to "screw off!" when I'd tried to reason with him. We didn't know what to do. But it was obvious that we couldn't go on like this every day.

Justman thought Vye was suffering from stage jitters and would be easier to get along with as time went by. But the next day was the same. The third day started out even worse.

I drove into Salida during our lunch break and placed a call Murvyn's agent in Beverly Hills. I explained the situation.

"God Is he behaving like that again?" said the agent. On hearing those words, I knew we were cooked.

"What do you mean, *again*?" I asked.

"Look, Murvyn just came out of Atascadero State Hospital after treatment for a nervous breakdown. It sounds as if he may be having a relapse."

"Well, we can't go on like this," I said.

"If it's as bad as that," Vye's agent said, "of course I won't hold you to our contract. That is, if you have to let him go...."

"Jesus," I said. "He's been in every scene so far. That's three days of production down the drain."

The agent's silent reply was like a giant shrug. Then he said, "Look, Jack, when you tell him, be careful. He can be sort of, like, well you know...violent. I mean when he hears something he doesn't like."

That evening I knocked at Murvyn's bungalow.

"Come!" bellowed a voice from inside.

I opened the door and was met with a bizarre scene.

Vye sat on the edge of the bed, stark naked, very hairy, illuminated only by the light of a TV screen, staring at the set with the sound up loud. *Very* loud.

"Can we talk?" I shouted over the TV.

Murvyn didn't look away from the screen or touch a knob.

"Sure, talk," he said.

I was uneasy, first because I wasn't used to having a business conversation with a hairy naked man, second because I had to shout to be heard over the TV, and third because I was afraid that when I told him what I was going to tell him he was going to come after me and that great hairy body was going to try to strangle me in a gorilla's chokehold.

"Murvyn," I yelled. "I'm afraid this isn't going to work out."

"I know," he said. "I figured. Gimme a ticket to New York and a car to the airport and I'm outta here in the morning. Okay?"

That was it. No blood. No sweat.

During the production meeting that followed, Bobby Justman was all for throwing in the towel. Vye had been in every scene we'd shot so far. Bobby figured that with the schedule he'd made, which accounted for every hour of production time and was already "iffy," that by starting all over again three days behind schedule—with a big hole in our cast and without ideas about who would fill it—we couldn't complete the show for the money we had. If we canceled everything and went home, Bobby figured, we'd lose less than $10,000. If we didn't cancel now, we'd lose it all.

But The Three Musketeers wouldn't listen. Murvyn Vye wasn't going to put us out of business. We tossed aside Bobby's advice and the next day wiped out one posse member by recasting one of them from a small to a big role. Richard Reeves made an instant change from good guy to bad guy, became our sharpshooter, and we restarted our production. When the first day of shooting began we were already three days behind schedule.

Considering everything else that happened during the production, we were lucky. After taking up residence in Arthur Franz's cottage following their first love scene, Doris got in a tiff with Arthur during the last week of shooting and walked off the movie. We wrote her out of one scene and shot her last sequence with Franz having a conversation with her boots. The editor laid in Doris's off-screen dialogue from a wild track. With innovations like that we made up the three lost days and completed the shoot on schedule.

The best our agent Ben Benjamin could do for us was a flat sale of all rights to United Artists. It didn't take much snooping for them to find out how much money we had invested in the picture, and good guys that they were, they let us off the hook for a cool $150,000. This benevolent payment (with Ben Benjamin foregoing a commission) allowed us to recoup our investment but not make a penny.

We paid back all of our investors at par. At least nobody got hurt, least of all United Artists. *Running Target* was a modestly successful theatrical release in 1956 and became a television standard for years to come. By buying into a finished picture at low cost, facing no risk of a failed production, UA made out like bandits.

The message to us was, never use your own money—a wise insight I was destined to brush aside more than once in the future. Too bad we don't always live by the hard lessons that experience teaches us.

The Eagle Boy

From the day I walked into Slavko Vorkapich's cinema studies class at USC, I'd been blessed to fall under the influence of some of the most creative people in Hollywood. As all such relationships develop, one person led to another, and soon I found myself surrounded by a group of congenial friends who shared a variety of skills and the same professionalism. From the small clique of The Three Musketeers, I'd become a part of broader family of equally likable personalities, a chain linked by likeminded friends and filmmakers.

I never met director Milos Forman, and I hadn't yet heard his meaningful words: "Hollywood doesn't exist. Behind every door in Hollywood is a different Hollywood. It all depends on which door you open at which time." Without knowing it, I simply lucked into knocking on the right doors at the right time.

Joseph Strick was a kid my age who had the urge to make his own movies—along with half the rest of the inhabitants of Hollywood. Like most of us, Joe started at the bottom, shooting short films showing the glories of small towns as perceived by different Chambers of Commerce. The company was called Home Town Movies. Does that tell you anything?

But everybody has to make a buck, and Joe never forgot his passion to direct quality movies. Then he met a successful screenwriter who had a yen to dabble in documentaries. His name was Ben Maddow, who had helped us Musketeers with polishing the script for our first feature, *Running Target.*

Ben told Joe that if he wanted to become a filmmaker the best way to learn was to go out and shoot some film on a subject of his choice. It was the same obvious yet profound message that Ben Sharpsteen had given to me during my first meeting at Disney Studios. I'd picked trap-door spiders. The subject of Joe's first step into the self-taught school of film was very different.

With a war surplus combat camera—a 35mm Eyemo—and some black-and-white stock, Joe chose as his subject a hangout of bodybuilding enthusiasts on Santa Monica Beach. Strick mounted his camera in an old suitcase with a little window for the lens to look out through and another little window with a mirror viewfinder on top. After a few weeks of sitting around on beach benches holding his suitcase on his lap, occasionally glancing down into the hole to make sure he had it pointed in the right direction, Joe built up a long row of exposed film cans in his closet. He knew his footage had a unique perspective but he needed help in putting it together as a coherent film.

He took his footage to Irving Lerner, and our chain of fellowship acquired another link. The Lerner-Strick collaboration turned Joe's vision into the zany spoof *Muscle Beach*, a romp of huffing, puffing bodies told entirely with picture, song, and lyrics.

Strick's next plunge into the world of the documentary was a collaboration with Ben Maddow in 1960. It was called *The Savage Eye,* and the story was conceived as a modern-day look at Los Angeles as it would have been seen through the eyes of 18th-Century British artist William Hogarth. He had looked upon London as a seamy underworld of vice, prostitutes, and shady characters—sound like Los Angeles? It did to Joe and Ben.

A young cameraman named Haskell Wexler—another link about to be clipped into my chain of film associates—had just moved to California, where he hoped to crash the union barrier. *The Savage Eye* was to be shot off-the-cuff whenever one of the producers happened to be available, and Joe asked Haskell and me to trade off in the cameraman's role to fit their schedules. Joe wanted a gritty style for a daring movie, and we gave it to him with black-and-white film and natural illumination as we found it in seedy skid row locations.

I mention this film because it was the first step of my long walk in the movie business with Joseph Strick, the most helpful producer any filmmaker could hope to have. Later, as a director himself (*Ulysses, Portrait of the Artist as a Young Man, Tropic of Cancer*), Joe understood the problems a director faces from the proper perspective and was always supportive, whereas some producers are so wrapped up in money issues all they see are the number of script pages shot per day, dollars spent on overtime, and financial spread sheets.

I also mention this movie because of an embarrassing incident during the filming that I'll never live down, so it might as well be made public as a part of the record of many failures among a few successes.

To help us find dramatic episodes to include in *The Savage Eye*, we'd had our car radios re-tuned to receive police calls. It was a little job that any good radio repair man could render, surprisingly simple when one considers its possible benefits to a criminal. Joe had the idea that if we patrolled skid row in the wee hours, maybe we could catch some authentic police action as it happened. (Remember, this was the seamy side we were out to film.) Joe wanted it coarse, sordid, and nasty—in short, Hogarthian.

When the radio call came that would beget my immortality according to Joe, we were closer to the crime scene than the nearest police cruiser. "Code three," the radio said. "Man with a gun. Robbie's bar. Fifth and Main."

We were at First and Main when we picked up the call. Joe was driving, Ben Maddow was beside him in the front seat. A cop assigned to keep us out of trouble sat in the back seat and I was beside the cop with the camera in my lap. Driving nearly within the legal speed limit, we soon came up behind a police car creeping along with its red lights flashing and siren howling. (That's what "code three" meant—red light and siren.) Not wishing to pass the emergency vehicle on its way to an emergency, we followed behind at reduced speed. After a couple of blocks we realized that our poky leader was taking us on a course directly toward Robbie's Bar.

"What the hell's going on?" Joe asked while glancing at his speedometer. "Twenty miles an hour with red light shining and siren shrieking?"

"Man with a gun call," our mentor cop replied. "Doesn't want to be the first to get there."

In spite of our turtle-paced approach, adrenaline was pumping fast as we pulled to a halt in front of Robbie's Bar. I was ready. I dashed out and raced ahead of the cops, who had pulled to a slow stop just ahead of us. They were still disengaging themselves from their car as I edged into the bar.

Inside, a couple of burly patrons had disarmed the gunman and were doing their best to hold him. The gunman was fighting furiously, shouting curses, and creating a wild scene of violent action. I switched on my newsman's camera light and started filming.

The cops looked in behind me, saw that the situation was safe, rushed forward, pushed the heroes aside, grabbed the guy and began working him over with their nightsticks. The would-be murderer fought back, but with a cop on each side he got nowhere. The policemen frogmarched him, kicking and yelling, toward the door. Then the guy saw me filming. The sight of my camera seemed to flip a switch in his brain. Infuriated by my presence, shouting profanities, he lunged at me as they went by. He kicked at my legs and swung at me with his fist. It glanced off my shoulder and barely missed my chin. The cops gave him another couple of belts and his reaction was to shout louder curses at me as they dragged him toward the door.

Still with the viewfinder glued to my eye, I followed them onto the street where the criminal braced himself with spread legs wedged across the patrol car's open door. He wasn't going anywhere in that cop car without a fight. The cops had to soften him up a bit more with their nightsticks before they could shove him in. Then they pulled away with a squeal of tires as other police cars screeched around corners and swerved to a stop in front of the bar.

I dove into our car and flopped down behind Ben and Joe. "Great stuff!" Joe yelped. "Finally, after a week!"

I checked the footage counter. Damn! I'd shot so much on our crawling approach that I'd run out of film on the perp's first swing. "Yeah," I said. "Wouldabeen, if I'd had some film in the camera."

* * * * *

Haskell and I eventually got other tough action for Strick's film, and somehow Joe had the heart to forgive me that most unforgivable of cameraman's blunders. He went on to produce several films I directed, including *Ring of Bright Water* and *The Darwin Adventure*—a personal favorite but a film that hardly anyone one has seen.

* * * * *

The first movie Joe produced for me was a documentary called *The Legend of the Boy and the Eagle.* With that, we now take a step backward by a link in the chain of film-making friendships.

In 1958, Disney producer Jim Algar hired Swiss cameraman-director Ernst Heiniger to make a movie about the Grand Canyon. It was a project of which my university mentor, Slavko Vorkapich, would have heartily approved: Ernst was using only the symphonic composition *The Grand Canyon Suite* by Ferde Grofé as his inspiration.

By this time I'd been working steadily for Disney on tv shows for eight years, usually with a crew of only seven or eight, some of the shows taking six months to complete, sometimes working on two or three shows simultaneously. And I also did some second unit shooting for Disney on features like *Big Red*, the story of an Irish setter with Walter Pidgeon starring. But I wasn't a staff member and got none of the benefits staff members enjoyed. I was still an independent producer and had to negotiate a new contract for every show I did.

One day Ernst Heiniger called me from Arizona. "Jack," he said, "I'm stuck with shooting a series of beautiful postcards of the Grand Canyon—the weather, the clouds, the river, the atmosphere. It's all gorgeous, but dead. I've got to get some life into it. The place is full of wildlife—but it's wildlife you don't see. I need some help with the animals."

I rounded up some tame specimens representative of Grand Canyon wildlife from friends, trainers, even a roadside zoo, and a week later I met Ernst with a car and trailer filled with a family of cougars, a bobcat, and a coyote. We met at a remote area on the north rim where we could work without bother from the tourist crowds who made such a circus of the usual canyon overlooks.

A golden eagle and the man who owned her, a friend from my commercial fishing days named Ed Durden, came a few days later. Ed had one of the most remarkable relationships between a man and an animal I've ever known. More of that later. Ed worked as an aerial spotter for the fishing fleet out of Santa Barbara, California. He flew mostly at night, locating schools of fish and directing the seiners when and where to drop their nets. For his services he took a share of the catch just like the crewmen on the boats.

Ed had been fascinated by the big birds all of his flying life, and he frequently encountered them high in the sky. He found that he could sometimes ease his plane over close and fly formation with an eagle for awhile.

During one flight he spotted a nest in the top of a tree, got a permit from the Fish and Wildlife Service, and returned with a climbing rope to take an eaglet. He named her Lady, and when she was ten years old, Ed bought a house on the ridge above Santa Barbara with a view of the Pacific Ocean and the Channel Islands one way, and the Santa Ynez

Valley the other. He moved his family there solely because this was a perfect eagle's eerie and he knew it would make Lady happy.

Every nesting season of her adulthood, Lady produced a pair of eggs. They were infertile, of course, but Ed didn't want to deprive Lady of the satisfaction of motherhood. He always replaced her clutch with fertile eggs of about the same size and color, usually those of a barnyard goose which Lady carefully incubated.

Baby geese fall into the category that ornithologists call "precocious." They are up and ready to go practically at the moment of hatching, whereas eagle chicks are nestbound for many weeks and take a lot of feeding and brooding by their parents before they are ready to leave the nest. The difference of behaviors was perplexing for Lady, who behaved toward these odd little hatchlings as instinct told her.

Ed would put out a pan of mash and a bowl of water as soon as the goslings hatched, and Lady coped as best she could. The scurrying little goslings imprinted on Lady and thought she was their real mother, so between soggy meals of mash they also nibbled the tidbits of meat she pulled off a chunk and daintily handed to them from the tip of her beak.

It was Ed Durden and his eagle, Lady, who helped Ernst Heiniger and me bring life to Ernst's images of *The Grand Canyon* and make it an Academy Award winner in 1959.

I had prepared a large cage at the edge of the canyon to house Lady and protect her at night from possible predators. During the day until she was in front of the camera she was happy wearing her jesses (leather anklets and leash) and perched on a block under the pines.

To fly Lady over the vast spaces of the Grand Canyon presented some risk. It was winter, not eagle nesting season, so there was no chance of wild eagles attacking her, but it was unfamiliar territory, a strong gust of wind could quickly carry her miles away, she could get lost, or something else unexpected could happen. After giving her a few days to get accustomed to the area, Heiniger felt we were wasting time. He was hyper-anxious to begin filming, and he was not an animal person, not sensitive to their special needs.

"Let's set up some portraits just to get started," he said. "She doesn't even have to fly. Just perch her on that tree limb with the canyon in the background and I can shoot some beautiful close-ups."

Ever one to please, Ed had no objection. He brought Lady to the limb on his gloved fist.

Lady settled, shuffled her feathers, stretched, and looked wonderful.

Heiniger set up his camera and rolled some film.

I suppose Heiniger, who had an outstanding career as a cameraman, had shot with animals before—dogs, cats, horses, who knows? But he had little conception of the edginess even tame wild animals can often have. As his camera rolled, Heineger began making quick little gestures and odd squeaks and grunts with the idea of getting Lady to react with interested looks and attitudes. In this he succeeded very well. She cocked her head cutely, stared hard, zeroed in. It tickled Heiniger and encouraged him to make more odd gestures and noises.

I looked at Ed and saw that he was uneasy.

I nodded and Ed stepped between Heiniger and Lady. Heiniger looked away from his viewfinder crossly.

"She doesn't like that," Ed said. "I can do things to help you get you those attitudes, but with you being a stranger, it's not a good idea for you to do it. Make her an enemy, and we've got a problem."

Heiniger laughed and brushed-off Ed's concern. "It's okay," he said. "It was just getting good. Did you see that intense look in her eyes? Just a few more shots and I'll have enough."

"That intense look is exactly what I'm talking about," Ed said. "She's suspicious of you."

Heiniger made a dismissive gesture and went back to his camera and funny noises.

Ed shrugged.

The next day when Ed removed the jesses and Lady was to take her first flight over the Grand Canyon, she soared straight overhead. She hovered up there for a moment, and she had an angry look in her eye. Ed was prepared for it. He stood behind Heiniger with a straw broom in his hand. Lady came down like a bullet, wings half-folded for speed, talons extended and aimed at Heiniger's head.

Only the broom saved him.

While Lady was climbing for her next attack, Heiniger ran for his car and closed the door.

Up until this time, Heiniger had been almost jealously possessive of his camera. He didn't want me to touch it. I couldn't even help him carry a tripod.

But Lady wouldn't allow him to shoot another foot of film. Hereafter, I was Lady's cameraman.

That night when we lay in our tents a violent thunderstorm flashed and crashed over the canyon. Thousands of waterfalls were pouring over the cliffs. Lightening made a nearly constant glow. Over the percussive almost continuous explosions of thunder I heard a wild sound and stuck my head out of the tent flap.

There at the edge of the precipice, with his arms spread wide to the heavens and toes over the void, Heiniger was dancing in the pouring rain, shouting with exhilaration, daring the bolts, defying frustration. By making himself the perfect target, Heiniger was challenging the world.

* * * * *

Such was the history of my relationship with Ed Durden and Lady seven years later when I accepted a Disney contract to produce a pair of TV films in Arizona. One of the hour-long shows was about a Navajo sheepherder who lost his dog and trained a coyote to do the job. The other was about an old prospector who found an orphaned pronghorn antelope fawn and raised it to return as a young adult to its herd.

Shortly after I arrived in Sedona to set up the productions, my friend, White Bear Fredricks, came down from his home at the Hopi pueblo of Oraibi with some sketches and a story he thought would make a good movie. I'd met White Bear through an old Glendale High School pal, Bill Beaver. Beaver (the name was Scottish, not Native American) was as absorbed in Indians as I'd been in natural history, and every year, the day after school was out for the summer holiday, Beaver was on a Greyhound bus bound for the Hopi reservation where he had been adopted by a family in the pueblo village of Shungopavi. A couple of winters Beaver brought a Hopi "brother" home to Glendale with him where he attended classes with us. Later, Beaver married a Navaho girl, has a dozen Navajo sons, daughters, and granchildren, and still owns and runs Sacred Mountain Trading Post on Highway 89 south of Tuba City.

White Bear's story came from the oral history of the Hopi. The tale was of an orphaned boy of twelve named Tutuvina who lived in the pueblo of Wupatki a thousand years ago. Tutuvina resided with his uncle, who was the religious leader of Wupatki. Like everyone else in the village, the boy wore a necklace of blue turquoise nuggets, the symbol of village membership.

In those times, men from every Hopi village took an eaglet from a nest in the spring and raised it to adulthood. Golden eagles have always been sacred to the Hopi, who believe that the magnificent birds have the power to communicate with the gods. In the old days, the eagles were sacraficed to the gods. Golden eagles are now protected by federal and state laws. But to accommodate Indians of all tribes to whom eagles are sacred, the carcasses of eagles that have been killed by collisions with wires, wind generators, illegal shooting, cars, all other things that kill eagles, are impounded by the U.S. Fish and Wildlife Service where they are kept frozen, and the carcases and feathers are available to Native Americans for religious ceremonies. (USFWS application form: "Because of the large demand and limited supply, qualified applicants can expect to wait up to four years for an eagle carcass and there are now over 3000 people on the waiting list for the approximately 1,500 eagles received at the repository every year.")

The summer solstice is that day of the year when the sun reaches the end of its journey to the north and turns around and starts south again. The solstice is a time of determination, a day in which, according to Hopi belief, everything that is to happen in the coming year is set in motion. On the night of solstice, the sacred eagle that has been raised for this purpose is sacrificed in a holy ceremony. Downy feathers plucked from the eagle carry messages on the wind to faraway gods.

As the legend goes, Tutuvina was awarded the important duty of raising the eaglet. He devoted himself to the job, and the other boys in the village were envious. Why had Tutuvina been chosen? Why not Crawling Wolf, the leader of the village gang?

As time went on, Tutuvina spent more and more time with the young eagle. His uncle saw what was happening and told the boy, "Take care of the eagle. Feed her well. But to fall in love with the eagle will only bring you grief."

But Tutuvina couldn't help himself. The eagle seemed to have a power over him.

On the night when the men put on their *kachina* masks and came to take the eagle to kill her, Tutuvina went ahead of them to the rooftop where the bird was tethered and untied her. She flew away.

As punishment for this grievous act, which put the whole village into jeopardy, Tutuvina was tried by the elders. His turquoise necklace was snatched from his neck and he was sentenced to be banned from the village for a year. Everyone knew that a boy alone in the wilderness could not survive and that it was a sentence of death.

None of the elders of Wupatki even turned their heads when the boys who had been jealous of Tutuvina chased him out of the village with a barrage of stones.

Tutuvina wandered in the wilderness for many days. His food ran out. He found a few berries. Even water was scarce. Finally, he collapsed in the desert.

But the eagle had been following and watching from high in the sky. When vultures landed beside Tutuvina and picked at his ears, the eagle dove down and drove them away. Tutuvina regained consciousness, and the eagle guided him to water.

Then she led him to her nest where he lived with the great bird. In the months that followed, the eagle taught Tutuvina how to hunt, how to spot game and stalk it. She taught Tutuvina all the secrets of the eagle people.

When a year had passed, Tutuvina returned to the village of Wupatki.

The people were shocked when he came back. They couldn't believe he had survived alone.

When he told them that he had lived with the eagle and had learned the eagle's magic, the boys laughed and taunted him. Tutuvina tried to show the bullying gang the secrets the eagle had taught him, but in their jealousy they refused to listen.

One day the boys grabbed Tutuvina and held him down. They tied eagle feathers to his arms. They cinched the rawhide tightly so the feather shafts dug deeply into his flesh. "You pretend to have learned from the eagles," they taunted. "Try these feathers for wings. If you know all the eagle's secrets, let's see you fly."

During the scuffle, Tutuvina snatched Crawling Wolf's string of turquoise and put it around his own neck. With that, the boys chased him, throwing stones. To escape, Tutuvina climbed to the top of tall pillar of stone.

With his toes over the edge, Tutuvina looked down on his tormentors. He spread his arms with their skimpy fringe of feathers. He flapped his arms like wings, and laughed at them.

They yelled and threw more stones. Then Tutuvina launched himself into space. As Tutuvina fell on his outstretched arms, his friend the eagle swooped down out of the sun and flew beside him.

They soared away together. And even today, it is said, an eagle is sometimes seen flying over the peaks and wearing a necklace of blue turquoise nuggets.

Since that day, every year, an eagle dance is held in Hopi villages in memory of Tutuvina and how he became one of the eagle people.

* * * * *

My first challenge in filming the story of Tutuvina and the eagle was obtaining Hopi tribal sanction to make the movie. I needed it not only to get the cooperation of my native American cast but also because it was the right thing to do. The Hopi Tribe was divided between traditional and modern political factions. I needed the support of both, and they seldom agreed on anything.

Approval hung in the balance. White Bear used his influence as respected tribal leader, and I attended several meetings to put our case before the Tribal Council. One of the long-hairs from the traditional side had qualms about letting an Anglo outsider like me get so close to tribal tradition. I respected the old man and his skepticism. If I were in his place I would have had the same doubts.

But White Bear was an important voice among the Hopi, and the Council respected his authority. White Bear had recently helped author Frank Waters write a thick volume, *The Book of the Hopi*, which was acknowledged to be the bible of Hopi religion and lore. Now he was engaged in a study of the ancient pictographs which were found engraved in rocks throughout the Southwest.

When I had been exploring the Arizona back country in my old Jeep, I'd once driven far off the beaten track into a wild canyon and blundered onto a huge trove of prehistoric symbols pecked into the stone. When I told White Bear about it, he was anxious to see the place.

On our way back from a Hopi council meeting, I took a long detour and drove him there. In an alcove of huge boulders of the type whose exterior is covered with a thin natural coating known as desert varnish, which when chipped away revealed a lighter colored rock underneath, were hundreds of beautifully preserved pictographs. White Bear was overwhelmed and found all sorts of meanings in the symbols chipped into stone.

As I drove him back through the desert to his home at old Oraibi, I noticed White Bear staring at a point high in the sky.

"Stop!" he said. I hit the brakes.

"That cloud," he said. "Look at it."

I gazed into the clear blue Arizona sky.

"Cloud?" I said. "What cloud?"

"Exactly my point," he said. "Now you see it, now you don't."

We sat staring into the empty blue. Then White Bear said, "There." He pointed. "Close to the sun. Don't you see it?"

There it was: a single white dot, small but clear.

"Watch it," White Bear said. "It comes and goes. Have you ever seen such a thing?"

As I watched, the cloud materialized into an opaque shape. Penny-sized, it hung there, then began to fade again.

I looked at White Bear. His face was full of awe.

"What is it?" I asked. "What's happening?"

The white dot came and went again.

"I don't know," he said. "But something's going on." He looked at me. "I want to go home. Hurry."

I left him at his traditional stone house in Oraibi. With its first dwellings built sometime around A.D. 1000, the Hopi village of Oraibi was said to be the oldest continuously-occupied town in America. White Bear said goodbye and hurried into the dusk without looking back.

The next word I heard from him was that we had been granted permission by the Tribal Council to make our film. White Bear's explanation was that the cloud we had seen had also been observed by others. It was a signal from the zenith. (The Hopi recognize six cardinal directions rather than the four we go by—North, South, East, West, the Zenith—straight overhead, and The Nadir—underground—straight down.)

The little cloud was a response to questions asked by the Hopi elders. It appeared and reappeared in synchrony with questions as a high priest asked them. The message from the cloud was that all was well, that I could be trusted to interpret the Hopi way.

It was the only time in my life that I had a cloud—or whatever it was the cloud represented—speaking for me.

* * * * *

I spent the next week visiting all of the day schools on the Hopi reservation, looking for a boy to play the part of Tutuvina. I sat in the back of each classroom, listening and watching. I was looking at physical appearance, demeanor, intelligence, and self-confidence, as there would be nothing else to show me how good an actor the boy might be. Eventually I cast an engaging twelve-year-old named Stanford Lomakema, from the day school in the village of Shungopavi, as the eagle boy. Stanford spent the summer of 1966 filming with us, living with White Bear and his wife Naiomi in Sedona.

The little white cloud was watching over me again that day. I couldn't have found a better person—Stanford *was* Tutuvina.

* * * * *

While we were filming *The Boy and the Eagle,* Ed Durden obtained a federal permit to remove a golden eagle egg from a wild nest. Lady, Ed's eagle, then hatched it. And when the fluffy white eaglet was a week old, Ed left Santa Barbara in his Luscomb airplane with Lady on a perch in the back seat and the downy eagle chick in a box. His ETA in Sedona was "around two P.M." We took the afternoon off and waited for him at the film compound out in the pinon-and-juniper hills south of the town.

Several hours later Ed's little plane appeared without a sound. He'd cut the engine to idle and was gliding down toward us out of the sun. As he passed overhead all we could hear was the wind through the struts. He had the door open and was looking down at us with a big smile. Then he shouted, "Send a taxi to the airport!"

That arrival was typical of Ed and his disdain for high tech. Ed always said that he flew "by the seat of his pants."

We had prepared for Lady and her chick's arrival by building a nest with a cage around it on a scenic overlook called Bell Rock. One panel of the cage was hinged to drop open so that Lady could fly freely to and from the nest.

From the summit all one could see was red sandstone cliffs and outcroppings with groves of pinon and juniper in the lowlands. An eagle could fly in circles around the promontory, camera following, and no harsh angle or obtrusive color of house or man-made construction could be seen—just mile after mile of spectacular wilderness.

Lady settled onto the nest as if she'd built it herself. She'd already adopted the chick she'd hatched as her own. The cage around the nest had been built as protection for Lady, not to keep her in—she would never abandon the baby—but to keep roving predators out.

This arrangement had a secondary benefit to us as filmmakers. In ordinary circumstances, a captive bird of prey could only be flown according to the conventions of falconry; that is, flown to a lure, tempted by food not to fly away. A falconer could fly a bird only when it was "sharp" or hungry. Once the motivation of hunger was exhausted, the bird couldn't be flown until it was hungry again. This would limit our photography to three or four flights every other day—a huge constraint on a movie production schedule.

From her nest on the summit, Lady could be flown all day every day without any fear that she'd grow weary of performing in the film business and take off for parts unknown. With her baby in the nest, Lady was as committed as if she had a notarized contract or a string on her foot.

I'd chosen Bell Rock for Lady's nest not only because of its beautiful view. But there was another factor that also influenced my decision: we needed to avoid setting up our area of operations within the nesting territory of a pair of wild eagles.

Golden eagles are secretive during the nesting months; you can be living on the same block and never get a clue that they are next-door neighbors. In view of this, I'd spent a few days hanging around Bell Rock with my binoculars before making a final decision about the location. I'd seen eagles a couple of times, but only from far away. I thought we were well outside the nearest wild eagle's territory.

How wrong I was....

We kept the side of Lady's cage closed for a couple of days while she settled into her new home. On the third day, Ed opened the door, Lady stepped to the edge, had a look around, and took off. She seemed to enjoy exercising her wings again. She soared around, gaining altitude, and then sailed out in lazy circles.

Suddenly, from high above, diving like a fighter jet out of the blue, another eagle came at her. Its attack from above and behind was as unexpected by Lady as it was by us, and she didn't see or sense its coming until it was almost too late.

Ed yelled, trying to warn her. "Lady! Look out! Behind you!" Of course it was useless. Lady was a part of Ed's family, but she couldn't understand English.

At the last moment Lady sensed, or heard, or saw, the other eagle coming—and reacted just in time. In midair she flipped upside-down and aimed her talons toward the attacker. The wild bird had only two choices—swerve away or be pierced by Lady's claws.

The wild eagle swooped up to get above Lady and gain the advantage for another dive. It came at her once more like a torpedo. But now Lady knew she was under attack and was ready; again she flipped over to meet the bird with her talons.

We all stood beside the nest on the summit watching this incredible battle. After four or five stoops and repulses, Lady began edging her way back toward the safety of her cage. Finally she made a break and flew straight and fast for the nest. Although we all stood conspicuously on the mountain peak, the attacker stayed right on her tail until it came within fifty feet of our production team. I've never heard of a wild golden eagle coming so close to humans.

Only then, when Lady was back in her cage, did the wild eagle veer and soar away. It had made a very determined statement: the eagle was defending its territory. There was a wild nest somewhere nearby.

That night we held a production meeting. It was clear that if Lady was attacked every time she flew, we couldn't proceed with filming in this area. She could easily be killed. This meant we'd have only footage of eagle combat—material for an exciting sequence, but not what was needed to complete the story.

Even if we wanted to act against our personal feelings and trap or shoot the native bird, that possible solution was eliminated by the law. We had two options left: carry on, or move our location.

Moving wasn't practical. Although I'd chosen this spot as the best location, and we could certainly find another place to build a cage, the problem was Forest Service red tape. It had already taken two months of negotiation to get our permit to build this nest and its protective cage. Another two months for another permit at another location was not possible.

Our eagle chick was growing fast. We were committed to shooting now. Hoping that the eagles would settle their own affair without our intrusion, Ed opened Lady's door another time. I was ready with a camera to film the expected dogfight.

One would assume that a wild eagle would excel over a captive-reared bird in the kind of aerial acrobatics we were witnessing. But this was not the case at all. Lady had been raised with a diet rich in vitamins, calcium, and the roughage required by birds of prey, and she had never been confined to a cage for long periods. Ed had exercised her regularly, and during the months each year when she was rearing goslings she flew at liberty. Perhaps as a result of her healthy upbringing, she was superior on the wing to her wild counterpart. At least that's the way it seemed to us.

A nesting behavior seen in many kinds of birds is called the "territorial advantage." Close to its nest, a bird of a given species and of equal physical strength has the drive and power to push away an intruding bird of the same species. The invader lacks the fierce psychological imperative of the "owner" and retreats under the stronger motivation of the nesting bird. But as the "owner" gets further from its nest and deeper into the territory of its neighbor, its drive and power diminishes. Then the situation reverses and bird number two takes over the territorial advantage. A balance occurs which normally keeps territorial birds occupying adjacent territories from hurting each other.

But here we had a man-made situation. The nests were only a mile apart. Lady and the wild bird had the same strong drive, but there was no space between them for a no man's land where nature's rules of warfare made a harmless balance. The "territorial advantage" did not apply. With two nests lying inside the critical zone, the fight could easily end in the death of one of the combatants.

The second time Lady flew, she emerged with a tentative searching of the sky. Again, the wild eagle attacked her and chased her right into the cage door. Lady's antagonists never flew more than one at a time, and it appeared to be the smaller male who was the more belligerent of Lady's enemies.

The situation was really too dangerous to repeat, but Ed thought he might have an answer. The wild bird was exceptional in that under the stress of the situation he had no fear of humans. He came very close to us during the heat of the chase. But if someone fired a gun when he was near, maybe the frightening blast would put him off.

Ed stood beside the nest with a shotgun under his arm as he released Lady. The flight followed the same pattern as before. Again the wild bird came near enough to make an easy target. It would have been simple to solve the problem by executing him, but this wasn't our intention.

Ed raised his shotgun and fired.

The blast from close range did teach the wild eagle a lesson. The next time the birds engaged, the wild male didn't come closer than half a mile from Bell Rock. The shotgun solution hadn't solved our problem at all; it only created a new one: from then on, we had the same fierce dogfights—but they took place at a greater distance.

By now we had located the wild nest. It was high on the cliff of Courthouse Rock, less than a mile south of Bell Rock. We could look across the valley with a telescope and see the female on a pile of sticks, apparently brooding eggs, as she spent most of her time on the ledge. Now she never joined the fray.

In the meantime we had work to do with the other two films on our schedule. We had a baby pronghorn that was growing up and had to be filmed at different stages of growth. We also had a litter of coyote pups that kept us busy for the same reason.

Ed was getting desperate. He decided to let Lady fly one more time in the hope that the wild male would decide that he'd made his point and lay off. If the male attacked again, we'd just have to move Lady's nest to another location.

Thinking it likely that the wild eagle would win his case, I found a site to build an alternative nest on private property where no Forest Service permit would be necessary. The background wasn't as photogenic and the changeover would set us back, but we could make it work. On what would be the last release unless the wild eagle relented, I set up a camera again to film the dogfight for the third time.

This time when Ed opened the door, Lady left the nest in a different mood. She took off more aggressively than before. She didn't pause at the threshold with any reservations this time.

Was she at last exercising her own territorial advantage? She flew straight out, and the male left the ledge on Courthouse Rock and flew toward her. Right away the two birds began spiralling up, each trying to gain the advantage of height above the other. Up, up, they went, until we could barely see them even with binoculars. They disappeared and reappeared, into and out of puffy clouds in the blue sky.

Clearly this was a different ball game.

"Keep them in sight if you can," Ed said. "I'm going for my plane. Give me a radio shout when I get back."

Soon we saw Ed's Luscomb climb toward us. The plane nosed up toward where we'd last seen the birds.

"They were headed due east," I told Ed as he flew overhead. "Higher than you are now, clear up above the clouds."

"Roger," he said.

A few minutes later, Ed came back on the air. "I've got them in sight," he said. "We're way over above Clear Creek, and they aren't stopping. Strong tail wind up here. I'm doing one-ten ground speed just to keep up with them."

Ed lost the birds in the clouds over the Mogollon Rim nearly fifty miles to the east. He came back worried and distraught. The disappearance of the bird that had been so much a part of his life worried him like the absence of a lost child. Ed hand-fed Lady's chick at sunset. We waited at the foot of Bell Rock, scanning the sky to the east until dark.

Ed was back at the nest at dawn. He waited all day, pacing and nervous, watching the sky. Still nothing. Another night went by. Another dawn came.

At noon on the third day of Lady's absence, we saw a dot in the high sky approaching from the east. The dot became an eagle soaring toward the valley from the direction where the two combatants had disappeared. It could be Lady, it could be the wild male returning to the nest, or it could be a wild bird "traveler." The eagle flew past Courthouse Rock and headed toward Bell Rock. It was Lady. She flew straight to the nest and landed beside her chick.

Now the truly remarkable part of this story became clear. Lady was hurt. She had talon gashes in her breast, but they weren't life-threatening. Most amazing of all, she was carrying a load of long cactus spines stuck deeply into her flesh. It looked as if she'd crashed straight into a clump of cholla.

Ed wrapped a blanket around Lady's wings to make her defenseless. Then he held her on the ground between his knees and pulled out the spines with pliers. She was furious throughout the half hour of this fight, screaming and trying to bite and claw Ed. But when he let her up, Lady forgave him immediately, as she always did when he performed the similar stressful procedure of trimming her beak and claws.

Lady didn't want to let her outrage focus on Ed. No, she took me as the scapegoat, aimed her talons, flew at me, and drove me into my car.

It was clear that the birds had clutched each other in midair and had fallen together to the ground where the battle had been concluded. Lady quickly recovered from her ordeal. The wild eagle never returned.

The wild female successfully fledged her two young eagles, and we completed our filming at Bell Rock without another incident of aerial combat.

* * * * *

I'd hoped that Irving Lerner would edit my eagle movie, and was disappointed that he was tied up with another project. Fortunately I found a substitute. A sound editor named Verna Fields was working as Irving's apprentice and accepted my offer to edit the film. With Lerner dropping in from time to time to look over our shoulders, Verna took on the task of sorting through the footage and making a film out of my raw material.

I've found that working with a talented editor when everything is cooking can be the most satisfying and enjoyable aspect of filmmaking. Seeing the movie come together from a collection of shots, without the daily frustrations and compromises of shooting, is for me sheer joy. When sitting in the editing room with a talent such as Irving Lerner or Verna Fields, a director can watch his material take on surprising new dimensions.

Verna not only made my footage coherent, she added new perspectives. Film is such a malleable substance, and I'm always astounded by the way a story's meaning can be changed completely by the simple rearrangement of a few shots. The editing phase of filmmaking sometimes gets short shrift, but it's as important as any other creative responsibility in the filmmaking process.

Joe Strick and I shopped our finished film during a difficult time for documentaries. They were out of style, nobody wanted them for theaters, and television was sour on the form. I was fairly sure Disney would buy it—the show fit into the format of their television programming and they were about the only people doing this kind of documentary at the time—but I knew if we could get a deal from another distributor the terms would be better. We tried everywhere, but nobody bit.

As a last resort, I showed the film to my friend Cardon Walker, who was the vice president in charge of operations at Disney. Card said it was the best thing of its type he'd seen. He called it imaginative, beautiful, inspirational—all those things I wanted to hear. With every new word of praise I saw more dollars being added to our profit. When Card made his offer, it was five times the money we had put into it—not as much as we'd hoped for, but the best we could get. We accepted.

Then my old nemesis Erwin Verity got into the act.

I made no bones about the fact that we'd moonlighted this movie at the same time we'd been shooting the two Disney shows in Arizona. But my company had contracted to make the Disney shows. I wasn't an employee with a requirement to put in eight hours a day for Disney. There was no exclusivity.

In a way, I'd taken advantage of the arrangement that Disney had made to exploit the non-union setup they enjoyed. But somehow Verity felt this was crooked. He didn't want my act of piracy, as he fancied it, to establish any precedents among his corps of handcuffed field producers. He tried to attribute Disney resources to my production, but I'd taken special care to protect us against that. Everything had been on the up-and-up, and there was no way Verity could scratch that itch.

Verity found out that we'd shopped the movie all over town and that Disney was our course of last resort. Somehow he came up with the precise amount we had in the show. Card's offer was withdrawn. Verity revised the numbers. Good friend that he was, he allowed us to break even.

If we'd held onto the picture for a few years, until documentaries went into another cycle of acceptance, we'd have done better. But who was to know then of the coming great wave of popularity enjoyed by nature documentaries? We made a flat sale, no participations. Joe got his money back. Through a contract clause that paid a bonus if the show went into theatrical release, my crew ended up making good wages for the time they'd invested.

With that sale, the project went out of my hands and animation director Ham Lusk was assigned to bring it down to television length. In 1967 Disney released it as a theatrical featurette and as a one-hour TV segment for their NBC series.

One aspect of the Disney edit was a curious irony. The use of tape splices by film editors, later the industry standard, was a new development at the time. The Disney editor wasn't familiar with the tape splices Verna had used, and before he'd touch the picture he ordered his assistant to go through our work print, cut out all the tape splices, and re-splice everything with the old hot-splicer system. This meant an automatic loss of four frames for every one of Verna's carefully considered cuts. In some fast action sequences, this meant all the difference.

Verna went on to bigger and better things. In the early 1970s she was at Universal helping a young new director complete a film that was having editorial problems. The man was Steven Spielberg, and the movie was *Jaws.* Steven was so grateful for Verna's help that he was instrumental in getting her one of the first high-level women's executive positions in Hollywood—as head of production at Universal Pictures.

The Legend of the Boy and the Eagle achieved some of the highest ratings ever for the Disney television series. When Lou Debney, who was in charge of scheduling, needed to boost the ratings or start off a new season with high marks, he always ran either *The Legend of the Boy and the Eagle* or *A Country Coyote Goes Hollywood*, one of my shows about the wild coyotes that live precariously on the edges of the city. It's something of a spoof with Rex Allen giving an often ironic narration. According to Lou, whenever Disney TV ratings began to sag, a rerun of *The Legend of the Boy and the Eagle* always brought the ratings back to the top.

* * * * *

Back at the beginning, I'd asked Stanford Lomakema to let his shiny black hair grow long for the part, in the way the Hopi wore their hair in the old days. When he returned to school in the fall, Stanford kept his long hair. His classmates laughed and teased him and called him a girl—just as the toughs of the movie had taunted the eagle boy.

But when the movie came out, it wasn't long before most of the boys in Hopiland were wearing Stanford's long locks. Thus began a trend, a part of the rising pride in the old ways.

The little white cloud's prophecy had been on the mark.

Home afloat during university years, *Kuuipo*, played the leading role in our movie, *Sea Theme*. We won the coveted ASC student film award, sold our class exercise to TV, and became motion picture entrepreneurs while still in film school.

Joan Couffer—two sweethearts (*Kuuipo*, the name of our boat, means sweetheart). In our sailing twosome the surprise view of any passersby was of a pretty girl all alone and commanding a salty schooner. I was below deck after a day on the fishing banks, sleeping off a dawn appointment with a tuna.

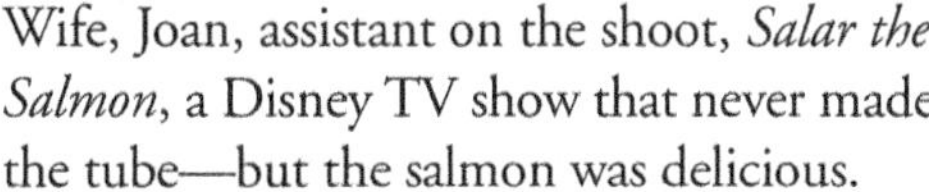

Wife, Joan, assistant on the shoot, *Salar the Salmon*, a Disney TV show that never made the tube—but the salmon was delicious.

Jean Allison, 1952, *Edge of Fury*, The first feature film for both Jean, actor, and Jack, Cameraman.

Jean Allison strived to be the best and studied with Sanford Meisner's New York Neighborhood Playhouse. Unlike the usual story of aspiring girls who flock to Hollywood, hang around for a few years, and then go home disappointed, Jean scored quickly and appeared in most of the popular TV series of the time.

My first step into the movie business was to film an unusual main character. Trap door spiders aren't your everyday actor, but for me they "opened the door" in more ways than one. It takes less than half a second for this species to feel the vibrations of approaching prey, throw open the door, grab, and disappear.

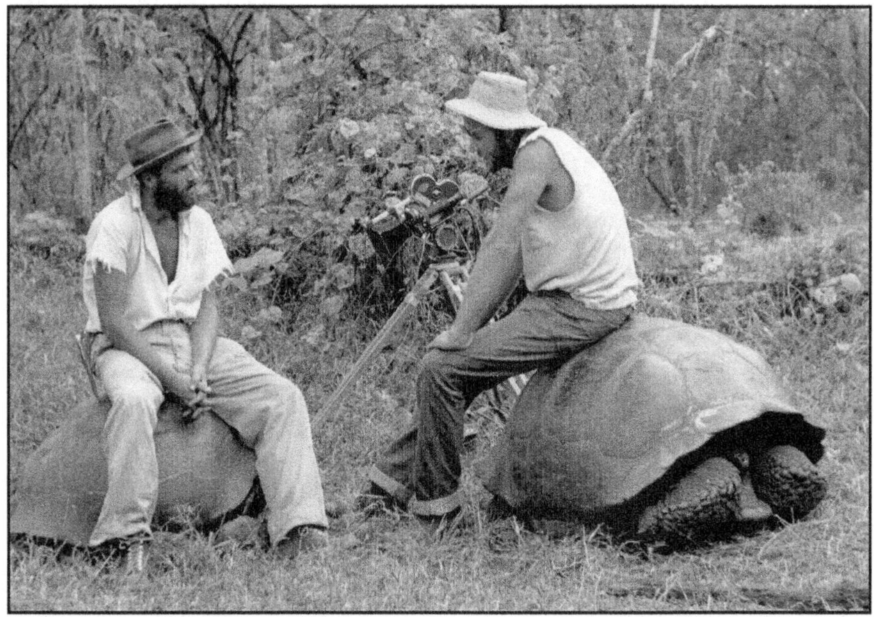

Jack (*right*) and Conrad Hall (*left*). Our year in the Galápagos Islands on a Disney assignment was one of the great adventures in our lives. (photo by Gus Angermeyer)

Highlander off Kicker Rock in the Galápagos. Life aboard a twenty-eight foot ketch was "rub-a-dub-dub, three men in a tub." When we changed over to a forty-footer, it felt like we had moved into a palace.

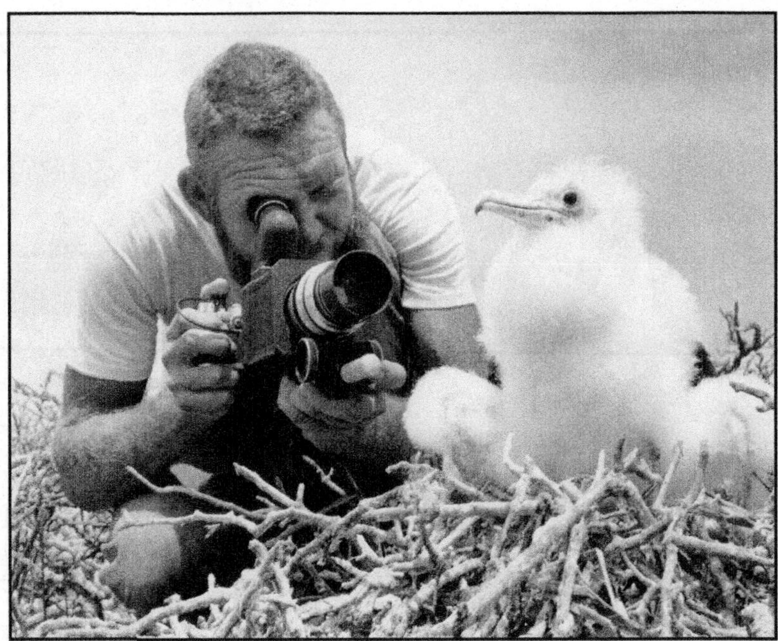

My beard came off when I got home. Conrad wore his for the rest of his life. (photo by Conrad Hall)

Conrad Hall. The white coraline coating the rocks was exposed by a huge undersea land upheaval. Our discovery of this event changed the charts of the Galápagos. The area has become a scientific benchmark for core studies on tectonic shifts and an important calendar to geologic changes.

Carl Angermeyer tamed a herd of marine iguanas like these that lived on his sheet metal roof. When they all moved overhead it sounded like an iron foundry at full production. That's me in the background. (photo by Conrad Hall)

We heard a "Mayday" distress call from the tuna clipper MV Queen Mary on the rocks a hundred miles away and set out on a rescue mission. After her desperate crew had managed to refloat her, we met the ship as she ran toward Panama for repairs. Drifting together in mid-sea we were hosted to a "thank you" celebration. Noting my lack, the captain took off his shoes and handed them to me.

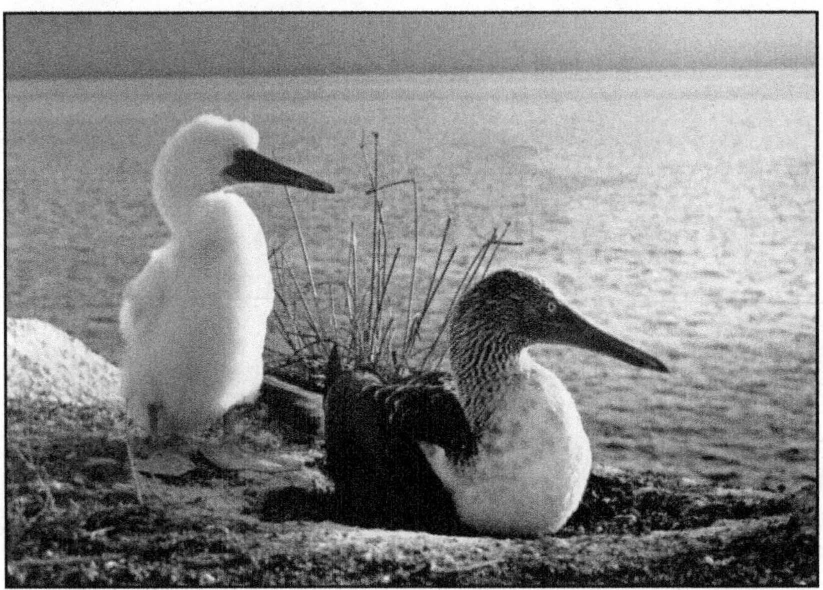

Blue-footed boobies—I can imagine the chick is saying: "Mama, someday will you take me there?"

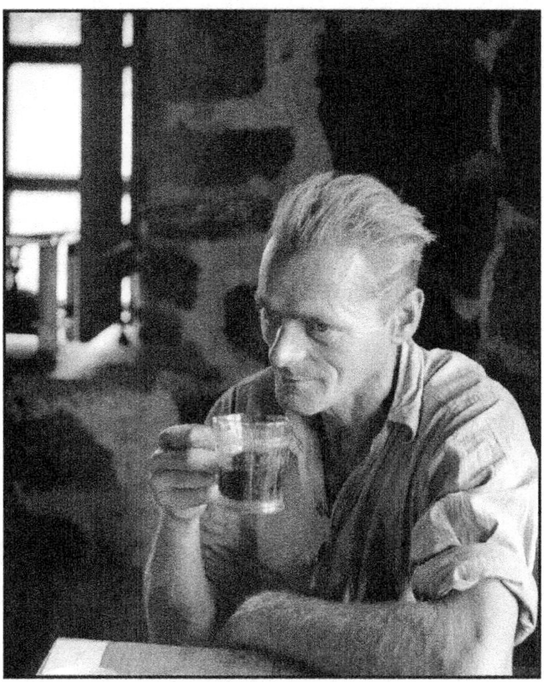

As a World War II commando Sandy had been a ruthless killing machine. Now a beachcomber, he wanted us to take him to the island of the "X" on his secret treasure map. Our problem—what if he finds the gold?

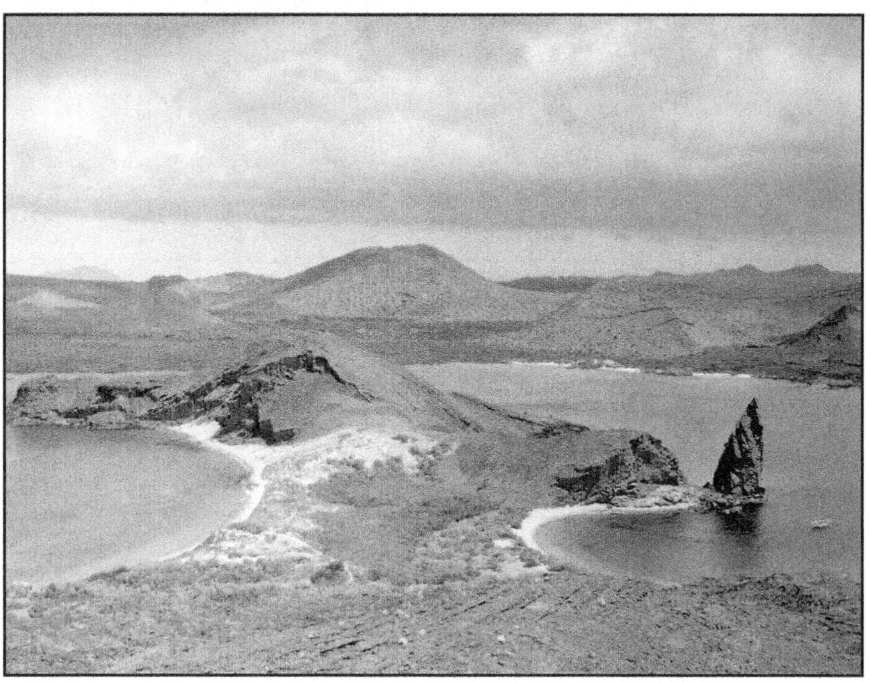

Sullivan Bay, named for Darwin's friend aboard the HMS Beagle. The buccaneers who preyed on South American ports came here to hide out and recondition their ships—and maybe to bury their gold.

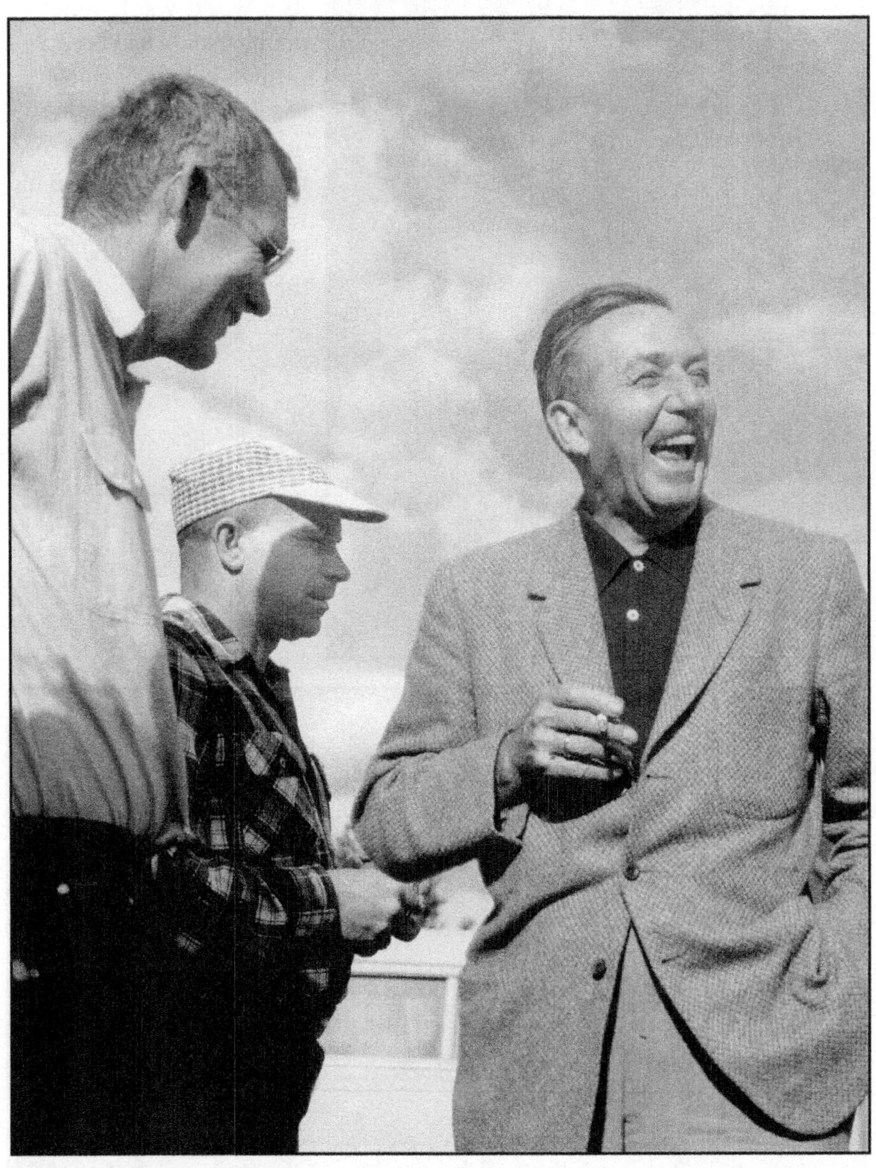

When Walt Disney visited us in Canada he brought enough questions for a quiz show. But Lloyd Beebe and I sent him home to Burbank with a big smile. (Photo by Bill Bacon)

Nikki, Wild Dog of the North—the malamute sled dog that grew up with a wild bear, but finally found his best friend was a man.

The Legend of the Boy and the Eagle told of a Hopi boy who committed the sin of falling in love with the tribe's sacrificial eagle. For his crime of releasing the bird, Tutuvina was banished to die in the wilderness. But the boy was saved and adopted by an eagle, who taught him all her secrets. The legend is sustained in pueblo villages every year by the eagle dance.

Cape Hallet, Antarctica. As a Disney correspondent, I held Navy officer's status with all its privileges—a far cry from my prior military caste as a dogface. A lesson from the Captain's table was that even persons of high station are really just the same as the rest of us—merely other small birds wearing the same feathers.

Without the animals, the Disney film *The Grand Canyon* was only beautiful postcards. The wildlife brought it life and an Academy Award.

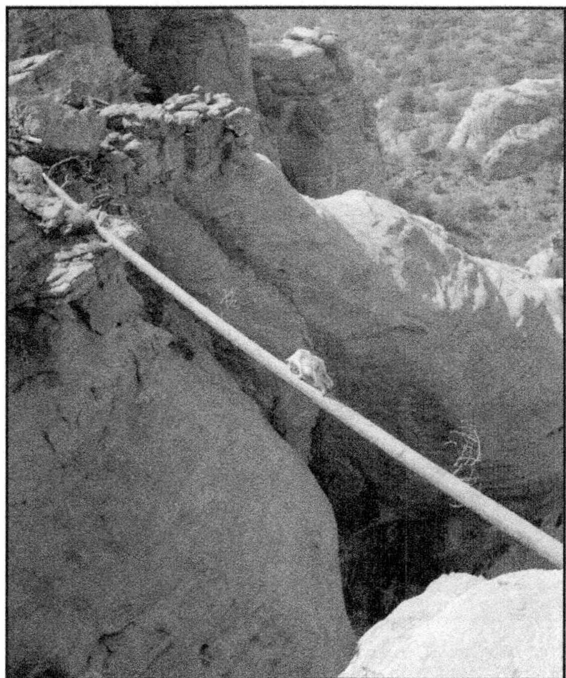

Animals don't write screenplays, but in the movie, *The Legend of Lobo,* Lobo suggested an important script change by showing his talent for traversing narrow footways. The wolf was allowed to cross the high "toothpick" only after proving its safety by walking a hundred times across a similar log mounted on low saw-horses. The training problem was slowing down his trot—he made it look too easy.

Although wolves closely resemble some breeds of dogs, dogs are separated from their wild kin by thousands of generations of domesticity. Wolves still retain wild traits and do not respond to classic dog obedience training.

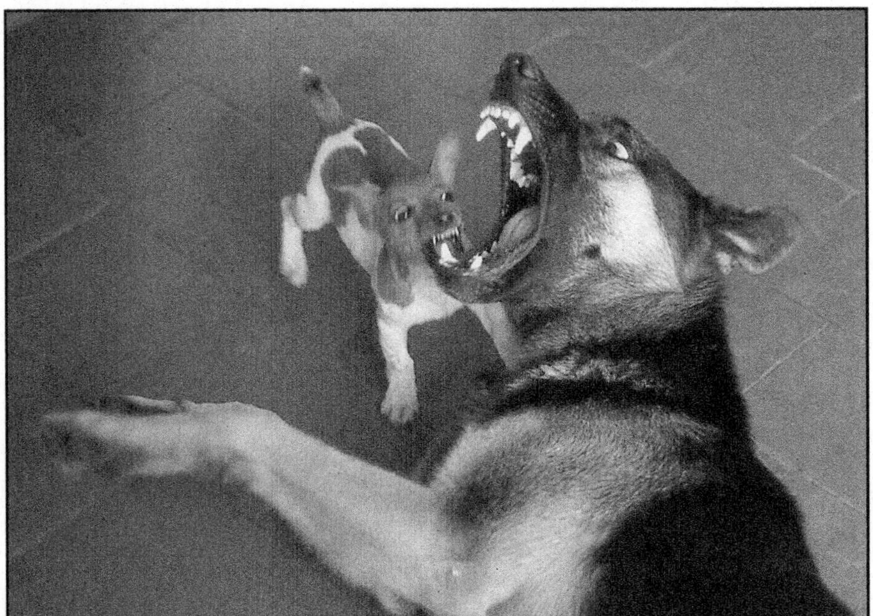

To film fighting animals, it's often best to catch them at energetic play and later add the sounds of growls and snarls.

Two sequels were made following the original *The Incredible Journey*, but neither one attained the popularity of the first. Could it be that the talking animals of the sequels took the edge off reality and spoiled the concept?

Mij had the cheerful personality of a happy otter. He was never out of sorts and ever ready for a romp. But Mij always wanted the last word of a scene—the rather charming "What? What? What?" vociferation that Bill Travers played off of to make it seem he was having a two-way conversation with an otter.

I've said uncomplimentary things about the character of an otter. How could anyone say this face is dull?

Bill Travers and Virginia McKenna played the key roles in *Ring of Bright Water*. They fought a shark in Scotland—but the shark was filmed in California. This "movie magic" is S.O.P.—standard operating procedure.

Found in a poacher's snare, a herdsman brought the foal to Sieuwke. Like so many farm women of the day, she was "mum" to all sorts of hurt or orphaned wild animals…but not many other wives raised lions and leopards.

Liposuction or a kiss? Baby giraffes raised by humans make strong bonds. When work on the movie *The Last Giraffe* was over and Sieuwke had to pass the youngster's care over to another keeper, we allowed for a month of gradual "get acquainted" transition.

I'd been inside the tent with Susan and Nigel, operating a hand-held camera, when the staged flash flood hit. A powerful wall of surging water engulfed the tent, and the simulated catastrophe came close to the real thing.

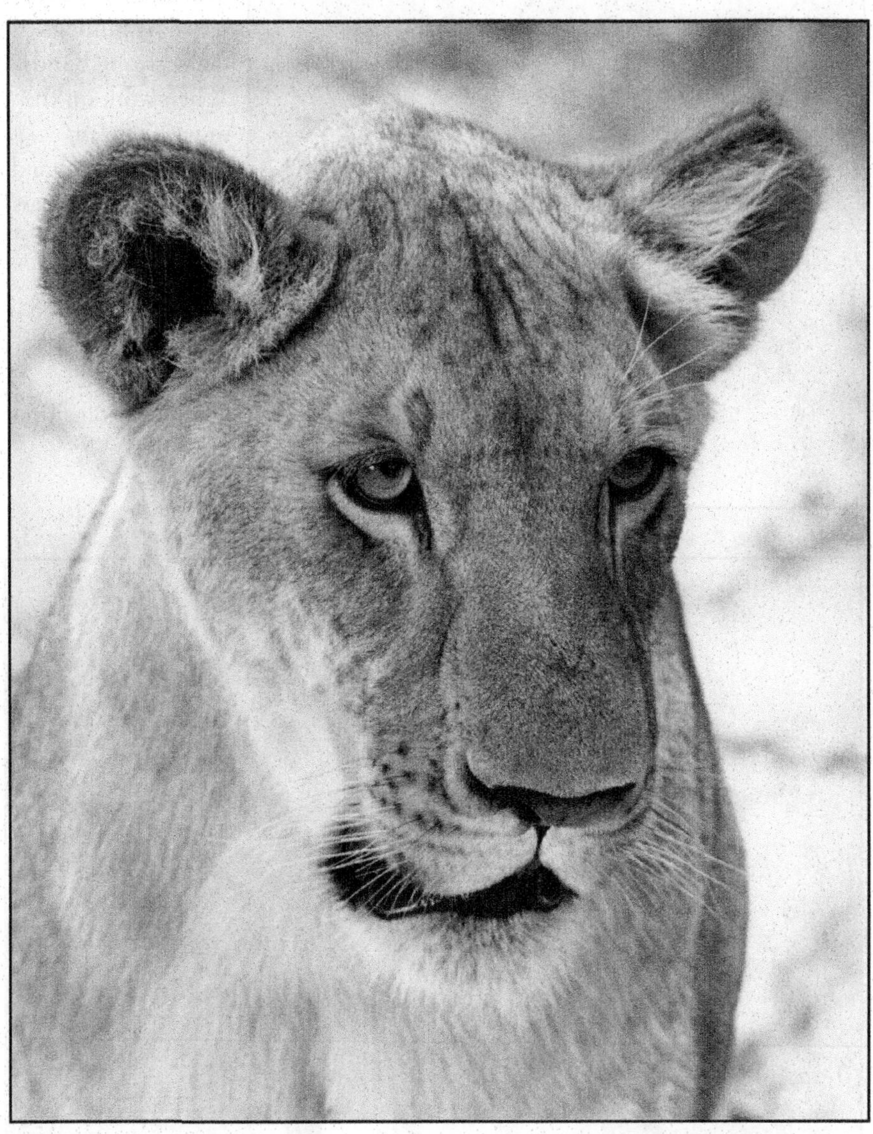

The lioness, Arusha. Her grandmother was Sieuwke's wild orphan named Sheeba who was a star in the movie *Born Free*. Arusha played the part of Elsa in the film *Living Free*, and her daughter, Asali, was a star in the *Born Free* tv series—a proud theater family.

The gift of Emperor Haile Selassie, "The Lion of Judah," as he was known. In honor of his exalted title, the Emperor kept a pair of adult lions in the palace gardens, thus these little princes and princesses were true royalty. But only one, Dennis (we called him Dennis the Menace) really felt himself to be the King of Beasts, for even as a kitten he was already showing his penchant for rule.

It wasn't easy for Susan Hampshire and Nigel Davenport to play happy close to the lions, but good actors they were, and soon made it look as if they all grew up together.

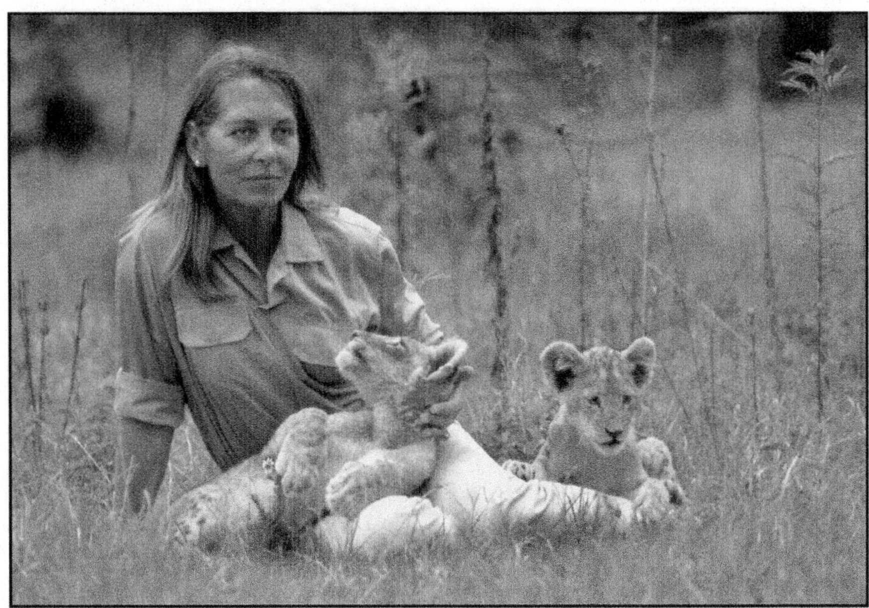

A moment of calm is only an intermission and the urge to play will soon erupt again. Sharp teeth and needle claws don't penetrate the thick hide of a cub's birth mother. But a human foster mum often adds another Band-Aid after a play session.

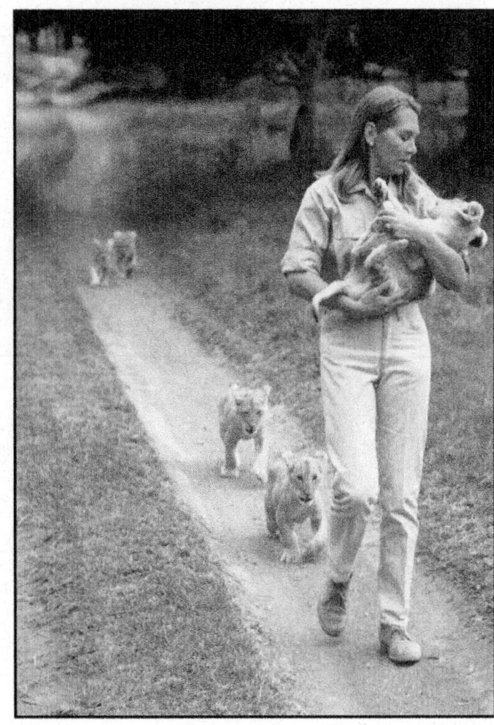

The cubs stick to position on their daily walk. Judy, Francis, and Ace bring up the rear, Homerus gets the privileged place in Sieuwke's arms, and Dennis the Menace leads the Pride.

There's no warmer pillow than a lion—and you don't have to worry about a thief sneaking up to pick your pocket while you sleep.

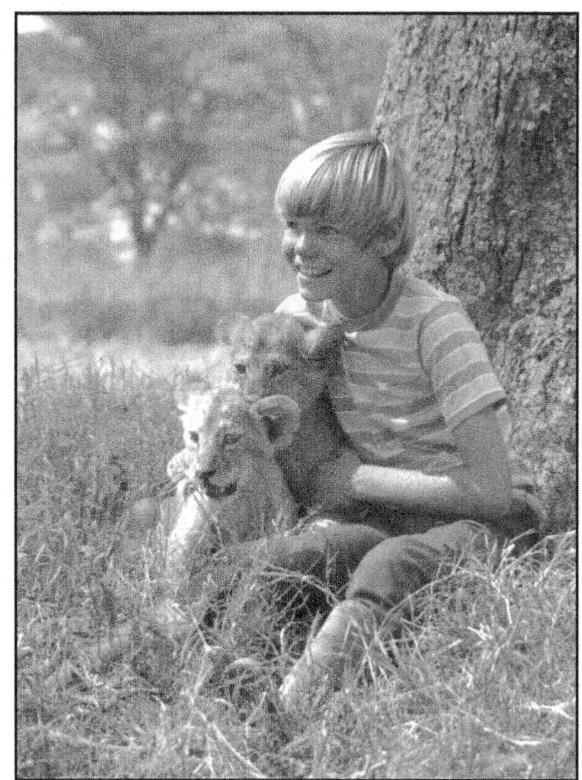

A lapfull of lions. Son, Mike (the Menace), had a strange kinship with Dennis the Menace, as two of a kind so often do.

I had many happy times when shooting Jonathan Livingston Seagull…

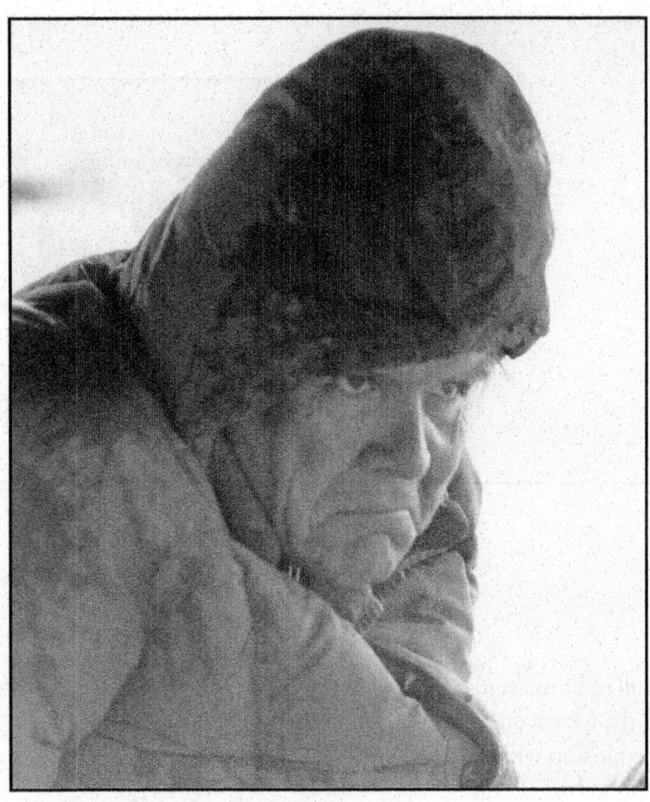

…and then there were the other days. (Photos by Elliot Marks)

Having taught Jonathan to glide in the even flow of wind from a stationary propeller, Gary Gero created a new twist in bird training.

Even star trainer Gary Gero can't teach a seagull to do tricks that are beyond a bird's physical ability. Inventor Mark Smith launches the propeller plane that will climb high and then loose the seagull glider to do the loops and barrel rolls that no living gull can really do.

Jonathan and his mentor, Chiang, who guided him in the pursuit of perfection—learn, improve, and defy tradition.

Of Dogs and Wolves

I was 37-years-old, had been working for Disney nearly exclusively for eight years and had just gotten my first co-directing credit on a Disney feature. The picture was *Nikki, Wild Dog of the North*, and it had been a big success when it was released in the summer of 1961.

Our base of operations for that film, which was more than a year in production as it included all of the seasons—winter snow and summer green—was a remote Canadian forestry experimental station on the Kananaskis River east of Banff National Park. The station with half a dozen log cabins had been closed and we leased the empty property from the government. There was even a large barn that made a perfect studio. It could hardly have been better for our shoot if we'd built it from scratch.

Joan was with me throughout the production, having reluctantly left behind the new house we'd just built in California. We'd only half-finished furnishing one home, now she was faced with furnishing and setting up housekeeping again. But it was a beautifully-constructed two story log house that had been built by German prisoners of war—we found swastikas and Nazi graffiti hidden in a couple of closet corners—and she jumped energetically to the task.

Joan became pregnant while we were in Canada and we looked forward to the birth of our first child. But before we returned home to California she miscarried a little girl. It had been a long time coming—we had been married for 11 years, and we were very sad.

* * * * *

Nikki was a malamute sled dog who grew up with a black bear cub. We had to see their continuity of growth, from puppyhood and cub to adults—another reason we spent so long on location. We also worked with mature elk, moose, a grizzly bear, wolves, and wolverines, all of which were met by the two main animal characters.

For me, the highlight of that film involved the grizzly. He was a mature Kodiak—the largest sub-species of the type—and his character name was Makoos.

At the time we made *Nikki* no grizzly bear had been raised to maturity and grew up tame and workable in films. Since then, several have been, and I've filmed them with pleasure and amazement at their docility. But an untamed grizzly is one of the few wild animals that actually lives up to its reputation of ferocity. One swipe of grizzly's paw can nearly tear a person's head off.

Makoos had an important role in the film as the main animal bad guy. (There were also a couple of human baddies.) For the grizzly sequence, we built a large filming compound in a flat-bottomed ravine with fences hidden behind the surrounding hills. The posts were twelve-foot-high logs, and the walls with overhang was the heaviest guage chain-link wire made. The filming enclosure was about an acre of aspen and Douglas fir forest. Several camera positions with portholes for the lens were at stategic places.

We borrowed Makoos from the Calgary Zoo where he had been raised. Never in his four years of life had he been outside the cage he'd grown up in. His feet had never touched earth, only concrete. We trucked him from the zoo in a sturdy cage of iron bars with a sliding drop door which we backed up to a similar door in the 20 foot square holding pen attached to the large filming compound. This would be his home when we were not filming, and he lived in this cement-floored cage for a week of familiarization before we set up a camera.

My right-hand-man on this shoot was Lloyd Beebe who has since then shot and directed several of the *True Life Adventures* including *Charlie, the Lonesome Cougar* and *The Vanishing Prairie*. He manned a camera at one point of view, I was at another, and we hoped for something unusual. It often happens when photographing wildlife that there is a special and unrepeatable reaction the first time an animal is introduced to a new situation. The situation can never be exactly duplicated because once the thing is done, it can never again be done for the first time.

Our fingers were on our cameras' start buttons, tense with anticipation, when the gate to Makoos's den was hoisted open.

Nothing happened.

Makoos sat in the far corner and stared warily at the open door and the earth and forest beyond—something he'd never seen before. Suspiciously, he seemed to study the situation.

We relaxed at our cameras, hands in pockets with disappointment, and shook heads at each other.

After half an hour, things slowly began to happen. Sniffing and cautious, Makoos moved to the open portal. He stood with his forepaws on the sill, put his head outside, and looked around. I could almost feel the wheels turning in his head as he absorbed the new vibrations. It was the first time in his life that Makoos was seeing a countryside without the sharp pattern of wire or bars before his eyes. Here were rocks and trees, leaves and soil, all strange things, unknown and not to be trusted. With great nostrils flaring he tested the air and withdrew again to the far corner of his den.

He returned to the doorway. Clearly this thing puzzled him and aroused his curiosity. He reached out gingerly and put one foot on the ground. He recoiled in alarm and reared back, returned to his corner. But something egged him on and he came back to the doorway. Again, he reached out with a paw and touched the ground. He snuffed and huffed with excitement—the first time in his life he'd felt the soft touch of earth.

It didn't seem to hurt, and Makoos pawed at the dirt, digging into it with the long curved claws of one paw. He brought the claws up to his face, smelled the earth and tasted it. He reached out with both paws and raked in a few bucketfuls of earth with easy strokes. Using two claws delicately like crab's pincers, in the same way a person holds a cigarette between fingertips, he picked up a golfball-sized clod and placed it on the back of his wrist. He studied the dirt with concentration and sniffed it. All seemed safe enough. Now he stepped out, guardedly looking into the shadows beneath the trees. He glanced back to the known safety of his den. He walked out further with growing curiosity, stepping lightly, sometimes shaking his paws at the strange new feel of earth and leaves.

He discovered the surrounding mesh of the large enclosure and followed it completely around. This exploration seemed to reassure him, as if he didn't have to cope with the new and frightening experience of being completely free. He moved to a small tree amd stood, heaving himself up to stand like a man on two legs. He leaned his forefeet against the trunk, and the tree bent with his weight. His paws slipped off and the tree snapped back.

He looked at it with puzzlement, and tried again.

The same.

Like watching a child discovering a new toy, I could see the amusement grow in the big bear. He snapped the tree again and again.

Then began a comedy of utter joy. The monster Kodiak went wild. He became a ridiculous clown. He threw himself at the saplings, ripping off their bark, holding them down and stripping their leaves. He dashed from one end of the area to the other, rolling in the dirt, digging, huffing at imaginary foes, cuffing stumps, rolling rocks, tearing down bushes and small trees. He leaped and turned like a player in some Gargantuan ballet. He rocked on his feet, back and forth, jumping first on his forepaws and rolling back to land on his rear. In a few minutes he completely destroyed the carefully manicured natural setting within our stage. The ground was upturned as if it had been plowed. It looked like a war's aftermath. At last he grew thirsty and retired to his den to rest.

In that half hour, which could never be duplicated, we had unexpectedly filmed the ending of an important sequence. We had no preconceived notion of the action that Makoos would give us with his first introduction to earth, rocks, and trees.

But by taking Makoos's action out of context, by adding a sound track of angry snorts and furious bellows, we had filmed a scene which would show not the true pantomime of a happy grizzly's gambol but an epilogue of frustrated rage, a temper tantrum to come after Makoos had been stuck in a hollow log, rolled down a hillside, and smashed into a pine tree. The scene wasn't in the script—Makoos had written that part of the scenario for us—but we had the ending to a new sequence almost before we began.

* * * * *

Through working with natural traits, trainers have learned to coax animals to perform special actions in films. You could call them "tricks," but in the training business we don't. The phrases "conditioned response," "behavioral reinforcement," and "operant conditioning" are all highfaluting terms used to describe the same thing: modifying an animal's instinctive behavior to get a good film performance. Often a trainer notes an idiosyncrasy in an individual animal that can be used to fit a specific movie situation.

Another animal that should have had screen writing credit was the star of the movie, *The Legend of Lobo.* The part of Lobo was played by a wolf named Shadow. His eccentricity seemed so far removed from anything relevant to our story that for months I overlooked his esoteric talent. Several times Shadow's trainer, Al Niemela, mentioned the wolf's gift, but I always shrugged it off.

"Shadow has the habit of walking things," Al said. "In the hills, he'll go out of his way to walk a narrow ridge. In town, he walks the curb. He even wants to walk the white line on the highway. It's just odd."

I thought little of it. I told Al that it was interesting, but I didn't see how we could use it. But not wanting anything to go to waste, I did say casually that he should work on it. Then I forgot about Shadow's excentricity.

A few weeks later Al told me that there was something he thought I ought to see.

He took me to a highway bridge on the trail where he and Shadow had their afternoon walk. It was a very ordinary bridge, twenty feet high where it crossed a creek, with a cement handrail less than a foot wide. Shadow approached the rail casually. He stepped up where the railing began and started to walk across the span.

A motorist drove by. He glanced to the side as he passed, stopped at the end of the bridge, and looked back. Then he drove away, shaking his head.

Shadow moved along with steady concentration, Al beside him, scolding when he became careless. At the end, the wolf jumped down and received a goody.

I sat down on the curb and shook my head. It had been an interesting performance. But how would it fit into our story? There were no highway bridges in Lobo's range.

"Do it again," I said, and watched as Shadow gladly obliged.

In the story Lobo and his mate kept their puppies in a den hidden on an isolated plateau surrounded by deep gorges. The wolf hunters on Lobo's trail could never find the way to his den. In the original script, a concealed passageway was accessible only via the trite device used in a hundred old "B" westerns: the secret path hidden behind a waterfall. I'd always had doubts about this overused and corny device. The inaccessibility of the mesa was not convincing. If Lobo and his mate could find this place, why couldn't the wolf hunters?

I watched Shadow cross the bridge railing and an idea began to form.

"It's very good," I told Al. "Let's go back to the compound and see if he'll walk a log."

"Log?" Al said. "He loves to walk logs."

And thus began the story of how Shadow's liking for walking extreme narrow pathways rewrote the script.

After weeks of training Shadow to walk on a two-foot-diameter log set up on three-foot-high sawhorses, changing the log to eighteen-inch-diameter, then to one foot, and raising the height of the sawhorses, he made the traverse a hundred times without a misstep.

In the meanwhile a set was built by winching a one-foot-diameter log across a deep chasm that cut through the edge of a high stone mesa—Lobo's otherwise inaccessible denning place.

The "bridge" to Shadow's den was seventy feet across and a hundred feet high. Shadow crossed it so nonchalantly that Al had to do a bit of retraining—slow him down—so it didn't look so easy.

This sequence that Lobo's special talent had made possible was the suspenseful high point in the film.

Lobo's eccentricity "wrote" the scene.

10

The Incredible Journey

Stormy Palmer, senior editor of the *True Life Adventures* series, was the first person at the Disney studios to read a serialized magazine story called *The Incredible Journey*. It was about two dogs and a cat who lose track of their owner and have to find their way home. He knew it would make a wonderful movie and went straight to Walt with it.

I was in the projection room with Erwin Verity and James Algar looking at footage I'd shot for *The Legend of Lobo*. Walt dropped in and watched most of the footage with us. After talking about *Lobo* briefly, Walt switched over and began telling us about this wonderful new story he'd acquired. He wanted Algar to write the script, which he said would amount to little more than putting numbers on the paragraphs. (He was right.) He wanted me to direct.

This would be a large step up the ladder for me. It was going to be a big feature, and the book (the original magazine serialization preceded the book) was an immediate best seller. None of us *True Life* field producers had yet been able to move out of the naturalist-photographer niche. We were generally regarded as nature freaks who wrestled with snakes and twisted tiger's tails but wouldn't have the slightest notion how to deal with actors who had two legs rather than four. It never seemed to occur to anyone in the director-hiring department that unlike animals, human actors sometimes did as they were asked to do, and therefore might be easier to direct than animals. Of course I also knew the reality that people—actors in particular—have sensitivities far more subtle than your everyday animal and thus require special skills to direct effectively. Appeasing edgy personalities was something I thought I could handle.

But when Walt began talking to me in the projection room as the director of his next big feature, I could feel Verity begin to squirm. He tried to draw Walt's attention to my lack of experience with human actors. I knew what Erwin was thinking—that my being graduated into a new category would screw up his whole system of control. He wasn't worried about losing me as much as what the other *True Life* field producers would think of my upgrade. They might see the hope of a break in their own status which had remained flat for so many years.

At the end of that first meeting I sensed that Verity's cool reception of the idea of me directing *The Incredible Journey* had already put the boss' idea on shaky ground. Sure enough, the next time I talked to Algar he told me they'd decided to have someone experienced with directing people do the people part of the show. I'd be responsible for all the animal work—which was half of the movie—and share the directing credit. It was the same lousy deal I'd had on *Nikki.*

There was only one of the old-time *True Life* producers whom I felt would level with me on my next question. Winston Hibler, the senior member of the corps who usually narrated the shows, had become a friend. I stopped him in a studio hallway one day. "What do you think, Hib? I've been working for Walt Disney Studios now for eight years. I'm not on the staff. One picture leads to another, but each time I have to negotiate a new contract. It's as if I'm starting all over. Do you think I'll ever get on staff and be entitled to the same benefits you guys get?"

"No," Hibler said bluntly. "It's not in the cards."

Hib didn't go into his reasons, and I wasn't yet savvy to them—that if I moved up, I'd be stepping on the toes of the established studio producers who were calling themselves the directors of the wildlife shows.

(All of the studios and most of the independents have contracts with the various Hollywood guilds and unions. Only directors, writers, and actors—not producers or cameramen—have residuals built into their agreements and are entitled to payments for each television showing. In a successful series like the Disney show, these payments go on for years of syndication and reruns.

What Hibler was telling me, but not in so many words, was that if I were a member of the Directors Guild, I'd be getting the coveted residuals and other benefits—thus cutting the Disney staff producers out of a big chunk of income.

"So I'm stuck as an outsider," I said.

"Yep." Hib said. "I'm afraid so."

* * * * *

In spite of that setback, I took the deal on *The Incredible Journey* and had a wonderful time. The best dog trainers in the business at the time, Bill Khoeler and Hal Driscoll, and cat trainer, Al Niemela, made the animal work easy. Several Siamese cats played the part of one of the leads. Many of them were specialists: we had a doorknob cat, the only one in our kennel who seemed to have the ready ability to open doors; a cat who didn't mind getting his paws wet who became the fishing cat (who was also the swimming cat); a stalking cat; and a snarling cat who arched his back like a Halloween character and bared his fangs on command.

We were on location in Washington state for five months. I had a congenial crew and lived in a comfortable house situated on the spectacular shores of Sequim Bay on the Olympic Peninsula. I had only to step through the door to dig up bucketfuls of delicious clams. Rhododendrons bloomed profusely. The surrounding forest was cool and quiet. Crab and salmon were plentiful.

Most importantly, Joan and our newborn son, Mike, were with me, and my mother made a long visit. It would have been nearly impossible for me to be away from my new son for such a long time.

The book's author, Sheila Burnford, stayed with us for awhile and became a close friend. You could say that I had everything—well, nearly everything. All I lacked was the chance to advance my career at a time when I felt I ought to be moving ahead.

We based our production at Lloyd Bebee's farm that had a stream running through it and photogenic wooded hills and grassy wildlands.

Early in production, Erwin Verity visited me to sort out a business problem. It seemed he'd made a six-day week deal with the dog trainers. I'd always worked on the studio schedule of a five-day week. I figured that I'd been working for Disney steadily for ten years; if I'd spent all those years working six days a week, it wouldn't have been much of a life.

But Verity didn't figure he was getting his money's worth if I was shooting five days when the trainers were committed to six. He wanted me to change my schedule to conform to their deal. I refused. Verity was furious. With the threat of being sacked hanging around my neck, I stuck to my guns.

During his four-day visit Verity was our house guest and took all of his meals with us. When he departed, he left a twenty-dollar bill on his pillow.

* * * * *

When I saw the first print of *The Incredible Journey* I was stunned. I liked the movie reasonably well, although the "people footage" I supposedly lacked the talent to direct was ordinary at best.

The thing that shocked me was my screen credit. I had been led to believe that I would receive a co-director's credit, the same as the one I had on my last feature. What I saw on the screen was the old meaningless title of Field Producer.

Verity getting his revenge for my five-day weeks? Probably.

In fact it was the best thing Verity could have done for me. His little coup was the proverbial straw that broke the camel's back.

At the end of the screening I looked over at producer Jim Algar. Always the nice guy, he begged off. He had no explanation and muttered some platitudes to try to soothe me.

This doublecross pushed me at last into doing what I should have done years ago. I made an appointment with Joseph Youngerman, Business Manager of the Directors Guild of America. I spilled the beans, told him everything about the way I and my wildlife filmmaker pals had been used. For the first time I saw clearly all the angles that went with the orchestration of the screen credit of Field Producer. This uniquely Disney title seemed to have been invented only to allow a few insiders to collect our rightful director's credit along with its valuable benefits.

When he heard my story, Joseph Youngerman picked up the phone. I sat across from him as he placed a call to Bill Anderson, the Disney vice president in charge of production. I heard only one side of the conversation. It went like this:

"Good morning, Bill. I've got Jack Couffer here in the office with me."

I could almost hear Bill's reaction: "Uh-oh!"

"That's right," Youngerman said. "The wildlife guy. He's been telling me about what he's been doing for you for the past ten years."

There was a slight pause as Anderson reacted to this, then:

"Well don't you think that's pushing the edges of the Disney contract with the DGA a bit far?"

Another pause while Bill considered that question.

Then Youngerman said, "Well, he's joining the DGA here and now." He looked across his desk at me for confirmation. I nodded.

Right," Youngerman continued. "As of today, he's a DGA member and entitled to all our benefits."

A long period of silence from Anderson's end, then:

"Do you know what I'd like to have you do, Bill? I'd like for you to pay Jack's Health and Welfare and contribute into his DGA Pension Fund retroactively from the day he began working for you."

Bill thought that over.

"That's right, from day one," said Youngerman. "If you can do that, then we might be able to avoid any difficulty with this situation. Uh huh. You agree in principle, then. Good. How much do I figure it would be? I'll have to work out the exact number, but just off the top of my head I'd guess around fifty grand."

I heard only silence as Youngerman listened, then: "I know, Bill.... Yes, it *is* a lot of money. Yes, I suppose we could settle on that figure now, to clear the whole thing up. Good. We can agree on a flat fifty thousand then. You'll have a check in the mail tomorrow. I think you're being very wise, Bill. And speaking for Jack, I'm sure he'll think you've been very fair."

And that's how I joined the Directors Guild of America. On the day I became a member I was instantly heavily vested in the best pension and health and welfare plan in the industry. It was the finest thing that anyone ever did for me in the movie business, and since then I've regarded Joseph Youngerman as the greatest union management person in Hollywood.

* * * * *

I was certain that this would be the end of my long association with Walt Disney Studios, but it was worth it. I was ready for new horizons.

But it didn't happen that way. My move only created a new attitude about me. Now my old employers treated me with new respect. I wasn't offered a big feature right away, but henceforth when I was called in to do a TV show, I did it as a director. The weekly Disney series was popular and each show went into many reruns. Until those residual checks began coming in, I never realized how much I'd been screwed all those years.

That hadn't been my only brush with Disney brass that I thought would end my career at the studio but in the end enhanced my position. This tiff also had me in one corner opposite Bill Anderson. In 1955 when NBC decided to go on the air with a daily kid's show to be produced by Disney, the studio launched into panic mode. The new series called *The Mickey Mouse Club* would have to gear up to produce an hour's worth of television five days a week.

In their scramble for instant product, they asked me if I had any ideas. Remembering back to *All in a Day's Work*, the series that went no further than the pilot, my partners in Canyon Films and I came up with a variation on the theme. *What I Want to Be When I Grow Up* was the working title of the series we said we could produce.

Through its Disneyland amusement park the studio had connections with Trans World Airlines, who were heavily invested in a big exhibit and ride at Tommorrowland. For the first segments of our new series, we suggested shows about a boy who wanted to be an airline pilot and a girl who wanted to be a stewardess. It was a concept that pleased the Disney folks in that it provided a double payoff: while getting free production facilities from TWA they could also get indirect advertising for Disneyland.

Canyon Films got the go-ahead to produce the TWA shows. Sterling Silliphant, our old friend from USC film school who hadn't yet made it to the big time, came aboard as writer. We visited TWA pilot and stewardess training facilities and worked with Silliphant to develop the scripts. We had an office in the Disney animation building, right up there with the top brass. Everything along the development road got the green light. A budget and shooting schedule with an imminent start date was approved.

Then I got a call to check in with Bill Anderson. His secretary suggested that perhaps all the partners of Canyon Films ought to come along.

Anderson seemed tense when we entered. The purpose of the meeting, he told us, was that the studio had decided to take over the production of *What I Want to Be When I Grow Up.* Our idea, along with our pre-production work, had developed into too good a thing to hand over to an outside producer.

Because of the rush to production, only a sketchy deal memo had been written; more detailed contracts were in the works. In the meantime, we had proceeded as if everything we'd agreed upon was signed—a system that had worked in my past assignments. On a prior occasion I'd already completed a six-month-long Disney shoot before contracts were finally signed.

To be given the shaft by Bill Anderson at this stage—after we'd prepared a production that would be a *Mickey Mouse Club* showpiece—was a bitter blow. It wasn't that the studio thought they could do it better, but rather because they could make more profit by doing it themselves.

I exploded. I threatened to break Anderson's furniture—the first recourse that came immediately to mind. He was picking up the phone to call security when Marv and Conrad and I stormed out.

We went from Disney Studios straight to our lawyer's office. Ed Mosk filed a lawsuit. Walt himself was called upon to give a deposition, a disagreeable nuisance that, for this well-protected man, just never happened. In Walt's testimony one answer sticks in my memory. When asked about some detail of our agreement, he responded with, "How would I remember that? Do you think I carry a tape recorder around on my back?"

I was sure this lawsuit would end my relationship with Disney Studios forever, but I was working for them on a new show a few weeks later. As with *The Incredible Journey* situation the reaction at the studio seemed to be respect for our having stood up for our rights. When faced with the reality that we weren't complete pushovers, Disney made a fair cash settlement so I had no lasting beef. In the end, no one at the studio ever mentioned the case to me. It was as if it never happened.

Anderson must have known we'd take the action we did. Probably the settlement cost was anticipated and calculated into the show's budget at the time they decided to pull the rug out from under us.

11

Ring of Bright Water

When *The Incredible Journey* upheaval put a temporary crimp in my long sojourn at Disney, Joseph Strick asked me if I could come up with a good feature project we could make together.

The Incredible Journey had been a big success. The public loved its sentimental style, and the dogs and cat in the movie could have been lying in front of anyone's hearth. Now, three years later, a Columbia release called *Born Free* was cleaning up at the box office. The genre of movies about animals had had its ups and downs. Now it was hot again.

At the same time, a nonfiction book about a lonely man and an adopted otter who find adventure in the Scottish Highlands had been riding high on the best-seller lists. It was such a popular book and had been around long enough that I assumed it had already been purchased for movie production, but I told Joe that I thought it would make a wonderful film and it might be worth looking into the rights status.

I was surprised when Joe called me in Canada, where I was shooting another couple of back-to-back TV shows for Disney, and told me to start writing the script—he'd just bought *Ring of Bright Water*. It seems no producer had touched it because the rather muted but obvious human attraction in the book was between the author (Gavin Maxwell) and a teenaged boy—not the most sanctioned relationship for what would obviously be a family film.

The solution to the screenplay adaptation seemed obvious to me: drop the touchy boy-adult infatuation and introduce Maxwell to a girl. Having a love affair with an otter was about as far as I wanted my movie to stray from everyday heterosexual experience.

When I finished writing the script which I was to direct, Joe wasted no time in setting a production deal with Edgar Scherick, who'd quit a high-level job at the ABC network to go into feature production.

The first thing I did when Joe confirmed that we had a deal to make *Ring of Bright Water* was to set about finding and preparing our animal star. Tame otters are not common, and none of the movie animal trainers I knew had otters. We would need several of these animals to act as doubles and train to different skills.

While one of my field producer friends, Hank Schloss, had been shooting a Disney TV show in Florida he'd seen a young man named Hubert Wells doing an impressive act with a dog and a leopard at a tourist attraction. When Hank had finished his show and returned to Burbank, the dog-leopard thing kept rumbling in his head. A Disney writer built a story around this unique animal friendship, and that had been Hank's next TV show.

Hubert was born in Hungary, the son of a forest engineer, a European occupation that in addition to managing trees, included looking after the wildlife within the forest. When Hubert was twenty-one the Soviets occupied Hungary and after fighting with the resistance, Hubert fled to Austria.

Fluent in Hungarian, German, and with four years of Russian forced on him in school, but not a word of English, Hubert applied for and received a visa to USA.

He spent three years in New York and Florida, where he worked as an animal keeper in tourist venues. He bought and raised a leopard cub and trained an act while working as a night watchman. It was while performing the perfected dog-leopard act that Hank Schloss found him.

Hank introduced me to Hubert. As it turned out, this was one of the more auspicious introductions in my career—as well as it was to Hubert's.

I hired Hubert to find and train our otters, and thus began a friendship that has lasted through six films and remains happy and respectful to this day.

* * * * *

Bill Travers and Virginia McKenna, who had made big names for themselves in *Born Free*, were our first choices to play the main roles in *Ring of Bright Water*. Their *Born Free* experience had changed their lives in more ways than one. In addition to confirming their already-established movie stardom, the relationships they had with the lions in that film had made them ardent animal rights activists, a calling to which they would henceforth devote their lives.

My first challenge in getting Bill and Virginia to agree to star in my film was to overcome the stigma of being a Disney guy. The original director-producer of *Born Free*, an ex-Disney *True Life* field producer, evidently hadn't met their standard before he was bought out and replaced.

Somewhat to Walt's original dismay but eventual approval, I'd written a book relating my experiences filming Disney animal shows—*Song of Wild Laughter*—which I gave to Bill and Virginia at our first meeting. My book must have cut some ice, as their attitude after reading it was that I was a kindred spirit. We got along very well.

Because my travels heretofore had mostly been to wild places, my sojourn to London to prepare *Ring of Bright Water* was a new and dreary experience. My producer-partner had just taken on a huge job which was to shoot in Tunisia; thus he was tied up with another picture, leaving me pretty much to paddle my own canoe. Joe Strick met me in London, introduced me to Betty Botley, a production assistant without whose help my canoe would surely have sunk.

Joe had a long-term lease on a flat in the heart of London that would serve as my office and home. It occupied three rooms above the ground-floor bank on the west side of Leicester Square. Every night, but especially on Fridays and weekends, the loud noise of many voices rose above the everyday din of automobiles and buses, and blasted through my bedroom, as the Odeon Cinema queue formed just below the window. Street entertainers played the line until the wee hours, and it took me until Thursday to recover from the lack of sleep I would have to face again on Friday.

I arrived in London just after Christmas in 1969 to prepare the movie to shoot in Scotland the following spring. I didn't know anyone in London. I was cold and lonely; it was a strange place and my only feeling of comfort was that at least everyone sort of spoke English.

My son, Mike, was six years old and had just started school. A move to London at this time wasn't practical, and Joan and Mike planned to be with me in Scotland when production started. None of us were happy about the months of separation, but work ethic, money, and the boost to my career prevailed.

The first bit of advice I received after signing Bill and Virginia was that I should go to Scotland, find locations, and absorb the atmosphere of the country. My production manager initiated all of the preparations he felt were necessary for my trip—he hired me a car and bought me a map. That was it. I didn't know London, but I'd observed that people there drove on the wrong side of the street, something that I'd never done. And I was used to maps on a different scale. On American maps you'd get all of the west coast—California, Oregon, and Washington—on a single page. My new map startled me at first: England and Scotland together—less than half the equivalent miles—were also on one page. The difference in scale could throw a navigator into a tailspin.

* * * * *

A little British car was delivered to me courtesy of Hertz, and I drove north out of Leicester Square after lunch, headed in the direction where I thought I'd find the M1 carriageway. But after making my first turn, I was lost.

It was nearly dark when I finally arrived on the main highway headed north, far behind schedule, weary, anxious, and pissed off at myself for being so inefficient and at the world in general. This trunk road didn't go through towns; it skirted past them. It got dark and I continued to drive. I was growing sleepy, I turned off into a village where I expected to find a motel and a bed.

It didn't take long to cover all the main streets. I soon realized that these villages didn't have motels or hotels. All they offered in the way of accommodation were rooms in houses with signs reading BED AND BREAKFAST. The windows in all those houses displaying these signs were dark, as it was by now past ten.

I headed back to the highway. "Maybe the next village," I muttered to myself.

Finally I could drive no further. I knew I had to stop and sleep somewhere, and I didn't fancy trying to snooze in this wee little car where my knees had been cramped up under my chin now for so many hours.

I banged on the door of a dark house that displayed a BED AND BREAKFAST sign. Finally a light went on. At last I heard footsteps approaching and the door opened. A little lady who was the perfect caricature of an English Bed and Breakfast proprietress stood in the portal. She took one look at me and said, "You poor man. You look exhausted. Do come in."

So far, these were the kindest, most welcome, and most compassionate words I'd heard in the two months since I'd arrived in the U.K.

* * * * *

I came into Oban, the place on the west coast of the Scottish Highlands that seemed the most likely base of operations, with only one possible contact. Bill Travers had a friend there, the Editor of *The Oban Times* newspaper. They'd met while Bill was filming *Wee Geordie*, the movie that made his stardom. Bill gave me a letter of introduction to Alan Cameron, and that was all I had to make my life easy in Oban.

The first thing I saw when I topped the hill above the seaside town was the graveyard. A rustic fence to keep sheep off the graves surrounded the plot. There was a stile and just inside the fence a modern addition to the old cemetery—it might have been one of those modernistic bus stop cupolas of glass and anodized aluminum imported from a sidewalk corner in Glasgow. Hanging from the roof was a sign: WAITING ROOM.

I'd reached my destination at last. I drove into the town which would be my home for the next eight months with a chuckle. A waiting room for a cemetery? Oh, well, those Scots. You never know whether they're joking or serious.

I called in at *The Oban Times* office and presented my letter of introduction to the owner and managing editor, Alan Cameron.

The book I represented and was to direct as a movie was a worldwide bestseller; its fame was certain. But here in Oban, *Ring of Bright Water* wasn't simply well-known, it was holy—almost as holy as the Bible itself.

Bill Travers had certainly introduced me to the right person—his intuition had been unerring. With two credentials—as the Director of the movie of the most famous modern book about the Scottish Highlands, *and* as a friend of Bill Travers, that was all I needed.

Cameron invited me to dinner at his house that evening. By now I'd learned enough about English manners to turn up in a jacket and tie. Not to have done so would probably have put me back on the street. Although Cameron had an American wife, he—and she, by now—were as thoroughly Scottish as you could get.

About the time we were having our pudding, I told Alan that my mother's family name was Craig. I hoped that by announcing my possession of a substantial dose of Scottish blood I would gain some status.

Alan looked down his nose at me. "Ach-aye," he said in a dismissive tone. "Crag…a lowland clan."

Okay, so I wasn't a Highlander—an important distinction that put me down a notch as a Scot, but still several notches above any other tribe of human beings.

The Camerons wouldn't have it any other way but that I move out of my hotel and into their guest bedroom, a relocation that I made that very night.

My next change of accommodation was to the empty third-floor rooms in the old stone building that housed *The Oban Times.* It took a week to sweep out the dust and wash the windows as this level hadn't been in use for a few years. There I had both a bedroom and some rooms that could be converted to production offices.

The building's walls were constructed of thick gray stone. It was February, and the hard granite seemed colder than the freezing air outside. As I was out roaming the countryside all day looking for locations, and huddled inside a sleeping bag in bed at night, I couldn't keep the fireplaces stoked, so the cold rooms didn't grow any warmer with my occupancy. The little heat that came from my body and the short-lived fires only condensed onto the cold walls, which grew strings of tiny silver balls of moisture. I was freezing.

At last I checked all of the electrical outlets throughout my floor, calculated the amps available, and bought multiple electric heaters for every room. I fudged just enough on power supply that I could turn on a single light bulb when necessary without fear of blowing a fuse. I left the heaters running continuously day and night. It took a couple of weeks for the temperature inside those rooms to rise enough to penetrate the stone by an inch—barely deep enough that it didn't feel as if I was placing my hand on a damp block of ice when I touched the wall.

When Cameron got the electricity bill for the month, he doubled my rent.

I leased a castle called Muckairn, situated on an arm of the sea, for Bill and Virginia, who would spend the summer of production there with their kids and a nanny. I knew they'd love the view with the rocks just offshore populated by a colony of seals.

Not far from Oban I found the location which would serve as Maxwell's home in the movie: a lonely croft cottage beside a little burn with a pond where the otter could fish for eels. Rocky hills stood on both sides of the burn, which wound down through a sandy beach into the sea. It was a lovely, wild, and lonely place.

Not far from the remote cottage I found a picturesque little seaside village, its rows of white stone houses with their gray slate roofs and stone fences snuggled against the foot of a cliff. With the island of Mull humped on the horizon, this place would appear in the film as the nearest village to Maxwell's cottage—Druimfiaclach—and the home of the girl who would change his hermitlike existence.

* * * * *

I wanted to meet Gavin Maxwell, the author of the book upon which my screenplay was based. It would be advantageous to have his approval of the script. Although this wasn't essential to the deal, it wouldn't be helpful to have him lambasting the production for having butchered his book—and Maxwell, a frequent newspaper contributor, was known to be touchy.

I called Maxwell's agent to see if he could set up a time and place for me to meet the author. I learned that Maxwell lived in a remote part of the Highlands, a secret location, with an invented name. (Camusfearna, the location of his house in the book, doesn't exist). Misleading clues to the place's fictional location abounded and were dropped into his book helter-skelter only as devices to maintain his treasured privacy. Maxwell had no telephone and could only be reached by mail or through messages hand-delivered by a Scottish friend and business manager who lived twenty miles away. Obviously he didn't like having visitors dropping in on him.

But eventually word came back that Maxwell would welcome me to his home on a certain date a month hence. A hand-drawn map was produced. A place on the road was marked with an X and with the note, "Park here," alongside it. A wavy line took off from the X. This was marked "Trail". The line connected to another X marked "House." At the bottom of the map was written, "Muddy trail—bring gum boots."

So that part of my expedition was settled.

As the date approached for my appointment with Gavin Maxwell, Cameron's wry observations of my future host didn't help my nerves. Maxwell's reputation as a hostile personality contradicted in every way his charm as a writer. You could say his nonfiction books contained an element of fiction in that he portrayed himself as a far more easygoing person than he was in real life.

I left Oban in a rainstorm, heading north on the road toward Skye. The place I was looking for—Sandaig, which Maxwell had fictionalized in his book as "Camusfearna"—was far off the beaten track, miles up a narrow road which curved inland into the hills, then came back to the sea.

I found the place on Maxwell's map that he'd marked with an X and labeled "Park here." It was a wide spot in the road, high on a mountain side. A mile below, at the foot of a steep winding foot trail close by the white-capped sea, I saw the familiar house exactly as pictured in the book.

It was late afternoon, the time when I'd been told to arrive. I would spend the night in Maxwell's house. He preferred to conduct business in the evening hours.

I'd brought not only a pair of rubber boots as instructed, but also a waterproof slicker. I put them on, stuffed the script and my overnight case into a plastic bag, locked the car, and started down the hill in a heavy rain.

The track was steep and slippery with many switchbacks. As I reached the halfway point the rain came even harder. Rivulets ran along the trail, cutting gullies that caved in under my footsteps, making the going harder. I came to an old plank laid across a steep-sided stream that was running full. A crude sign said BRIDGE UNSAFE. I took a chance and stepped gingerly onto the board. It creaked and bent, but didn't break. I made it to the bottom in half an hour. Going back would be a different story.

The first thing I noticed when I reached the flats at the bottom of the hill and approached Maxwell's house was a car parked in a shed. I'd wondered how he kept his house supplied. Carrying everything up and down on the footpath seemed a bit much, even for a hermit.

The rogue! I realized that the trail was a test. I think Gavin pictured all movie producers and directors as charicatures—pale, flabby guys puffing stinky cigars. If you survived the path down to his house without breaking a leg, you passed trial number one. Lose that one, and you might as well not have come at all. I resolved not to mention the difficulty of the hike. If he said anything about it, I'd shrug it off with something like, "You think that trail is bad? You ought to see the one to my house. You need crampons, rope, and a climber's axe to get there."

Maxwell came out with an umbrella to meet me. Contrary to what I expected, he was quite cordial. We headed inside and sat by the fireplace, where we each had a whiskey and exchanged small talk. Soon we were joined by a nice-looking lad of eighteen named Jimmy Watt.

Maxwell said the boy had been wonderful with his otter, Mij. He ran through all the lad's other splendid qualities as if reading off a list. It became evident that the main purpose of this evening's discussion was to promote this boy whom he wanted to play the same role in the film that he'd played in the book. This was impossible not only because the lad wasn't an actor, but the character had been written out in my adaptation. The excised boy's role was now being played by Virginia McKenna, who was every inch a girl. None of this was known to Maxwell, as the script he had yet to read was still lying in a wet plastic bag at my feet.

I listened, nursing my drink and becoming increasingly uncomfortable, as Maxwell continued singing the boy's praises and refilling his own whiskey glass. Occasionally I was able to slip in a word about having brought the script and wouldn't it be useful if he read it before we discussed the movie? I tried to sound reasonable and accommodating by suggesting that maybe he'd find some details that he'd want me to change. I even pointed out that now was the time I might be able to make a few minor alterations.

Maxwell replied that he knew I was probably tired after my long drive and that he would read the script after we'd had dinner and I'd gone to sleep. We could talk about it in the morning or perhaps the following night.

It was getting late. It had been dark in this high latitude, with the storm howling outside since about five. Then I saw car lights pull up near the house. Presently a man came in without knocking. It was Maxwell's business advisor, the one who'd set up this meeting. Nobody mentioned the odd fact that this gentleman had arrived at the bottom of a slippery footpath by automobile and that he wasn't wearing mud-covered gumboots.

He'd brought our dinner with him: salmon, venison, and wine.

After dinner, I begged out of another whiskey and said I'd like to go to bed. My room was up some creaky steps in the loft. The old frame house squeaked and howled as rain slashed against the boards and windowpanes. The wind wailed outside, and the building actually moved before the gale's heaviest gusts, swaying and groaning like an old wooden ship about to break apart.

The storm was one of the hardest to hit the coast all winter. It was as if Maxwell had personally orchestrated the weather to fit his scenario for my visit. I slept very little—the sound was louder than the boisterous crowd below my Leicester Square window on Saturday night—and the eerie howls seemed in my intermittent dreams to herald dangerous portents. Shingles above my head flapped like bird's wings, and at times I wondered if the roof was going to fly away.

Morning brought a lull in the storm. Maxwell was still asleep. I walked around outside, saw the now-abandoned otter pen where Mij had occasionally been locked out of the house, and chatted with Maxwell's amiable business manager and provider of our meal who soon departed in his car, heading back up the hill on the gravel driveway.

When Maxwell appeared in midmorning, his eyes were red and puffy. No one could read a screenplay in less than a couple of hours, probably three if you were in the condition in which Maxwell had been last night. He'd put away the better part of a bottle of scotch by the time I'd handed him the script and turned in. He couldn't have gone to sleep until well after one or two in the morning, and I could tell from his long face that I wasn't about to have a jolly time hearing his critique of my work.

The first things he attacked were minor production items of which he really had no filmmaker's background to challenge. There was a scripted sequence that mirrored a situation in the book. It built around one of Maxwell's experiences hunting basking sharks, eighteen-foot-long monsters weighing a couple of tons. Maxwell said it would be impossible for me to film such a thing, particularly in the exciting way I'd described it in the script, and certainly not with the actors in the midst of the action.

When I told him that I'd already filmed the basking shark in California using doubles and the sequence was written to fit existing material, I didn't think he believed me. But it was true.

Three months before coming to Scotland, I'd taken a jaunt down the California coast to San Pedro and had a beer with a couple of buddies from my years as a commercial fisherman. They told me that swordfish boats out of Morro Bay occasionally harpooned a basking shark for its liver, which had value as a source of vitamin A.

I drove north the next day. Tony Bertola, skipper of the plank boat, *Maid of Guadalupe*, said, "Sure, we been takin' more sharks than swordfish lately, anyways. It's a hassle, them bein' so huge ya know. But I been stickin'um for the liver. You want to come along and snap some pictures, that's okay with me."

I told Tony that it would be a bit more than just me "comin' along to take pictures," but when I told him what I had in mind, he agreed to a price for me to join the crew of the *Maid*, and I went back to L.A. for my camera and all the other things I'd need.

I found an old-fashioned wooden skiff that I was pretty sure could be matched later on with one in Scotland when we staged the action with actors as they pretended to battle the shark that I'd filmed in California. I bought yellow seaman's slickers with hoods to cover the faces of the doubles who would stand in for Bill Travers and Virginia McKenna. I hired a big fisherman friend of Tony's to double for Travers. I also hired a pretty stunt-girl double to play Virginia's role. She claimed to be able in a small boat and said she could row—aside from the vague physical similarity, those were the main qualifications for the job.

I knew that finding a basking shark from a boat on a given day was an iffy mission. I hired my friend Ed Durden and his plane (from *The Legend of the Boy and the Eagle).* Ed's occupation as an aerial fish-spotter for the commercial fleet would improve the odds.

Back in Morro Bay, it was dawn and time to get underway. All was ready, but where was our action double for Virginia? I'd made reservations for her at the motel where I was staying with my camera assistant. She didn't answer her phone. The receptionist hadn't seen her and couldn't find her. Rumor had it that she'd been at the bar until late and had left with a male friend.

I was desperate. I looked at Francesco, the deckhand of the *Maid of Guadalupe.* He was small and slight—if he kept the slicker's hood turned away from the camera to hide his face he could pass for Virginia.

The idea of being in the skiff with the shark close-by didn't faze him. But pretending to be a woman? No way!

Would twenty bucks ease the pain?

Nope.

Fifty?

"Hell no! I wouldn't do it for a thousand!"

"How about seventy-five?"

"Okay. But if you tell anyone, you're dead."

We set out into a gray overcast. That suited me fine as I knew the light would be easy to match on the notoriously stormy western coast of Scotland. The *Maid* dove into the swells of the infamous Morro Bay bar. Then we were on a gentle sea, the skiff tugging along at its painter astern like a puppy on a leash.

The radio crackled—Ed reporting a large basking shark cruising the surface about four miles north. He'd circle the spot until we arrived.

Harpooning the shark was everyday stuff to Tony and Francesco. We kept the big fish connected to the *Maid* as the doubles in their yellow slickers piled into the skiff and pulled close to the thrashing fins and tail. A short rope tied to a stone and hanging taut over the bow appeared to be the harpoon line. It looked as dangerous as...well, as dangerous as an angry two-ton, twenty-foot shark tied to a tiny skiff holding two intrepid fisherfolk.

In a few minutes I shot all I needed of exciting close contact between the shark and the skiff. Now all that was needed to complete that part of the sequence were shots of Bill and Virginia in Scotland being towed and splashed by a tightly circling motor boat.

Then Tony killed the fish and extracted the huge liver. We tied the carcass alongside and dragged it close to a deserted shore. Just outside the breakers, which would carry the dead shark to the beach, we cast it adrift. The tide was high, about to change, and I depended upon the lowering tide to leave the carcass stranded so I could film the essential shots of Bill and Virginia carving up shark steaks for otter food.

The *Maid* got us back to our car where we found our female stunt double waiting on the dock, embarrassed, contrite, and hung over. But this time, I did need her, if only for her hands.

We sped to the shark site. There high on the beach lay the impressive carcass. It looked even larger than it had in the water. I filmed my doubles as they walked to the shark carrying buckets and knives. Then I began shooting close-ups of hands and knives cutting through skin and slicing off chunks of meat.

I had my eye stuck to the viewfinder of my Arriflex, focusing on "Virginia's" hands and following their movements and shooting away, when I realized that her hands were being intercepted by a pair of big grizzled paws with red shirt-sleeve cuffs that didn't fit the script. The unexpected hands took the knife away from the subject hands and began slicing meat.

I looked up.

An elderly beachcomber had come upon our shoot. Seeing a pretty girl slaving away at man's work he was only being helpful.

* * * * *

Maxwell shrugged off my assertion that I'd already filmed the basking shark sequence and dove into the subject of his main objection to my messing around with his story: the new female character, he pointed out, was a gross fabrication. My alteration to his story, changing the young male character into a woman left no part for his protégé—a wrong turn from reality that he hoped I'd change.

While being as discreet as possible, I tried to explain my reason for this tweak in the truth, which had changed his story—heretofore unattractive to moviemakers—into a valuable motion picture property. Our talk was brief and it was clear that we'd come to an impasse on the main point. For me to hang around another night only to kill another bottle of whiskey with an unhappy writer seemed pointless. Maxwell had no legal or contractual grounds to enforce his wishes, and I had no urge to change my conviction. We shared a brunch of leftover salmon and venison sandwiches, and I pulled on my rubber boots and slogged back up the muddy trail to my car.

I drove up the road a quarter of a mile, pulled into the fork of Maxwell's driveway and turned around. I never asked him why he'd failed to mention this gravel road on the map he'd sent me.

* * * * *

Hubert arrived with six otters. Somehow he had found the only otter breeders in the USA, Mabel and Tom Beecham of Michigan. Their captive otters were tame and as amenable as otters can be, and the Beechams came with them. They had hand-raised their otters, but they weren't trainers. Hubie had already brought two of Beecham's pets to his California compound and spent four months training our pair of stars.

Though they are among the hardest animals to train, the otters under Hubert Wells' supervision did well. As an example of the kind of difficulty Hubert faced, and in answer to that question most frequently asked of animal cameramen—"How do you get them to do all of those things?" Here's what Hubert did to make an important otter trait possible to film.

The most aggravating thing about filming an otter is that the curious little animal is never still. Except for the rare moments when it's asleep, an otter is constantly on the move, sniffing here, looking there, charging off first in one direction, then another.

There were many moments in the movie when in order to interact with the humans in the film, Mij (the name of Maxwell's pet) had to be still. How does an actor talk to an otter that's all over the place? To carry on a conversation—even a dialogue as one-sided as a man talking to an otter—the listener needs to be sitting calmly and "reacting" to what his human co-star has to say.

Unlike many animals—a dog, for example, with its many expressions—an otter's face is more or less fixed in a frozen mask. Still, an otter's bright-eyed expression registers engagingly when you can get a good look at it. So two problems had the same challenge: the fidgety animal had to remain still long enough to engage in a dialogue, and it had to be still long enough so we could get a good look at its face and see how charming it was.

At certain times, especially if attracted by something moving or calling in tall grass, an otter pauses from whatever it's doing, sits high up on it's hind legs, and takes a look over the top of the grass to see what's going on. In that attitude, it's often still for several seconds—not a whole minute but long enough.

That was the attitude I wanted Hubert to train our otter to take on command. Not only would he be required to sit up and look, he had to do it where and when we wanted him to do it. That was the ringer.

As a first step, Hubert adapted a classic method used by old-time lion and tiger trainers in circus acts. In trainer's jargon it's called "pedestal training." Sit a big cat on a pedestal and teach him to stay put; it helps a lot as a way to control the cat and to save the necks of lion trainers.

Hubert pedestal-trained the otter by feeding him on the top of a miniature pedestal, a foot-high block of wood four inches in diameter. At the same time that the otter was learning to take his meals atop the block of wood, he was also learning through repetition that the brief ring of an electric buzzer meant dinner time. When the otter got used to eating every meal atop his pedestal—a matter of a few weeks' training—Hubert began holding a tempting piece of fish high enough over the otter's head that it had to sit up on its hind legs atop the pedestal and reach high for the delicious treat.

When the otter got accustomed to that exercise—coming to the buzzer, feeding atop the pedestal, and standing there looking around waiting for the next tidbit to arrive—Hubert began to shrink the pedestal.

Gradually it was reduced until it was only a piece of cloth, unobtrusive to the camera but still a marker for the otter. The disc of cloth and the buzzer could be hidden in the grass or on a set, and we used Hubert's ingenious training method for many of the most effective otter scenes.

Spring came late the year of our shoot. On the first scheduled morning of filming, half a foot of newly fallen snow lay on the ground. I was there with a full crew, a bit nervous, faced with shooting a sequence in the snow that had been written to look like the middle of summer.

With sudden inspiration, I imagined a new scene: shoot the unforeseen new snow just as it happened. The solution to our problem was obvious: incorporate the new situation into the story. With my experience in filming wildlife shows, I was used to dealing with the unexpected, when success depended upon the filmmaker's adaptability. So a new sequence was created by nature in the moment.

The otters went wild in the snow, a favorite medium for play. They tobogganed down hills on their bellies, then raced back to the summit to sled down again and again. The unexpected bonus scenes were worked into one of the most charming sequences in the film. By the time lunch was over the snow had melted and we were able to proceed as planned—with the gift of a wonderful new sequence in the can.

Back in USA school was out. Joan and Mike packed for their flights to London and on by train to Oban. I had rented an old stone croft cottage on a farm in a cozy-looking valley between grassy hills. Stone fences surrounded our house. Sheep and highland cattle grazed the pastures, and a bright stream cascaded through the meadow. Rooks pecked at the slate roof and wild greylag geese floated on the pond. It had looked picturesque and beautiful the sunny day I closed the rental deal, but living in it was anything but picture perfect.

We soon discovered that the heating system was of a type I'd never seen or heard of before. Water pipes ran through the wood-burning stove in the kitchen so the fire had to be constantly stoked to provide warm water. A fireplace in the sitting room, with rusty iron flues that ran helter-skelter to the other rooms, took the edge off the chill, but even with the fire blazing we were seldom without sweaters.

After Mike was born, Joan had discovered that she was a nester, and this was anything but her idea of the perfect nest.

I was out shooting every day, up at dawn and back home after dark. Joan and Mike were left all day with a cold house and a damp, soggy countryside.

I'd been advised that it was foolish to take a film unit to the west coast of Scotland. The area was notorious for week after week of steady rain. We'd be wiped out, I was told. As a precaution, a number of interior sets were prepared where we could film under a roof on rainy days. At the end of the production we shot all of those cover sets that weather had never forced us to use.

* * * * *

The editing was completed at our Soho cutting room in London, a short walk from my Leicester Square digs. Gavin Maxwell never visited us during the filming, but he had written a few dubious comments about the production in the newspaper. Joe Strick thought it was worth the risk to show him the film now and let him get any gripes off his chest before the release, when bad press would be more damaging.

The screening was arranged and Maxwell showed up in London with his business manager in tow. They were accompanied by a stranger, Maxwell's solicitor. He was beetle-browed, clean-shaven, chin with black whisker roots—a more ominous-looking character I couldn't imagine. I said something to Joe about typecasting him as a Fagin in our next horror flick.

Most movie pros are used to the sterile ambiance of an empty theater. But even for filmmakers used to looking at films without audience participation, a screening with only a handful of viewers always poses obstacles to enjoyment. Audience reactions are friendly and supportive; movies play best with a house full of receptive viewers. When one's neighbors are laughing, the emotion is contagious.

By contrast, a large, nearly-empty screening room, no matter how comfortable the chairs, has the atmosphere of a morgue.

Sitting in the middle, surrounded by rows of empty seats, Joe and I felt like convicted jailbirds waiting for the executioner. Introductions had been cold and businesslike. Maxwell and his friends skipped a couple of rows and took seats behind us. These guys just *knew* they were going to hate the movie.

As the lights dimmed Joe and I looked at each other. Ever supportive, Joe winked and whispered. "Don't worry. They'll warm up."

"I'm not so sure," I said. "Maxwell looks cold enough to spit ice cubes."

The film began to roll. Except for the sound coming from the speakers, we sat in silence. I listened in vain to catch a word from the muffled whispers coming from behind.

Then I picked up Maxwell's words: "He doesn't look at all like me. And never in a thousand years would you catch me in a hat like that."

So he wasn't going to give us a chance. Maxwell was set to nitpick every detail.

A few mumbled whispers, a heavy sigh—or was it a groan?

Then I heard a chuckle. Oh, oh! Someone was warming up.

Twenty minutes into the film, the voices from behind had lost their secretive whispers. The cold atmosphere had changed. There were outright exclamations. Approving chatter emanated from the rear. Laughs came at all the right places.

When the lights came up, Maxwell was rubbing tears out of his eyes.

* * * * *

Edgar Scherick's company, Palomar Pictures, still needed to secure a commitment from a releasing organization. Joe and Edgar decided that the Disney company could do best with our movie. I sent a print to my friend Cardon Walker, the head of production at Disney.

Back at the beginning when Joe and I had first approached Bill Travers and Virginia McKenna about starring in our film, Bill had insisted on one script change. In my adaptation, I'd made only two fundamental changes to the book. I'd substituted Virginia's role for that of Maxwell's young male friend, and rather than end the story on a downbeat note with Mij's death, I'd changed that as well.

In my version, which I thought was preferable for a family film, Mij disappears near the end of the story. He's gone for weeks and Maxwell thinks he's dead. Then at the final curtain, Mij comes home with a wife and babies in tow. He'd been denned-up with the female while she had his pups. The script ended on an upbeat note.

Bill Travers was adamant about sticking with the ending of the book. He felt that the killing of animals by humans was a wrong that should be addressed. *Ring of Bright Water* presented a chance to show the inhumanity of people who killed animals—the message that Travers, in his new role as an animal rights activist, was preoccupied with telling to the world. Travers would star in the film, but only on the condition that I change the ending.

Edgar Sherick reluctantly agreed to Travers' ultimatum, but he had his own conditions. He made a side deal with me. He'd accept the change, but only if I'd shoot the original finale as well—and shoot it cleverly so that Travers wouldn't be aware that the ending of the film could be cut either way.

During the editing process, Joe and I decided we had to take the honest approach. We knew that Edgar's ending (which was to drop the otter's death scene and let Mij live) would be the more popular one, but we'd made a commitment to Travers that couldn't be broken. We knew that killing the adorable otter was going to turn off a part of our audience, but that's the price we'd agreed to pay to our obdurate star. Sure, we wanted to be players, but not at the price of a double-cross.

We cut the picture Travers' way. Mij was killed, and many a tear flowed in cinemas all over the world.

But by incorporating an upbeat stroke we could still bring some relief to the ending: the film fades out as Mij's mate and her babies return to the pool beside Maxwell's cottage. In this way, Mij is dead, but his blood will live on in the youngsters he had fathered.

* * * * *

Our compromise ending wasn't enough for Card Walker. When he called me immediately after screening the picture, he was sincerely angry. "Jesus, Jack! When you killed Mij, I could have wrung your neck. Do you realize that by killing that otter you cost yourself millions of dollars? Halfway into the movie everyone has fallen in love with Mij. Disney can't release a movie that'll give every kid in the audience nightmares."

I didn't tell Card that we had the material to re-cut *Ring* with the original cheerful ending.

As it was, *Ring* was a huge success when it premiered in the summer of 1969. People cried, but they went to see it in multitudes. In its opening week, it broke house records and received only good reviews.

Joe and I held a big piece of the net profits, but in the end, the millions Card Walker said I'd cost myself wouldn't have materialized anyway. Cinerama Corporation, with whom Scherick made a releasing deal, played our film in its first run with a weaker but far more expensive film, one in which they had a big investment. People went to see *Ring of Bright Water*, but to see it, they had to sit through the main bill, *Krakatoa, East of Java*. The profits were fiddled by an accounting trick called cross-collateralization; thus *Krakatoa* took the biggest part of the box-office coin.

There is in Hollywood something called "Creative Accounting." Our movie made so many dollars that we should have gotten a healthy share, but there were no net profits, only gross profits to which we weren't entitled. We never saw a penny.

12 Jonathan Livingstone Seagull

In 1973, I was nominated for an Academy Award in cinematography for my work on *Jonathan Livingston Seagull,* which had been shot two years earlier. I was in Africa working on *Living Free* during the time the Awards ceremony was taking place in Los Angeles. I hadn't thought of attending the ceremony. If there'd been even a remote chance of winning, I'd have gone, but I knew there wasn't. But to me, this nomination was the most generous gift my peers could have bestowed upon me.

Seagull just wasn't the kind of movie that gets Academy Awards or even nominations. Nominations are presented to movies with strong dramatic stories and performances. Both blockbusters and sleepers get awards, but there hadn't been a nomination for a film in the general nature of *Seagull* within my memory, if ever. My photography was what one would expect to see in a fine documentary. It was nice-to-look-at outdoor photography, but hardly the wonderful series of sometimes complicated, always artful lighting setups within the interiors of buildings that requires the more technical kind of filming so rightly appreciated and nominated by my brother cameramen.

My lighting kit and crew had consisted only of reflectors, a small generator, a handful of lamps, one gaffer, and a grip. I'd broken some new ground by using emulsions in unconventional and imaginative ways, but as I said, this was the kind of movie that just doesn't garner Academy Award nominations.

I'd never been an insider among the upper crust of Hollywood social circles. I had a few friends who were, and many of the people I'd worked with were regulars at the famous places where one went to see and be seen. But Hollywood socializing wasn't my bag.

Hall Bartlett, the Producer-Director of *Jonathan Livingston Seagull*, lived in that circle, and as the picture was nearing completion he put things in motion that he hoped would bring critical attention to his movie. He bought full-page ads in the trade papers touting me and the photography. He wanted me to join the Academy of Motion Picture Arts and Sciences, an invitation that had been open for some time but which I'd never acted upon. And he pressured me to seek membership in the prestigious Hollywood cameramen's club, The American Society of Cinematographers. I did, and my pals Conrad Hall and Haskell Wexler nominated me. I couldn't ask for more distinguished sponsors.

I'd always felt that another of my gifts to the *Seagull* picture was at least as important as, if less noticed than, my photographic contribution. Hall Bartlett had written the script, and in the style of the bestselling book he gave voices to the seagulls. As I saw the movie coming together in the cutting room, I realized that this device wasn't friendly to my taste. Those often pretentious lines were spoken by well-known actors and actresses, but having them come out of the mouths of birds just didn't work for me.

I showed Bartlett the workprint of my film *The Legend of the Boy and the Eagle*, sure he'd see a corollary to the seagull movie. One sequence of an eagle in flight was a particularly effective parallel to parts of *Seagull.* There were no narrative voices, only music and the exotically haunting voice of Yma Sumac coupled with the images, told a strong story point. I also showed Bartlett the film collaboration by my chums Joe Strick and Irving Lerner, the zany spoof called *Muscle Beach*, a romp of huffing, puffing bodies told entirely with picture, lyrics, and song.

Hall Bartlett saw what I was trying to tell him and went his own way with it. He made a deal with singer-songwriter Neil Diamond to write an album for *Jonathan Livingston Seagull.* It was the half-dozen or so sequences in the film that were accompanied by Diamond's music that made those parts of the picture fly for me—and I believe for most audiences.

The Academy Award for cinematography that year was won by Sven Nykvist for his outstanding work on *Cries and Whispers*. Other nominees were Owen Roizman, Robert Surtess, and Harry Stradling, Jr. I was honored to be on the list alongside such talents as these.

13

Living Free

Perhaps you will remember from the beginning of this book about my arrival in Africa and meeting Sieuwke Bisleti. She had signed-on to rear the lion cubs for the film I was to direct called *Living Free.* Now we have caught up again with that point in time, and the five baby lions that came to be known as Sieuwke's Cubs arrived by air in a small wooden crate from Addis Ababa in Ethiopia. They were the gift of Emperor Haile Selassie, "The Lion of Judah," as he was known. In honor of his exalted title, the Emperor kept a pair of adult lions in the palace gardens, thus these little princes and princesses were true royalty. But only one, Dennis (we called him Dennis the Menace) really felt himself to be the King of Beasts, for even as a kitten he was already showing his penchant for rule.

The first night Sieuwke got the little two-week-old cubs she took them to bed with her. The more they got to know her smell, the closer they would bond. They were so tiny, and the nights so cold, that Sieuwke didn't want them to catch colds. A hot water bottle wasn't enough—they needed body heat.

She named the cubs Homerus, Ace, Mace, Judy, and Dennis. That first night in bed, Dennis tried to suck Sieuwke's nose. There on her face he found something sticking out—he wanted milk. That was too much. She decided they'd just have to keep warm at night by snuggling close to each other in a modified human baby's crib that she kept near her bed, so she could hear any distress calls during the night.

To get the cubs used to the experience of riding in a car, Sieuwke drove them back and forth from her house to the film compound in a minibus every day. This part of their education was important: we wanted riding in the vehicle to be a pleasure for the cubs, something they would look forward to each day when they had to report for acting duties on the set. They soon grew to love the minibus with all its excitements. They raced each other when they heard the familiar hoot from the car that meant "time to roll." Then they all tried to scramble into the side door at the same time, pushing and shoving, each to claim a window from which to stick out a head, feel the wind, and watch the scenery passing by.

The sight of a minibus tearing down the road with five little lions' heads sticking out of the windows gave many a tourist a double-take. But to the best of my knowledge this phenomenon caused no serious accidents.

My friend, head trainer Hubert Wells, who had dealt so well with the otters, arrived with nine older lion cubs from California. They would play Elsa's cubs in later stages of development. By switching around between three age groups of three lions each, we would be able to film within a period of only a few months a progression of growth that covered a couple of years in real time.

It's easy for people who already feel an affinity toward animals to lose their hearts completely to lions. Perhaps it's not rational, this love one develops for an animal, but through our close associations with domestic animals—a dog, horse, or cat, for example—many of us know the feeling.

Although lions are wild and bear no hint of the long process of domestication of, say, a dog, which carries in its genes an inborn familiarity that comes from centuries of association with humans, lions are also highly social animals. They live in close family groups called prides that sometimes number more than a dozen individuals who live and work cooperatively. They help each other in the hunt, and mothers run day care centers for the offspring of other lionesses—not unique social traits in wild animals, but a rarity nonetheless. Maybe it's these sociable attributes that make lions so compelling to humans—or possibly it's their appealing and expressive faces. Some people say it's the human fascination with predators that forms this attraction.

After spending months working with the lions and virtually reliving the lives of George and Joy, Bill and Virginia had become personally involved with the young lions they helped to raise. They felt that to react truthfully with the animals in the film, it was necessary to be as close to the lions as George and Joy had been, and they threw themselves into the roles without fear.

At the end of production, George Adamson offered to take over the company-owned lions and train and habituate them to live in the wild. He already had a remote base camp where he was rehabilitating other captive-reared lions. Bill and Virginia supported him with fervor. If the company didn't turn the big cats over to George, what did they intend to do to assure the future welfare of these animals they had grown to love?

Because Sieuwke's lions were happily ensconced and well taken care of at Marula, they never became a part of the argument and bitterness that followed.

Producer Carl Foreman's answer to the Adamsons and to Bill and Virginia was that the film lions should be returned to the zoos and animal parks where they had come from. Paul Radin took the side of his producer partner.

A quarrel of great philosophical disparity erupted with a lot of ugly recriminations. Foreman ordered the *Born Free* lions shipped back their origins in Europe and America, and the issue was settled by action if not consensus. It was this event, involving animals they had grown to know and love, that was to spark the lifelong anti-zoo activism of Bill and Virginia, which later continued through their son.

If the producers had any idea at the time about how successful their film would be, and what stars Bill and Virginia would become as a result of the sympathetic roles they played, perhaps Carl and Paul would have listened to the impassioned pleas of their acting team. But Carl, at least, didn't really expect the movie to be a hit.

Carl Foreman hadn't enjoyed the Africa experience and it had turned him sour. (Paul Radin, in contrast, fell in love with Kenya and built a house there.) Probably due to the many production hassles during its making, Foreman didn't particularly like *Born Free.* One irony that became a Hollywood joke was that Foreman hated the original score that John Barry wrote for the movie. He disliked it so much that immediately after hearing it he commissioned another composer to write a different piece of music.

John Barry had this to say about it: "I had big disagreements with the Director [James Hill]. He thought he'd made a very meaningful movie, an intellectual statement about freedom. I saw it as a lovely family entertainment. So I said to Carl Forman, the only way I can do this is by doing almost a satire on a sentimental Disney kind of picture."

Forman hated the new score even more than the first, and finally went back to the original only because time ran out. John Barry's *Born Free* score became one of the most popular pieces of movie music ever written.

* * * * *

Because the producers had not acceded to the wishes of Travers and McKenna for a more sensitive placement of the movie lions at the end of production, the stars refused to appear in the sequel.

I had just finished working with the couple in *Ring of Bright Water* and what began as a warm professional relationship had evolved into a close friendship. When I accepted the assignment to direct the sequel to *Born Free*, I knew nothing about the wrangling that had gone on over the lions and assumed that Bill and Virginia would be in the cast. I accepted an invitation to spend a weekend with them at their home in Dorking, south of London, expecting to talk about the new movie we were going to make together. I was floored when they told me they had already been approached by Carl Foreman and had told him they'd have none of it.

I was deeply troubled by this unexpected turn of events. I couldn't imagine a sequel to *Born Free* without Bill and Virginia in the lead roles. At last, in deference to the respect and good feelings they had for me, Bill and Virginia agreed to appear in the sequel, but only on the condition that neither Paul Radin nor Carl Foreman would be present in Africa while the movie was in production.

Then, making a huge bungle, Paul turned down Bill and Virginia's terms—a lack of foresight that hit me hard. Virginia's role was recast with Susan Hampshire, who had just won fame as Fleur in the popular British TV series *Upstairs, Downstairs*. Lovely Susan was a good choice to play Joy Adamson and would probably have carried the role beautifully if she'd been the original Joy, but to step into the shoes of a character already known and loved by a large—and presumably repeat—audience, was a tough hurdle to leap.

At the same time, Nigel Davenport was being considered by the producers to play the role of George Adamson. Nigel had impressed Carl in a feature called *Virgin Soldiers*. I had never met Nigel but had seen his work and felt the actor lacked the warmth and engaging charm of Bill

Travers. I thought Davenport was so wrong for the part that I didn't take Foreman's suggestion seriously, and began leafing through the casting directories and talking to agents in search of the perfect male lead. After a couple weeks of interviewing actors, I felt betrayed when Carl told me that he'd already signed Davenport to play the George Adamson role.

A nice enough man, Nigel had a stiff physical carriage along with a stern and stony countenance that was just the opposite of his warm-faced predecessor's portrayal of easygoing George Adamson. To this day I can't imagine a more unhappy choice, and I'm sure my intuition was right. As good an actor as Nigel may have been, he was terribly miscast as George Adamson.

14 Swimming To Elephant Rock

For the house that would pass for the Adamsons' home and the main location in the film we chose an old homestead on an island in Lake Naivasha. It was made habitable by chasing out a colony of bats. I moved in, preferring the beautiful solitude of Crescent Island to hotel living.

Joan, and Mike (now nine), came to spend the months of July and August with me there. Mike quickly made friends with Kamau, a boy his age who tended a herd of sheep on the island. Each boy had his field of expertise, which was happily shared. Mike soon qualified as apprentice shepherd, while in hours of truancy Kamau turned to fisherman-in-training.

I was involved in preparing the lion compound and scouting locations. The pressures of filming hadn't begun, thus we had ample family time together. But Joan declared that this was the last time she would accompany me to the "ends of the earth." This visit to Africa finally sunk the foundering ship of a marriage that had previously gone off course, run onto a few reefs, and sprung many leaks. Years of packing up her nest and traveling to remote places—a life that Joan hated and on which I thrived—at last drove us completely apart.

On the day that my crew finished building the lion pens, Joan and Mike left to return to America, home, and school. Hubert Wells, who was bringing his big cats from America, was due tomorrow.

* * * * *

Sieuwke's cubs were growing fast. By the time actors and crew were scheduled to arrive the cubs would have passed through that appealing phase of kittenish antics—the period when they are charming clowns and can best be described as adorable.

To assure myself that I didn't miss anything, I began shooting brief sequences with the cubs at play. These were informal sessions for which I didn't need a crew, only Sieuwke to help with the cubs. It was a casual way of edging into production, and the kittens benefited through gradual exposure to a work schedule that would grow rigorous when the crew and actors arrived.

At this time my friend, Joe Strick, accepted my invitation to enjoy an African honeymoon with his new bride Martine. I organized a three-day safari for us to visit Samburu Game Reserve in the northern part of Kenya. It would be my last chance to get away before the start of intensive filming.

It was late in the day when arrangements for the charter flight were completed. On the way home from the production office I pulled my Land Rover into the lion compound where I saw Sieuwke on the grass playing with her cubs. I sat down, joining in some gentle roughhousing with the lions, and soon we were laughing together over their funny antics. They played with us and each other with equal zeal, mauled us with oversized paws, pulled at our hair with tiny teeth, tumbled and fell, pawed the air, pulled each other's tails, and nipped our ears.

In a moment of respite from claws and teeth, while the cubs rested on the grass to gather steam for the next round, I told Sieuwke about noting the sadness in her face on the first day I'd seen her. For a month we had each been busy with our work; this was the first time anything personal passed between us.

"The sadness is still there," I said. "But I think you're winning the battle."

"Quite honestly, I needed the work," she said.

I remembered that Paul had seemed surprised when Sieuwke accepted the assignment without hesitation. "Don't you think you should discuss it with Francesco?" he'd asked.

"Paul," she'd said, "with things as they are, my husband couldn't care less. Francesco has left me."

She'd made no pretense. There was no hint of pride that might cause her to try to make it seem that *she* had left *him*. She was clearly heartbroken, defenses down, on the edge. Her self-esteem must have suffered a severe blow.

"This was just what I needed to get back on my feet," she said to me now. "It couldn't have come at a better time."

I smiled when I recalled my surprise when I'd seen her face harden. "But don't you dare take advantage of my situation and offer half the salary you would otherwise have given me," she'd said to Paul.

Sieuwke wasn't shrewd—and I'd never bet on her in a poker game. Her bargaining tactics were as open as a book.

I could identify with what Sieuwke was going through. My wife and I had not actually pulled the plug on our relationship back in America. We had discussed the inevitability but decided to keep up the pretense for a while longer. Right or wrong, we thought it would be better for our son to have the advantages of a few more years of family life. But we were only going through the motions. In reality, I knew our marriage was over.

"Thanks to you and Paul," Sieuwke said. "This involvement with the animals came at just the right time. Amazing…something unexpected comes out of the blue, turns everything around, and pulls one up out of the dumps."

"Spoken as a fatalist?" I asked.

Sieuwke nodded. "If a fatalist is a person who doesn't make plans, who accepts life as it comes day by day, then yes, that's what I am."

I realized that Sieuwke's life had been more unsettled than mine, subject to unexpected events over which she had no control. At this very moment, while I was contemplating my first broken marriage, she was suffering through her third.

I found myself telling her about my honeymooning friends and our upcoming safari to Samburu Game Reserve. In all her years in Kenya, Sieuwke said, her safaris with her husband had always been to hunting areas, not to the parks and reserves.

I was surprised to hear myself telling her that as an unattached male tagging along on a honeymoon trip I was sure to end up feeling malapropos. A feeling of giddiness came over me. I couldn't believe the dramatic effect of the thoughts that were ricocheting through my head. I felt like a teenager again. With my heart pumping wildly, I asked Sieuwke if she'd like to join us.

She accepted without hesitation.

The next morning, the four of us were picked up literally in our backyard by a twin-engined Cessna. We flew north along the edge of the forested Aberdare Mountains and skirted Mount Kenya, which on that rare day showed its teeth of jagged ice. We flew on into the wild semi-arid Northern Frontier District toward the tree-lined windings of the river Uaso Nyiro, its sandy banks shaded with tall dom palms. Our pilot brought us in low above the stream, following its meander, and by the time we landed on a rough dirt strip we had already seen hippos, elephants, and giraffe.

At the lodge nestled beneath flat-topped thorn trees, Joe and Martine had a bungalow to themselves. Sieuwke and I were shown to separate cottages. The space between our rustic doors was soft with luxuriant grass. The river ran slow and shallow before us; birds called across the water. That afternoon we went on a game-viewing drive. I saw animals I'd seen before only in pictures or at the zoo. Elephants, gerenuk, oryx, and the oddly beautiful vulturine guinea fowl were common. I had dreamed since childhood of this experience, of visiting Africa. Until this moment I'd never realized how much I wanted to be here.

That evening we had drinks on the lodge terrace and watched crocodiles haul themselves onto the bank below our chairs. Between serving cocktails the waiters were kept busy chasing monkeys away from the guests' hors d'oeuvres. Then we retired to our rooms for showers and a rest.

Later, after dinner, I sat alone on my veranda overlooking the river, trying to resolve a problem in the script. But my attention kept wandering to the spectacle of this enchanting place which was coming alive with new animals as the natural history program shifted from daytime activity to creatures of the dusk.

Then I felt a presence behind me. Before I could turn, soft hair crossed my forehead and I realized it was Sieuwke bending over me. "I had a marvelous time today," she said as she leaned over my shoulder and brushed my cheek with her lips. "Thank you."

I was smitten.

"Life is really rather beautiful, isn't it?" she said.

As I was to learn later, that thought was Sieuwke's refrain. It epitomized a facet of her character that endeared me to her. It wasn't that Sieuwke never suffered the blues; she did of course, as we all do. And when Sieuwke was dejected, so was I; emotions are contagious. But she had the rather unusual ability to bounce back from the most trying or depressing times. She was a happy person, ever the optimist, always looking for the good aspect of a bad situation or the redeeming feature in an unsympathetic personality.

Sieuwke warmed my heart with those words, making them real and believable: "Life is really rather beautiful, isn't it?"

* * * * *

It was still six weeks before cast and crew would arrive in Kenya. We had built cages, Hubert and his assistants and the lions were getting acclimated and training was underway. I'd heard of a place called Lake Hannington that I thought would make a good location for a sequence with the cubs. It was a remote byway, seldom visited and reached at the end of a long and stony trail. In three four-wheel-drive vehicles, one carrying camp staff and gear, another Hubert, my camera assistant, and lion cubs, and the third Sieuwke and me, we followed a vague track through thick bush country. The wandering route criss-crossed innumerable vague paths so we were often obliged to ask the local tribespeople which obscure track was game trail and which was road.

Sadly, that romantic state of remoteness has changed over the years. The paved approach to Lake Hannington, along with its new name—Lake Bogoria—is quite different today. But the objective at the end of the road is still the same amazing place.

As our caravan topped the last summit and the lake came into view, my car stopped almost spontaniously—as if the sudden spectacle that appeared before us was a physical barrier. At the bottom of the sheer black face of a 2000-foot-tall escarpment lay a shimmering surface of brilliant color, of luminous depth and vivid pink. It was the season when flamingos gather, and we had arrived during one of the greatest amassments in years. Skeins of pink motes drifted between us and the dark cliffs, solid masses of pink undulated in moving waves from the shore far out into the blue-green shimmer where thousands more pink dots speckled the surface. The entire mass was in movement. Birds were taking off, landing, flying away, coming back, circling, climbing, dropping. We heard a babble of voices muffled by distance—the chatter of thousands of flamingos all mixed into one great chorus.

We had come to film a sequence depicting Elsa's orphaned cubs lost in the immensity of Africa. This awesome background of brightly colored birds and black cliffs was the perfect setting. The dramatic effect I imagined required the angular golden light of late afternoon to highlight the pink flamingos against the black background of the escarpment. But as luck would have it, we arrived in the company of a slow-moving storm. Fierce thunder squalls rolled in close behind us and cut off the sun. The production company's bad fortune became our personal windfall: the lingering clouds provided the welcome excuse to lay off work until the storm went away.

We set up our tents and lion shelters beneath flat-topped trees near the lake and awaited a change in the weather. A short distance down the shore, billows of steam erupted from geyser vents, and at the end of each meal our camp staff carried dirty dishes to the edge of a bubbling geyser and used the hot runoff to scald them clean.

I was used to rough camping, so this was a new experience for me. With a cook and staff to look after the chores, with hot geyser water on demand for showers, bedding aired every day, and laundry washed at the asking, it was a luxury camp unlike anything I'd known before. We had wild animals of many kinds close around, and unusual-looking, traditionally-garbed people wandering past, as interested in us as we were in them. There was little of the urgency of time under which a film unit is usually obliged to work; and being there with Sieuwke, I was very happy.

Not far from the camp site, a noisy stream boiled down from the range of hills we had descended in getting here. Colored by silty runoff, it looked like creamed coffee running through the rocks. Although not appealing to the eye, the water was known to be free of the hateful parasite that causes a disease called bilharzia. Common across much of Africa, the worm made it wise to know your waters well before plunging in.

During a break in the storm, we drove back to the swimming stream where it ran through a series of hot springs. As it bubbled past the submerged geyser vents, the stream changed from a cold hill torrent into a tepid bath.

Leaving the others soaking at the hot springs, Sieuwke and I let the current carry us downstream. With only our heads sticking above the surface, the turbid water wrapped our bodies in an opaque blanket. At one river curve, a gallery of curious Njemps tribesmen watched us drift past. We floated on through a narrow gorge into a private world of solitude. Wild fig trees with their snakelike roots coiling onto the cliff overhung the canyon. Ahead of us, with its feet in the stream, a mound of gray stone was worn as smooth as an agate pebble by a few million years of river current. The huge boulder was sculpted into convoluted shapes, and the bumps and hollows resembled the limbs and body of a great elephant. Climbing up the trunk of Jumbo Rock, we fit ourselves into the declivities as snugly as moss fits a boulder. Alone under the great African sky, thoughts of work as remote as our youth, cradled by the sculpted stone, we allowed ourselves to be caressed by the warming sun.

Getting back up the current to our car and clothes was another thing. But happily, the local people had left the scene. We had only our own giggles to go with us in our scramble back over the stones.

Later, with rain beating on the car's drum metal roof, roaring down hillsides in cataracts and cutting gullies across the road, we drove back toward camp. Then the downpour stopped abruptly; silver rays pried through clouds that lay heavily against the escarpment. On a knoll close beside the track a ray of sun probed like a theatrical spotlight. Into the silver shaft, a huge bull kudu loomed from the bush. Most spectacular of antelopes, the kudu's horns curled in long corkscrews. I eased the Land Rover to a stop. Then the magnificent buck strode away and disappeared into a new rain squall.

That evening the storm cleared and we all sat on camp chairs around a fire, balancing whiskey glasses on the arms and munching cheese toasties. Someone threw a dry thorn tree bough onto the coals, and its sharp spines caught fire before the heavier limbs and lit up in hundreds of tiny lights. Sputtering like candles on a Christmas tree, snapping and sparking against the backdrop of the night, the little lights burned down and became red twists of glowing ember. Then they broke loose from their stems and shot upward, the dying sparks soaring away toward the far-away stars.

Later I lay awake listening to the jaws of a large grazing animal—probably a waterbuck or a zebra, although I imagined it was our kudu—close outside the tent, munching noisily on the grass. I fell asleep with the wild sound in my ears, perhaps the most contented man on earth.

* * * * *

After we had completed our work at Lake Bogoria and were driving back to Naivasha, I was troubled. Even though my relationship with my wife was finished, I was still married. Although my nine-year-old son would hardly know the law and manners of society, his disapproval was alive in my mind, shaking a finger at me. I was loaded with guilt, pestered with self-blame, assailed by doubt.

I didn't know if I fell in love with Africa and there happened to be a woman, or if I fell in love with a woman and I happened to be in Africa. Or was it simply a double love affair at first sight?

I pulled the car to the side of the road and turned to Sieuwke.

"There's something I have to say."

"Yes?" she said.

"I just want you to know that there's no future in this."

Sieuwke laughed and shook her head. "Does it matter?" she said.

15

Bushy Island

But there *was* a future. And it had already begun.

When Sieuwke and I met, she was living on her husband's ranch. She also owned a small hill next to the farm we had leased for the *Living Free* headquarters.

In years past when Lake Naivasha was high, Sieuwke's property was called Bushy Island. Now, after years of drought and lowered lake level, her land only lived up to half its name—bushy it was, but an island it was not. Now it was a peninsula. A border of papyrus stood along the shores, and a tall grove of yellow-barked fever trees made it shady and cool.

Sieuwke and I chose to live on Bushy Island during the months-long production of *Living Free.* We talked about building a house here some day. With that in mind, we wanted to learn the animals' habits before we built *our* house on *their* land. To help us absorb the land's vibrations, we set up our tent in a clearing close to the summit.

The property was a wildlife paradise. A wide variety of birds were drawn by the lake waters or the thickets which the name suggested. Monkeys combed the treetops for seeds; bushbuck, impala, reedbuck, dic dic, and waterbuck trampled winding trails through the bush. Sometimes cape buffalo moved through, so one had to keep an eye out for these dangerous animals. Servals, jackals, mongoose, genets, even an occasional leopard, stalked the paths at night. By far the most conspicuous animals were the hippos that grunted and snorted from the lake during the day and came out after dark to graze the hill for its succulent grass.

The nearest electrical lines were a mile away. This meant we'd have a bit of inconvenience—no pump for running water, no electric stove, lights, radio, TV, hot water heater, none of those taken-for-granted comforts of modern life. We set up our camp as if we were on permanent safari, and bent to the tasks of that lifestyle.

We hired four diggers and they picked and spaded a well near the bottom of the hill. The shaft went through three feet of soil and then hit rock. Boulders too big to hoist out were dealt with by lighting fires on top, then dousing the hot stones with cascades of cold water and roping out the shattered, sharp-edged chips.

Two fuel drums served as water tanks, and one of the ex-diggers was given the permanent job of carrying pails up the hill and keeping the drums full. One drum was balanced on stones over hot coals, and the same man's chores included collecting dead firewood.

The shower pail hung from a tree limb. It was surrounded by a screen of bushes and woven reeds that you could see out through, but not in through. Even with the water near scalding hot, our shower when the evening wind was whistling through the cracks was bathing of the most chilling kind—definitely not the stuff of romantic adventure.

Kerosene lanterns were another thing. Years later, when we finally had built our house, brought in power lines and installed an electric pump, refrigerator, hot water heater, and wall sockets with plug-in appliances, the kerosene lamps with their warm yellow glow were the one thing we missed.

We never considered bringing a noisy diesel generator to Bushy Island. Our excuse was that the animals wouldn't like it. But we knew that it was us, not the animals, who would find it disagreeable.

16

Pure Joy

Sieuwke had known Joy Adamson for years. Their shared interest in raising lions, and the fact that they lived in the same community made occasional encounters inevitable. But despite their proximity to each other, they had never developed a close friendship.

Much of what Joy had written in her famous books—*Born Free, Living Free, Forever Free,* and *The Spotted Sphinx*—had happened a number of years before. The author now lived apart from her game warden husband, who preferred a lonely lifestyle, sharing his camp in a remote corner of the wild Northern Frontier District with the lions he was rehabilitating.

Joy's home, which she called Elsamere in honor of the lioness about whom she'd written so successfully, and Sieuwke's husband's ranch, Marula, were on opposite sides of Lake Naivasha. Halfway between the homes of these two lion ladies we had set up the production headquarters for *Living Free.*

With a month still to go before the start of shooting, Joy invited producer Paul Radin and me to tea at her house amidst tall trees and lovingly manicured lawns. She led us to her sitting room for coffee. I was surprised to see throw rugs and chair covers of lion skins in the home of this famous lion lady. The walls were decorated with memorabilia of safaris, photographs of lions, paintings of traditional people, and curious tribal artifacts. In a conspicuous spot on the wall I noticed a large framed photograph of a pile of boulders, which I recognized from a picture in one of her books as Elsa's grave.

George and Joy Adamson had become famous through Joy's book and its movie adaptation, and the whole world thought they looked like

Bill Travers and Virginia McKenna, the real-life husband and wife who portrayed them in the film. Like most other fans of her books and the *Born Free* film, I had always visualized Joy as the same lovely young English woman portrayed by Virginia in the movie. I'd heard that the authoress was actually Austrian, not English, but somehow the image of Virginia never left my mind.

Upon meeting Joy I was reminded of the differences between Hollywood and the real world. My first surprise was that Joy not only didn't look like Virginia McKenna, she didn't speak like her either. Virginia had the pleasing locution of a cultured English lady; the real-life Joy Adamson spoke the language with an Austrian accent so thick it was difficult to understand her. Joy had a round flat face which reminded me of Bert Lahr wearing the makeup of the cowardly lion in *The Wizard of Oz.* But there the similarity stopped. Joy was hardly a coward—as I would soon find out.

Naturally, Joy was curious to know how I would translate her work to the screen, and I was as interested in her as she was in me. As her story was autobiographical, it was important that I have as complete an understanding as possible of her remarkable personality. The better I knew Joy and her husband, the more truth I could bring to the film. That was the take I had from my experience with documentaries. But *Living Free* was not a documentary.

I also looked forward to meeting Joy's husband, George, whose passion for lions, it was generally agreed, had been the inspiration for Joy's writings. George was the expert upon whom her facts depended. I had been told that George was the passive mentor, an introverted personality, the complete opposite of his loquacious wife. By all accounts George was taciturn, quiet, unperturbable—the grand old man of the African bush.

Unfortunately I was unable meet him on that day. He was at his camp in the remote Kora Game Reserve, where he indulged his pastime of rehabilitating captive-bred lions to live in the wild—the theme of Joy's books. I knew that George had taken several of Sieuwke's hand-reared young lions, taught them to look after themselves, and released them into the wild.

I had the feeling during that first brief meeting that Joy was holding back, sizing me up. Our talk didn't approach any aspects of her life with the depth I'd hoped for.

Thus a couple of weeks later when a courteous black man in servant's clothes handed me an envelope I had no notion of the import contained in the hand-written message inside. It was from Joy Adamson.

> *Dear Mr. Couffer,*
> *You will attend a dinner at my home on November second.*
> *Please arrive promptly at seven.*
>
> *Sincerely, Joy Adamson*

Well, she did say "Please."

While Joy's letter writing lacked the winning style of her books, it did say everything she wanted me to know.

On the appointed date I drove through the stone gates to Elsamere and parked under the fever trees. The sun was going down across the lake. Joy was hosting a house guest I was soon to meet: the bushy-browed proprietor of the prestigious publishing house that bore his name, William Collins, Ltd., which is known today as HarperCollins. Billy Collins was Joy's business manager as well as her publisher. He would continue to use his informal first name even after he was knighted years later.

I was delighted to hear that George was also visiting. Joy told me that one of George's tame lions, Boy, had been injured in a fight with a wild lion, and her husband had temporarily moved to Naivasha with the hurt lion to simplify veterinary treatment. George had set up his tent in Joy's garden, where he was now at rest on his folding camp cot.

Joy's was a large and comfortable house containing three bedrooms. I wondered if her husband's choice of living quarters was an arrangement he preferred so he could keep a close eye on the injured lion—or if some other consideration was at play.

Upon my arrival, George was summoned and we all went directly to the dining table. That's where the impending inquisition took place, not in the comfort of the sitting room over pre-dinner drinks before the fire.

Joy was much more talkative than at our first meeting. I watched as she passed plates as if in a hurry, gesturing broadly to her guests, instructing her servants in a curt tone. She was charged with all the nervous energy for which she was renowned.

George sat in silence at the other end of the table nodding agreement when called upon to verify some statement. His small pointed goatee beard, pipe, and humor-wrinkled eyes gave him the aspect of a benevolent wizard.

Joy picked my brain at the dinner table: How would I film this? What did I intend to do about that? She kept me on my toes, testing me, doubting me. I seldom knew if she was satisfied with any of my answers.

She made it clear that she thought my education would be incomplete until I visited Elsa's grave at Meru where the lioness heroine of *Born Free* had been buried with great sadness beneath a huge pile of boulders. Joy insisted that in order to fully appreciate the Elsa phenomenon I should accompany her to the grave. She hoped that if I stood close to Elsa's bones, I'd be moved to insist that the movie scenes which took place at the grave should be shot at the actual site.

Joy told me that the producers wanted to construct a simulated grave in a spot near the main filming location. If I took her side, it would help to resolve this disagreement.

I understood Joy's sentimental wishes and was sympathetic to them, but I knew that the simple facts of logstics and economics would prevail. Moving the entire fifty-plus person crew more than 100 miles into the bush where there were no accommodations, for a set as simple as a pile of boulders, just wouldn't play.

But Joy thought that the vibrations emanating from Elsa's grave would somehow transpose themselves into the film. She said that by filming at the actual site, the movie might absorb some of Elsa's mystic power. And she insisted that we take the survey trip together. It would be a three-day jaunt.

Joy showed me photos of a pile of boulders hemmed in by thick colorless bush. It was a claustrophobic setting, hardly a fitting place to stage an emotional movie scene. Vibrations it might have, but atmosphere? None whatsoever.

In fact I had already chosen the location, a hilltop on nearby Crescent Island with an inspiring view. I told Joy how I felt. I tried to express the importance of giving this sacred moment a pictorial significance, but she'd have none of it. My resistance to joining her on a safari to Elsa's grave annoyed her.

Did she sense my other qualm—that I simply wasn't keen to accompany The Lion Queen on an overnight camping trip into the African wilderness?

Looking back, after *Living Free* was released to less success than its more famous predecessor, perhaps Elsa's cosmic vibrations from the dead were the lift the film needed to bring it wider popularity, although I lean toward the theory that sticking with the original cast would have been more effective.

That night at dinner I made the mistake of being honest. I could have humored Joy and invented some evasion that might have put off the moment of truth. When I promised her that I'd instruct the art director to duplicate the grave in every detail, matching stone for stone with the original from a photograph, I could see that she thought I didn't "get it."

As if to test my credibility further, Joy now held court with her theories of animal-human communication through space. She told of several personal experiences of clairvoyance and recounted incidents when animals she had known had transmitted vital messages to her through the ether and across great distances.

I noted George's noncommittal silence, assumed the same attitude, and nodded at appropriate times. I only wished that, like George, I had a pipe to puff, the perfect smokescreen to hide behind.

Although I'm a doubter, I have no proof or care to prove that extrasensory communication between humans and animals doesn't or can't take place. Countless such episodes have been noted. I made no dissenting comment.

As Joy poured coffee for us, she really got down to business.

"George has employed a nice young man named Tony Fitzjohn," Joy said, "who has a marvelous way with lions. He's presently looking after the Kora camp but when George returns he can get along without a helper for a few months." She stared hard at her husband. "Can't you, George?"

Smoke from the far end of the table billowed out in a cloud and obscured the sage old gentleman.

Ignoring George's silence, Joy continued: "He's by far the best person in Kenya around lions, certainly better than anyone you could bring from America."

Puff, puff, nod, puff.

Again I saw that I was going to have to displease Joy. I explained that training animals for films is a technical specialty, not just an ability to keep them tame and happy.

"I don't doubt Tony's capability," I said. "In fact, I've met and like him. But I've already employed a top-notch California trainer."

I told her that I'd worked with Hubert Wells before and I had great confidence in his ability. I said that Hubert had already selected his staff assistants, but I'd pass along her recommendation. I knew, of course, that Joy wasn't suggesting Tony Fitzjohn as anybody's assistant.

Undaunted, Joy continued to push her candidate. Billy Collins shuffled his cup and suggested that it was really the privilege of the film company to select the crew. Given her business manager's advice Joy finally desisted, but her voice still tingled with irritation.

Then, unwilling to quit without the last word, Joy brought us all to attention with a surprising remark: "Well, I hope at least you won't have that whore working with you."

George puffed rapidly on his pipe and disappeared into an opaque cloud.

Billy Collins' large eyebrows shot up. He sighed, "Now, Joy. Let's not..."

I had the feeling that a thunderbolt had struck nearby.

"I'm sorry, Joy," I interrupted. "But I don't understand."

Collins seemed to know—and dread—what was coming. "Joy, please...." he said.

George remained invisible in his cloud.

"That whore," Joy repeated. "Sieuwke Bisleti."

I was befuddled by this woman and her flakiness. Her comment was so off the wall that I felt no outrage, as perhaps I should. In fact, I almost laughed at the audacity. "Sieuwke is helping with the cubs," I said.

"Well, I won't have it!" Joy snapped. "You'll have to find someone else."

Joy was in no position to dictate such details, but I had no desire to engage in a fight. I simply steamed and kept my mouth shut.

From out of his cigar cloud, George cleared his throat. No words came from the smoke.

Billy Collins shook his head. "Joy, you're overstepping your authority. I know you're only trying to be helpful, but Mister Couffer has every right to chose his own associates."

"We'll see about that," Joy muttered, smoldering.

* * * * *

When I returned from the dinner to our Bushy Island tent and told Sieuwke what Joy Adamson had said, she was stunned. As neighbors, Joy and Sieuwke had often met at the store or post office in nearby Naivasha town. They had only shared small talk, the usual neighborly chit-chat. But their common interest hadn't brought them together at all. They'd never had a sit-down talk about lions.

"I've always had the greatest respect for Joy," Sieuwke said in a rattled, dumbfounded voice.

Sieuwke said that aside from what the cats themselves taught her, she had learned as much about lions from Joy's books as anything else. She praised Joy's selfless conservation work, and said she'd never said a bad word about Joy.

So why had Joy attacked her in this incredibly insulting way?

Sieuwke thought for a moment. "I'm sure it all goes back to a day when I worked on *Born Free*," she said. "Paul Radin hired me to bring my lions with their cubs to the location for the last few shots in the movie."

Sieuwke described the setting near Dol Dol where a huge pile of dome-shaped boulders had been enclosed within a strong wire fence. There was little anyone could do to manage her untrained animals when they were released inside. They were tame but not trained. She baited the lions to a natural platform at the peak of the pile. They came readily and ate the meat she'd placed where the cameraman wanted it. Then the lion family lay down on the spot and looked beautiful—exactly as everyone had hoped they would.

"The camera rolled as the cubs played around their handsome parents," Sieuwke recalled. "And that was it. A happy family portrait—mama and papa lion, their three cubs, and all of wild Africa spread out before them. That, the very ending shots, was my sole contribution to *Born Free*."

But it happened that several journalists and publicity people had been invited to the location to witness the filming of the final scene. Although Joy was generally unwelcome on the set because of having ruffled Travers' and McKenna's feathers through her criticisms, in the interest of positive marketing for the film, she was brought to Dol Dol to meet the publicity people. Everyone played nice.

Sieuwke said that she was present only as an insignificant short-term member of the crew who happened to own the lions that were being filmed on that particular day. "I was definitely only small potatoes and I knew it. I didn't pretend to have played a larger role. I didn't want publicity; I wasn't out to grab the limelight.

"But a couple of the publicists latched on to me," she remembered. "I suppose they thought that an attractive woman who owned lions was something special, and they were groping for anything out of the ordinary to bring attention to a movie that had no big name movie stars attached to it."

Sieuwke was interviewed and photographed and thought she was doing her best for the cause. Joy was interviewd and photographed by the press as well. As it happened Sieuwke's story and picture was the one picked up by the media and she appeared in various magazines and newspapers around the world where Joy most rightfully thought she belonged.

"I wasn't particularly excited by my day of fame. But Joy must have never forgiven me."

I wondered why Joy had picked that particularly onerous epithet to throw at Sieuwke. Why "whore"? Not "busybody," not "meddler," not "lens louse," but "whore?" Sieuwke's reputation was pure. There were no rumors of trysts or midnight affairs with male companions either on or off the movie set.

I realized that Joy saw Sieuwke as a threat, as competition—there wasn't room in Kenya for two lion ladies. I explained this to Sieuwke.

"Me, a threat?" Sieuwke said. "You must be joking. How could I compete with Joy Adamson?"

Sieuwke cried; frustration and anger welled forth in tears. I told her that I wasn't interested in Joy Adamson's quirky judgments. I found Joy difficult to understand in more ways than just her accent, and that I had no intention of separating Sieuwke from her cubs.

* * * * *

I knew that Billy Collins was right in telling Joy she had no control over who I hired as crew. Because of Joy's past interference in the making of *Born Free*, this time around the producers had been careful to keep her at bay. She had only limited script approval and no contractual oversight of anything we did. Still, it was my feeling that as the true-life character in the biographical film, she should be treated with courtesy—although there were times when she made that difficult.

One reason I had looked forward to Joy's dinner invitation was to gain more understanding of her complicated character. It was inevitable that when filming got underway Susan Hampshire would ask me questions about her characterization. To portray a living person can be difficult for an actor or actress. How much to reveal? How much to invent? How much honesty? How much showmanship? Difficult questions.

I would have to tell Susan that I thought it would be best if she stuck with the characterization established by her predecessor, Virginia

McKenna, in the earlier film. When Susan did meet Joy, she thanked me for my advice and said she agreed one hundred percent.

Hubert, however, found Joy's presence on the set to be unbearable. Ordinarily easygoing and professional, he became puffed up and refused to work the lions if Joy was within ear-or eye-shot. He claimed that the aura she projected had bad effects on the cats—that the quick, nervous way she moved annoyed them.

It was likely that her mannerisms annoyed him more than she did the lions. After all, her explosive personality hadn't turned off Elsa in any way. But Hubert prevailed in this snit, and although Joy was always made comfortable when she visited the set, no one ever laid out a red carpet.

17

A Cub of a Different Mettle

A month before cast and crew arrived, the cubs were two months old. Hubert told Sieuwke to bring her babies to the compound to begin their film training. She thought she'd be taking them to the compound every day and bringing them back to sleep in her bedroom, then to the compound again the next morning. But to her horror, when she got to the compound, Hubie told her that henceforth the cubs would all be separated and live at the compound in separate enclosures.

As the mother to those kittens, Sieuwke exploded. "You can't do that to them," she said angrily. "They're a family. Little Judy mothers all of her brothers and they'll be lost without her."

Hubie was patient. "I'm hardly one to advocate unkindness," he said. "But once the cubs are separated, their focus will change. From depending upon each other, they'll quickly learn to rely on their human trainers." He went on to explain that with a different person feeding them every day, the cubs would learn to connect with people, not with other lions. Then any trainer would be able to handle any cub—a more practical working situation than each cub having a strong link with only one trainer. In spite of this broad socialization, Hubert was sure that a personal bond would happen spontaneously.

"The first change you'll see," Hubert said, "will be a partiality to either male or female trainers. Then an alliance will develop with an individual person. It's a given, don't ask me why."

Hubert was right, and Sieuwke soon felt jealous pangs as one cub after another turned his or her affection away from her and toward one of the other trainers. But Sieuwke was happy that her favorite, Dennis the Menace, always kept his heart open to her.

* * * * *

When Sieuwke and I walked through the bush for exercise outings with the cubs, we were constantly on the lookout for a surprise ambush. The game Dennis the Menace seemed to most enjoy was to lie hidden, then spring out and charge an unsuspecting target. The attack always came from behind, silently, and and although the cubs weighed only thirty pounds one of us usually ended up flat on our face while being mauled by little teeth and claws. This juvenile urge was as much a part of Dennis as his whiskers and claws; his genes seemed to tell him this was something that lions should do. In the wild, the activity would eventually be redirected through parental training into the hunting charge. Under Sieuwke's care, the attack from ambush was only a playful—if irritating and somewhat frightening—part of lion character.

* * * * *

Despite what one might think, food isn't always the best motivator for behavior. Lions aren't always hungry, and a lion playing for food has a hungry look in its eye. One useful training method comes from a lion's social sense. Lions in the wild are part of a strongly bonded pride. Handlers strive to become the pride leaders.

Hubert has spent all of his professional life with animals. He is analytical, methodical, calculated, accomplished. You might call his method the "scientific approach."

Sieuwke was completely the opposite. Her first reaction to working a lion under a trainer's supervision was one of doubt. Unlike Hubert and his staff, she never thought of herself as a professional animal handler—she'd never earned her living working with animals. She thought of herself only as Mum. Her approach to the husbandry of animals was that of a mother, not a trainer; and like a good mother her approach was intuitive.

Hubert's top assistant, Cheryl Shawver, was dead center in approach between her boss and Sieuwke. As a pro she was able to detach herself from some of the emotional aspects of dealing with animals, but at the same time she had Sieuwke's intuition.

Hubert's way of calling Arusha, the adult lioness who played the part of Elsa, and Sieuwke's way of calling her cubs were as different as day from night.

When he wanted to call a lion to a camera point, Hubert buzzed an electric doorbell powered by a battery in his pocket, an application of the training method called operant conditioning. Modern and high-tech, it worked marvelously.

When Sieuwke wanted to bring home her five children, she imitated the call of a mother lioness summoning her cubs. She'd learned these vociferations from her own lioness, and her imitation was true—at least the cubs thought so. I loved watching Suk walking through the bush, trailed by five cubs and talking to them in their own language, making the "baow" or the "unh-hungh" sounds that have such explicit meanings to a lion cub.

18

Rules of the Game

Sieuwke was far more familiar with the character of lions than I. I'd worked behind the camera with lions before—American mountain lions—cougars. Compared with the killing potential of an African lion, a cougar is a wimp. An African lion—a real lion, and when I use the generic name that's the kind of lion I'm referring to—can break the neck of a zebra with a single twist of its jaws. Cougars kill smaller prey.

A lion moves with the speed of light and can hide behind a blade of grass. As the director of a shoot, when taking the responsibility of working with lions in the company of a film crew and performers, I was constantly aware of this ever-lurking potential for danger. No matter how well-trained, tame, and disciplined a lion might be, the possibility for a mishap is always there. It's always the unexpected that causes an accident.

Hubert's trained lions were docile and friendly. Hand-raised by humans, they loved everybody and everyone loved them—but we had to train ourselves to realize that one miscue could result in a tragedy.

Two lions I used in films were later shot for killing people. One was the most docile and obedient big cat I'd ever worked with. I met him when I was shooting a Disney TV show called *Race for Survival* in Naivasha, a far-fetched story of bush pilot who was trapped in his crashed plane and sent his dog with a help message. On the way, the dog encountered a lion. Under the hand of his trainer, Giant—for that was the name of this majestic black-maned lion—broke all the rules and could be worked safely with children. But a year after Giant had been to Africa, left unattended in the supposed sanctuary of his enclosure in California and with his owner away for the day, a trespassing child wandered too close. The lion dragged him through the clean-out port between the bars. Giant was shot by the police. It was the only way they could retrieve the child's body.

The other lion to pay with a summary execution for behaving according to the urges of his kind was the handsome black-maned king I used in the *Born Free* TV series, which went into production several years after *Living Free* was released to theaters. We were aware of the quirky nature of this animal and always worked him within an enclosure and never with people.

After the series was over and we had returned this lion to his owner in Tanzania, he killed his caretaker. To execute a lion because of the carelessness of its keeper is hardly a fair shake, but that's the usual penalty.

* * * * *

When the two stars arrived in Kenya, they'd heard exaggerated stories about the difficulties Bill and Virginia had with lions in the prior film—Virginia's leg was broken when she was knocked down while playing on the beach with an overly friendly lion—and everyone agreed that the newcomers should have some get-to-know-you time before starting to work with the big cats.

Hubert was in charge of introductions. To make everyone comfortable our cast and crew gathered for a Saturday afternoon tea party under the fever trees at *Campi ya simba* (Lion Camp) with its tall wire lion enclosures. In a shady clearing of green grass and sunlit knolls, Sieuwke brought out her five babies. Now nearly three months old, the cubs were the size of cocker spaniels—but their personalities were still as soft as kittens. They had just been fed and would play rowdily for half an hour before settling down for afternoon naps.

Hubert gave Sieuwke the job of taking Susan Hampshire under her wing and putting her at ease with lions. Susan was immediately captivated with their kittenish looks and behavior. She got her initiation by playing on the grass with these five little animated stuffed toys, and quickly found that there was nothing to fear from them. But she kept glancing at the band-aids, scratches, and red splashes of anaseptic on Sieuwke's hands and forearms. Sieuwke explained that the wounds came from her carelessness while feeding the babies from a bottle. Kittens naturally paw at the breasts of their mother when nursing—a rhythmic movement which causes the mother to relax and let down milk. It's an instinctive part of nursing and when Sieuwke picked up a bottle, milk, and rubber teat, she usually protected herself from their sharp little claws by wrapping a towel around her forearms. But sometimes the towel fell off or a kitten got carried away, and Sieuwke got scratched in spite of the precautions. Bottle-feeding was nothing Susan would have to endure—and nobody, least of all the makeup person, wanted the star to have scratched-up arms.

I spoke to the group, emphasizing the professionalism of Hubert and his trainers, which had been one of the weaknesses of the *Born Free* animal team. As good as the original movie was, it had taken months longer to film than necessary because of the lack of filming experience of the two lady circus trainers, who were sent back to Germany with their lions when the shooting was only half done.

As good as George Adamson was with handling lions—and he was an expert—he had no movie experience, either. Nor did Joy Adamson have any practical ideas or methods for working with a lion in a movie. She had a very personal relationship with Elsa, the lioness she had raised—perhaps a closer and more loving bond than she'd ever had with a human. But that didn't begin to help her with the techniques needed to coax a movie performance out of a lion.

Personality differences between Joy and Bill and Virginia had kept Mrs. Adamson off the set during most of the shooting of *Born Free.* It was really only Bill's and Virginia's devotion to the project and their love for the lions that made the film the success it was to become.

Now that we were working with performers who didn't have that same attachment to big cats, more would be required of the director and trainers of *Living Free* to make it seem that the relationship was alive and well.

Susan truly fell for the charm of the lions. The kittens energized her maternal instincts, which were already in high gear—she was a new mother at the time and her three-month-old son came with her to Kenya. Susan couldn't resist cuddling the cubs, and she believed me when I told her that she could trust Hubert and his crew to keep her out of trouble when she was working close to the adult cats.

When it came to the adult cats, Nigel remained distant, and his fear of the lions was always there, hovering at the edge of his performance. When he was close to a big lion, no matter how tame and friendly it was—no matter that there were always two or three trainers just one step outside the camera view, alert and ready to move in at any moment—

Nigel always seemed to be looking sideways to see where the lion was. I always had the feeling that Nigel had to work at pretending to care.

But even Nigel couldn't be put off by these fuzzy little beasts.

While Ace and Judy were leaping and running together, clutching each other, wrestling and rolling in the grass, Dennis (the Menace) began his favorite game. He stole away from the action and crouched in ambush. Instinctively, as he would someday wait for prey, he hid behind a tuft of grass, tail twitching, ears back, eyes fixed, tense, vibrating with the anticipation of his forthcoming charge. He waited as long as he could bear. Then, as his mates came closer, he blew it all in a premature burst. Ace and Judy were ready for his attack, and all three rolled together in a ball, squirming and growling, until at last they came apart, panting with exertion, ready for another nap.

Susan stroked one of the babies, and Nigel lay on the grass with the others and submitted to their sniffings and pawings, nippings and other declarations of affection.

Now that the cubs had broken the ice, Hubert said it was time to introduce the stars to the mature lioness who would play the part of the Adamsons' famous Elsa. Several scenes in the script called for Susan and Nigel to have close contact with the big cat.

Hubert led the full-grown lioness, Arusha, on a leash. She came along like some great tame pussycat, rubbing her face and shoulder against his thighs, using her big paws like hands to grasp his leg, trying to tackle him and have a little of the roughhouse game they played every day. But today was all work and no play.

Hubert tied Arusha to a tree and we gathered around to admire her. It would have been pushing too hard to attempt much close contact between Susan and Nigel and the lioness on their first day of introductions. The stars did stroke her back and allow her to rub her muzzle on their legs, a demonstration of her complete friendliness. But Arusha's intimidating size and the great strength one felt when she leaned against one's thigh were not reassuring. Still, it was a friendly gesture and the actors felt good about her passivity.

But in the end, Arusha got bored and yawned, unexpectedly showing her massive teeth, and thus somehow spoiling the whole illusion.

Hubert had made one thing clear to cast and crew from the beginning: as tame as the big cats were, they were not harmless. As with any accident, it would always be the unexpected that could cause harm. A big animal built to kill, who could break a cape buffalo's neck with one blow, was not something to be taken for granted. The potential for danger was ever present.

The greatest measure of safety came from the trainers who were always aware of the dangers and never more than a step away. If they saw any note of threat in a lion's look, or if a lion began to engage in overly exuberant play, one of the trainers would insert himself between the lion and the nearest person. Each of Hubert's crew carried an ordinary hickory cane at all times, an effective persuader in the event of an unexpected incident..

Perhaps the most important safety measure was that Hubert and his team could read the lions' every intent. Nothing escaped their vigilance.

All of this was discussed at our tea party. Hubert listed the basic rules—the do's and don'ts.

First came the don'ts. According to Hubert's dictums, one can do more things wrong with lions than one can do things right.

ONE: If a tame lion takes a part of you in its mouth—an arm, for example—don't pull quickly away. He will only be "holding," as in "holding hands."

TWO: If a lion approaches you, don't run away. That would only be an invitation, because it's a lion's instinct to chase anything that runs. A running thing is inherently regarded as prey.

I could see at this point in Hubert's lesson that the atmosphere was growing tense.

"If you can't run," Nigel grumbled, "and you can't even pull your arm out of its maw, there doesn't seem to be much you can do if attacked by a lion other than stand like a post."

"Good idea," Hubert said cheerfully and continued with his list of edicts.

THREE: Never kneel, sit, or lie on the ground in the presence of a lion. A lion will see these attitudes as an invitation to play. Handlers frequently use the device to recall a lion or to induce a charge. A lion simply can't resist the fun of running at and pouncing upon any prone or kneeling figure.

So much for the don'ts; now Hubert told us some of the do's.

FOUR: In the situation previously mentioned in Rule One, when the lion has your arm in its mouth, do shove it in further. The idea is, if a mouthful of arm makes the lion uncomfortable, he might let it go.

Nigel wondered if the same rule went for heads as for arms. Hubert assured him that the same principle applied for any part of the body.

FIVE: Be trusting—but trust the trainers, not the lions. "Do what we tell you to do with confidence," Hubert said. "Trust us, and you will never be afraid. The lion, at the same time, will know intuitively that you are unafraid and won't try to take advantage of your fear."

Finally, Hubert advised Nigel and Susan to spend time with the lions as often as possible. To achieve a suitable degree of bonding, frequent visits were more important than long intervals of connection; a few minutes each day with each lion or group of lions was enough. "Lead the cubs around on their leashes," Hubert said. "Be with them between shots on location, get used to them and let them get used to you."

All of the London technical crew eventually became comfortable working close to the lions. When the lions were standing by on the set waiting for their next shot, Hubert kept them staked out on their chains in the shade. We used no cages when filming to keep the big cats away from the crew, and Hubert wouldn't allow guards with guns standing by. If ever an attack or dangerous situation occurred, a trainer would quickly be in the thick of the action. In the commotion to follow, a bullet would be as likely to hit a trainer as a lion.

The trainers and I knew about the danger, but Sieuwke was the only one who had actually seen how quickly and unexpectedly a deadly attack can happen. It was in the early 1960s, when Paramount Pictures was in Africa to shoot the film *Hatari!* starring John Wayne. The movie was about catching wild animals for zoos. Sieuwke was invited by her friend, the professional animal catcher Willy de Beer, to visit the set in Tanganyika, which today is called Tanzania. Willy was supervising the exciting action during which wild animals were roped cowboy-style from a speeding car.

For these shots, John Wayne or his double sat on a chair screwed to the front fender of the catching car as it sped across country, dodging holes and stumps, trying to get alongside the running rhino, giraffe, or whatever they were after. When an animal was close, the catcher reached out with a noose on a pole and lassoed the head.

These were dangerous and thrilling chases, but when an angry rhino was noosed, that's when the real excitement began. The battle sometimes grew so fierce that to maintain picture continuity a crew of metal workers were on stand-by, ready to pound out the dents made to battered cars by charging rhino horns.

Another friend of Sieuwke's, Kenya game catcher "Carr" Carr-Hartley's sister-in-law, Diana Hartley, was hired as an aide to Willy de Beer. She'd worked on other films and was an experienced animal handler. On the day of Sieuwke's arrival she took Suk under her wing and showed her around the compound.

"It was the first time I'd ever been on a movie set," Sieuwke told me. "Someone said that the Director, Howard Hawks, was unhappy about putting his female star, Elsa Martinelli, into situations close to dangerous animals. But a scene in the script called for Martinelli to play a scene with lions close by, and Hawks was agonizing about how to stage the shot.

"When Mr. Hawks noticed me stroking one of the big lions, he came over and said, 'Marchesa Bisleti, I couldn't help but notice that contrary to the feelings of my star, you have no fear of these big animals.'

"I love lions," I said. "I've got a couple of my own."

"'Really?' Mr. Hawks said. 'That's very interesting.'

"He stood back and grinned as he looked me over. 'And I see, if you don't mind my saying so, that you've got an ass that's a dead ringer for my star's.'"

Sieuwke still didn't have any idea what was going on in this famous director's head.

"Then he said, 'I've got a scene coming up where Miss Martinelli, in her role as a professional photographer, has got to be close to a group of lions while she takes pictures of them. If you were wearing her clothes and a wig, I could shoot you from the back, cut in closeups of Elsa Martinelli, and get the scene.'"

Whenever the star was seen close to one of the dangerous animals, it was Sieuwki wearing a wig with her backside to the camera.

In between doubling assignments, Sieuwke helped around the animal compound.

It was on a day shortly after her arrival that she went with Diana Hartley and Mama de Beers to help with regular maintenance at the animal compound.

As they approached one of the lionesses staked out on her chain, Diana stopped and looked at the big cat critically. "Well, girl," she said to the lioness. "You look a bit out of sorts this morning."

Then, Diana, who knew this lioness very well, seemed to decide that everything was okay. "What's wrong, baby? Did you have a bad night?" she cooed. Diana clearly intended to walk up to the lioness and stroke her.

As she began to approach the lioness, Mama de Beers said, "Careful. Diana. I don't like her look."

At that moment, Diana stepped within the radius of the lioness's chain and the lioness leaped. Diana went down under the weight of the charge. The lioness held Diana in her paws for only a second as she bit into her neck. Mama de Beers, swinging her bag by its strap, hit the lioness. Sieuwke picked up a stick and hit the lioness on the head. She dropped Diana and backed off.

"I'll never forget the bewildered look on the lioness's face." Sieuwke told me. "As she looked at us with her big soulful eyes she seemed to be saying, 'I didn't mean any harm.'"

Seconds later, men with shovels and sticks arrived and drove the lioness to the other end of her chain.

But Diana was already dead.

* * * * *

Living Free didn't come close to achieving the box office success of its predecessor. When it opened, critques invariably compared the two and were equally balanced in liking. Some thought it better, others preferred *Born Free*, but all would have preferred to see Bill Travers and Virginia McKenna in the roles, and this was the thrust of the reviews.

My own feelings about the movie were mixed. My main gripe went back to the beginning and mirrored that of the critics—Bill and Virginia *were* George and Joy. The casting had thrown this movie to the sharks and wolves.

But again an old postulate proved to be true—the problems or conditions of the production have little bearing on the success or failure of the movie. The film was only a modest success, but the experience of making it had been one of the best and most enduringly happy of my career. I had fallen in love with a country and a woman, and each would be a part of me for years to come.

And I was easily able to weather any disappointment because I already had another iron hot in the fire and ready to go. I'd been working on the script of *The Darwin Adventure* for months. Now Joe Strick had made a production deal.

19

The Darwin Adventure

My work segued smoothly from the editing room of *Living Free* in Soho, London, to the production offices of *The Darwin Adventure* in Soho, London. This film would be shot and edited in England with a second unit shoots in Mexico, Panama, and the Galápagos.

By this point my marriage with Joan was more a parenting partnership, a relationship that we believed was the best thing we could do for Mike. Joan and I were living together as mother, father, and friends. Not as husband and wife. We agreed on our standing. It worked—better than wedded—as friend-partners in a worthwhile cause to which we could both happily make our contributions.

I had been living for three years in Scotland, England, Africa, and now England again, with only short visits back to USA. Joan and Mike had spent each summer with me, and Mike and I had enjoyed good family times together during those visits. Again, Joan agreed to come to England for the summer. This time, however, life would be easier. We had made a good friend of the author of *The Incredible Journey* when Sheila Burnford had stayed with us in Sequim. Sheila lived in Minnesota, but she had a cottage standing empty in southern England which she offered.

When I took the train from London to Lymington and drove into the Hampshire countryside to check out the house I was elated. I knew Joan would love it. The comfortable fully-furnished cottage was alone on the beach with a view of the Isle of Wight across the Solent. A forest reserve was around us on three sides (the New Forest, it's called—because, I suppose, it was new in the year 1079 when William the Conqueror declared it a deer hunting reserve). The beach was at our doorstep, ready for fishing, beachcombing, sand-castle building, stone-skipping, all of those joys of ten-year-old boyhood.

June came, school was out, and Joan, Mike and my mother arrived in England and settled in. I was shooting on the Darwin film each day and had an apartment in London. I made the two hour train trip to Lymington every weekend.

Mike was immersed in curiosity with natural history. When he set out a line of home made live traps in the New Forest, he discovered that he had a competitor—the game keeper of the large estate bordering our plot, which included a pheasant hunting club, had a set a string of steel traps for foxes. Mike's game, which happily was never discovered by the game keeper, although he must have suspected foul play, was to steal through the forest like an Indian, finding and springing fox traps.

Mike's own trap line, intended for hedgehogs, which were studied, fed, and then released to be caught again, ended up most often catching a feral domestic cat. These cats were as wild as any lynx.

Our house had a little-used screened back porch, and it was here that Mike established his cattery. The porch was off-limits to all but Mike and his cats which grew in number to eight or ten. When Mike cracked open the door to slip in with food and water a pandemonium of wildcats erupted. Cats were everywhere, bouncing off the walls, yowling here, snarling there, climbing the screens, ricocheting from corner to corner, and seemingly running on the ceiling.

They were anything but pets, but Mike had caught them, and having done that felt responsible for their well-being. The way things were going with his success as a trapper, it seemed my family would soon be dispossessed from the house by wildcats.

Then one morning when grandmother and Mike were walking the beach they found a scrawny, flea infested, worm ravaged, skin infected, abandoned, orphaned kitten. Mike loved it. It had to be rescued.

A trip to the vet who provided inoculation and sterilization produced a doubtful longevity prognosis, but an unexpected opportunity for the adult members of the Couffer family. Mike understood that a screen porch full of wildcats could not be transported to California when the summer ended. Thus a suggestion was made; open the screen porch door—and keep the kitten. The deal was struck.

The kitten—Kitten Little—thrived under Mike's care. When fall came and I drove my family to Heathrow for the flight to LAX, Kitten Little went into the baggage line snug in a cat crate to which she had been conditioned and felt like home.

Eleven hours later, at the LAX baggage carousel, Mike, Joan, and grandmother collected their luggage and waited. No crate, no Kitten Little. The conveyer belt stopped—empty. They waited for it to start again, growing nervous.

Then from across the huge baggage hall two men in uniform, one carrying the cat crate, walked toward them. Joan could tell from the long faces that bad news was coming.

"I'm sorry," the leader said. "There was a malfunction. The heating and air supply in the baggage compartment failed. I'm afraid your cat is frozen…dead."

Mike grabbed the crate, opened the door, and took out Kitten Little, stiff and cold. Crying, he put his face in her fur. "No! She's alive. I don't believe you," as he put the icy carcass under his warm sweater.

"I'm sorry," headman said. "I understand your sadness, son." To Joan. "We'll make restitution. Come to the desk. There's a form to file."

"But she's alive," Mike said.

After minutes of Mike's insistence and adult resistance, sure enough, a squeak and movement came from beneath the sweater.

Kitten Little recovered completely—well, not *completely*—maybe some brain damage occurred, as hereafter, for the rest of her long life, Kitten Little was more than a bit squirrelly.

* * * * *

The Darwin Adventure was a film of a different kind for me. Heretofore, my directing experience had been with movies in which animals played the important roles. There were good human actors in these films of course, but it could be said that animals were central players as even the titles of the movies often confirmed. There were animals in *Darwin*, but in impersonal, documentary, kinds of roles.

Many of the TV shows I'd done had human characters, but these roles were usually played by amateurs who had natural skills allied with the parts they were playing and to whom my best advice was invariably: "Don't act! Don't even try, just do what you would do in everyday life."

Darwin was different. I enjoyed working with skilled English actors. We were shooting from a script I had written, and it was fun to discuss motivations, characterizations, and mannerisms with these profoundly professional players. I discovered that my best directing technique was to begin shooting each scene with an unrehearsed run-through. The staging usually fell into place in a natural way, suggesting camera positions as the actors moved, and they always brought something unexpected to a scene. It was the same technique that I used when filming animals. The "something" was usually good. If it didn't work, at least it opened a door for exploration and discussion. It almost surprised me that I was able to move confidently and efficiently in this new dimension.

When one big complicated crowd scene was in the offing, Joe Strick asked me if I was comfortable to handle it. I said sure I was, and it came off very well. Working within the milieu of a period costume drama, horses and carriages, stately homes, and cultured English women and gentlemen was a huge boost to my ego.

Another plus for me was that a second unit shoot in the Galápagos (where Darwin's most important observations were made) was required. It had been 16 years since my first visit. I had kept up communications with my friends in the islands and I yearned to return. My friend Gus Angermeyer's son, Jonny, was living in Florida now, and I hired him as my assistant for this trip. We flew to Ecuador with six cases containing tripods, film, 35mm Arriflex camera, lenses, motor drives, batteries, everything I thought I'd need.

This time, we weren't required to sail our own boat. There was now a ship that sailed to the islands on a dubious schedule, and we had booked a cabin for the next voyage two months ahead of departure.

When we arrived in Guayaquile and made our way to the dock, we were told that sailing was delayed by a week while the ship underwent some repairs. That was no surprise in this Mañana Land, and to kill the time we did a bit of filming in the jungle. It would only be a week before the rusty hulk tied to the dock would be ready for the 800 mile voyage to the islands.

When we finally got underway, the ship's propeller stopped turning halfway to our destination and we drifted in the calm Pacific Ocean for a couple of days while greasy Ecuadorian engineers made a racket in the engine room. As our 1st Class stateroom was near the engine room, which was noisy when we were stopped and stiflingly hot when underway, we moved our mattresses to the deck and enjoyed the cruise under the sun and stars.

I hired Fritz Angermeyer and his fishing boat and went to the places where Conrad and I had filmed before. They were the same as I remembered them—the iguanas still plentiful, the sea lions friendly, the birds the same.

During our first trip Conrad and I had been hard-pressed to find a couple of the giant tortoises for which the islands were famous. (*Galápagos* means tortoise.) We finally came upon a couple in the forest near the top of the island of Santa Cruz.

In the years since then a remote place had been discovered. In four-mile-wide hard-to-get-to Alcedo crater on Isabela Island hundreds of giant tortoises have lived undisturbed since forever. Jonny and I organized a safari of friends who volunteered as porters to carry camera and everything we would need to spend three days in the crater. Fritz's boat landed us on a desolate shore early one morning and we climbed the hard ascent burdened with heavy gear.

When we arrived at the top and descended to the level bottom, Jonny shot a feral donkey and we ate donkey steak and donkey stew during the time of our stay.

We camped near a geyser with a view of steaming fumaroles and an expanse of green grass kept mowed by dozens of huge lumbering tortoises. More tortoises gathered at shallow ponds. The hissing from beneath the earth and the strong odor of volcanic sulfur projected an atmosphere and picture of earthly beginnings. Tortoises were mating, and their deep bellows added to the feeling of a prehistoric time.

It was the Pleistocene. The tortoises were fantastic—one of the biggest thrills of my life.

* * * * *

The Darwin Adventure was completed in London where it was a modest box office success. In America it failed to attract an audience. The distributors thought it would make a clever come-on to open the film where the famous "Monkey Trial" had taken place and lawyer Clarence Darrow had defended a school teacher named Scopes who had broken the law by teaching Darwinian evolution. The trial had taken place in Dayton, Ohio, in 1925.

Some thought this connection would stir local interest. Publicity dollars were spent in the area, and a *Time* magazine notation stoked hope that the USA premiere would be a success. Distributors place a lot of emphasis on a movie's opening box office numbers. If the first couple of weeks' earnings aren't up to expectations, the show is considered a flop and not pushed.

The Darwin Adventure died before it had a chance. Nobody came. Did the nimble-wits of the film distribution world really believe the Bible Belt was the best place to open a movie about Charles Darwin and evolution?

* * * * *

In 1973, I faced a summer without the prospect of a job. My son, Mike, at the age of eleven had been stuffed with stories and lore from my two trips to the Galápagos. He thought it was very unfair that I'd had all that fun and he'd had no part of it. I had to agree, so we cut a deal. If he'd keep a daily dairy, I'd take him to the Enchanted Isles during the three month school break.

This was the year that air travel to the islands was just beginning. The Ecuadorian Air Force made flights on an irregular schedule from Guayaquile to an old U.S. radar base that had been set up during World War II on Baltra, one of the smaller islands near the big isle of Santa Cruz. The buildings had been abandoned for years but the runway was still good. Seats on the flights were available, but departure dates were iffy. We hit it lucky and only hung around the city for a couple of days until a plane left. We stayed with my friend Gus Angermeyer and his wife Lucretia, backpacked and camped in the mountains and on remote beaches, took a long cruise through the islands with Fritz aboard his sloop, and had a wonderful time.

Mike kept his word and his diary was full.

When we returned home and I read his work I was struck with its language and boyish insights. During the trip we hadn't thought of our adventure as a cooperative book-writing event, but now I saw an opportunity—a book in two voices, father and son, sharing the same experiences and seeing them from different perspectives.

Our collaboration, *Galápagos Summer,* was published by G.P. Putnam and did well enough that we were asked to write more. We took off for each of the next three school summer breaks and made them working holidays. We wrote *African Summer, Canyon Summer,* and *Salt Marsh Summer* and then called it quits. Those adventures together made a bond that exceeded my hopes and expectations in every way. We became—partners, pals, co-authors, sharing in the profits both in money and every other way.

The publishers were considering issuing the four books as a boxed set, then bad luck hit. The winter was one of exceptional snow and ice, and the roof of the warehouse in New Jersey where Putnam's stock was stored collapsed and all of our books were destroyed. They were never reprinted, but the last one was selected by the Junior Literary Guild for the Outstanding Science Book for Children award.

Not bad for a couple of guys having the times of their lives on summer holidays.

For six months we lived in tents on Bushy Island, watching the habits and movements of the animals and learning where to site the house. Aware that we were building *our* house on *their* land we wished to interfere the least with our wild predecessors. We have never owned a mower. Grass on our hill is kept short by zebras, waterbuck, dikdik. hippos, and impala.

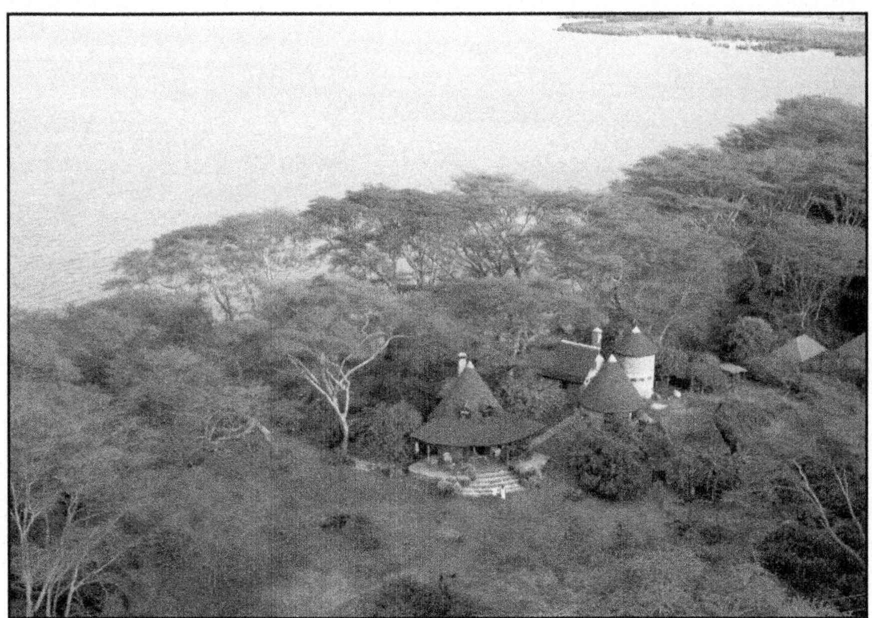

It was a different world when we came to Bushy Island. There were no fences then, and it could have been a thousand miles down The Great Rift Valley to the first wire.

Sheena, Queen of the Jungle. During times of drought our neighbors water their stock at Bushy Island. Samburu/Maasai warriors grow up with spears in their hands. Being paid for playing war games when Sheena and her tribe attacked the invading mercenaries was a bonus to top off all the fun they had.

Young Sheena. Twelve year-old Kirsty Lindsay was as fearless and empathetic with animals as her adult incarnation was supposed to be.

(Photo by Hubert Wells)

The art, architecture, and culture of the industrious Dogon of Mali has not changed for centuries. Never far from their ancestors who occupy the burial niches pocking the cliffs above the village, the Dogon can never forget older times.

Mali's Dogon tall mask dancers—maybe the last time so many will ever gather at such a ritual.

Hutu dancers of Burundi, the country which has since seen unimaginable genocide. We wonder if these proud people will ever dance so happily again?

Remembering the strange words from a film director many years before us, the crews of two huge dugout canoes greeted us with John Ford's shout urging his crew to "get the lead out." *Hubba! Hubba! Hubba!*

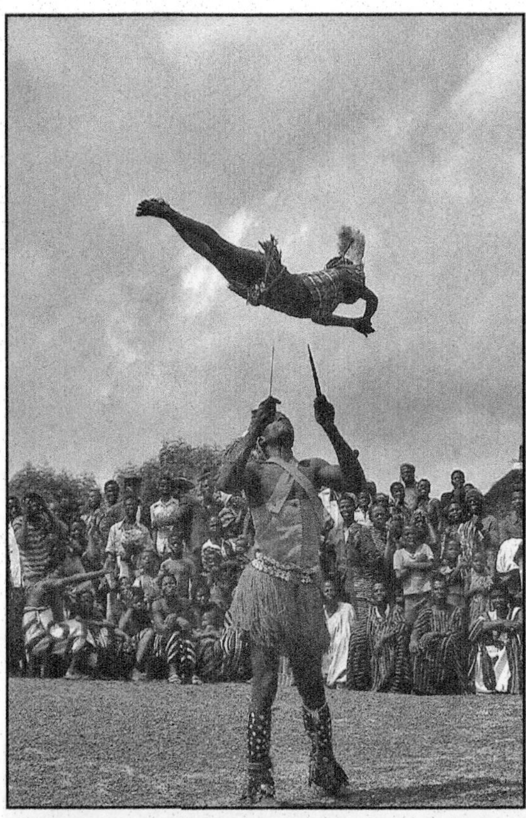

Knife dancers of Senegal. One man tossed the boy from high above. At the moment it seemed he was sure to be impaled, the knives magically disappeared and the boy was safe in the catcher's arms.

This is the way one usually sees wild wolves—running and far away. The sound of wolves howling under the mystic aurora in the far north is a thrill we'll never forget.

Again Sieuwke found herself raising cubs, this time wolves in the Yukon…

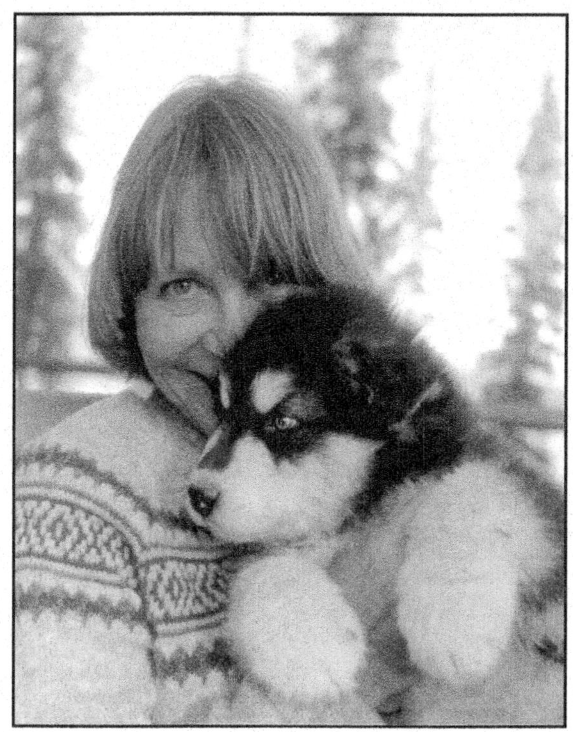

…and a sled dog pup named "Bigfoot".

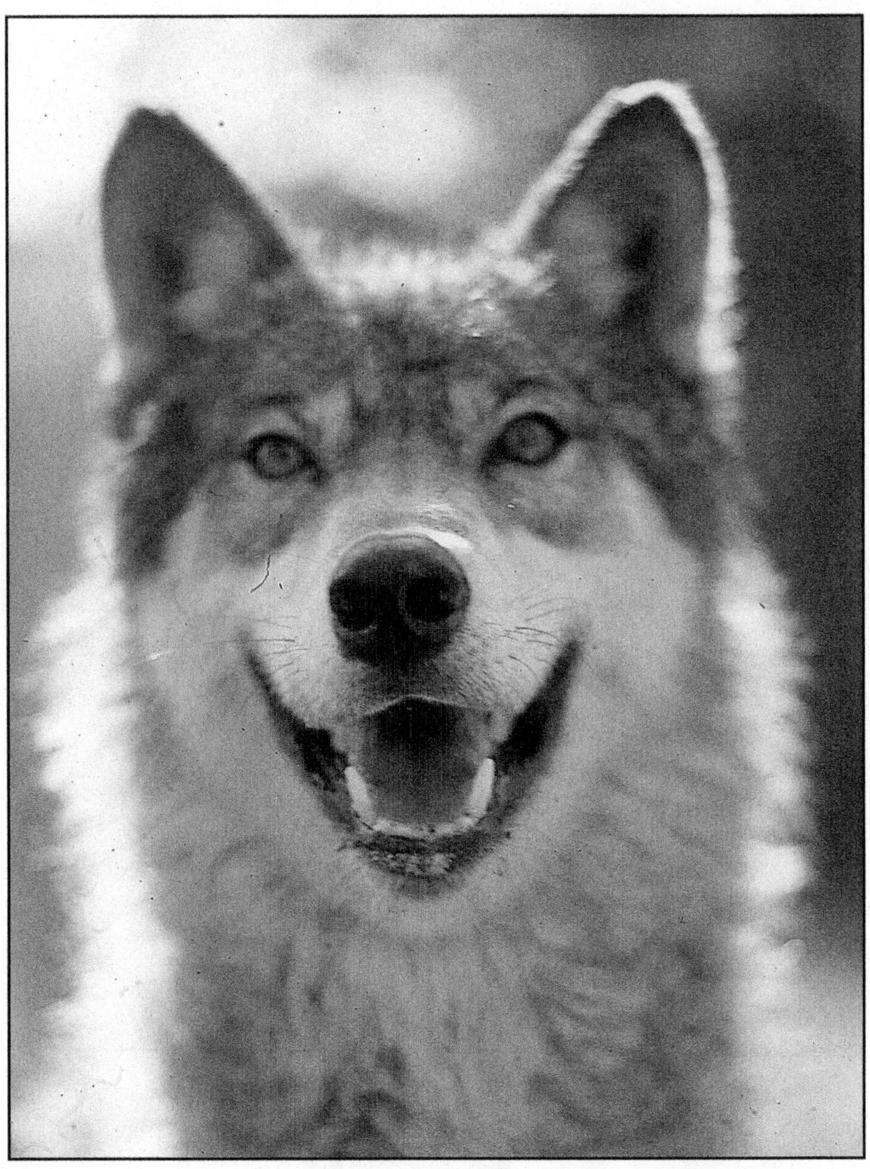

By picking off easy prey—the old or crippled caribou—wolves benefit the herds. There is an Inuit saying: "The caribou feeds the wolf, but it is the wolf who keeps the caribou strong." Now *that's* a happy wolf.

Farley Mowat (Charles Martin Smith) has been dropped by ski-plane. alone in the frozen Arctic. His mission—prove that wolves are decimating the caribou herds. What he finds is: *Sure wolves eat caribou. But when there are none around they live on mice.*

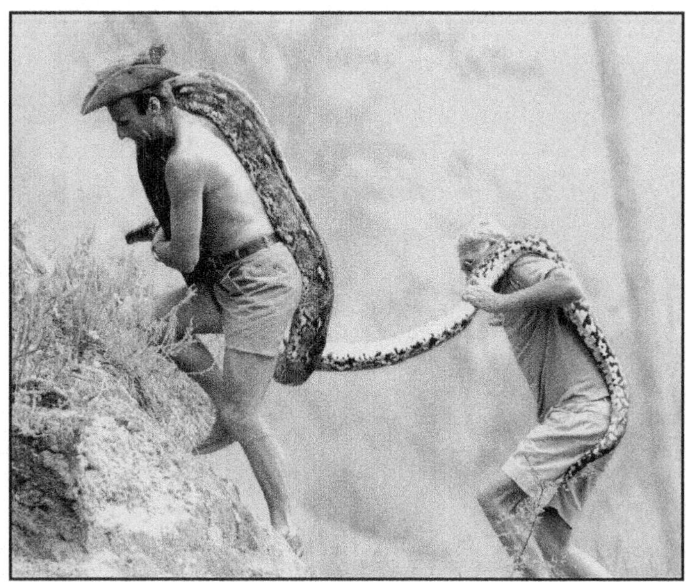

To think of a film director's job as sitting in a chair and shouting: "Roll 'em!" is less than half the picture. There are other days like this one—Hubert Wells and Jack lugging a lazy python to the set. (Photo by Wolfgang Suschitzky)

Using a moving pickup truck as bait, an elephant could be teased into "charge mode" and the attack prolonged by allowing the jumbo think he almost had us. This "riding the edge" was hairy stuff and it nearly cost my life. Here we are using the trick, but not the take that nearly got me. (Photo by Mike Couffer)

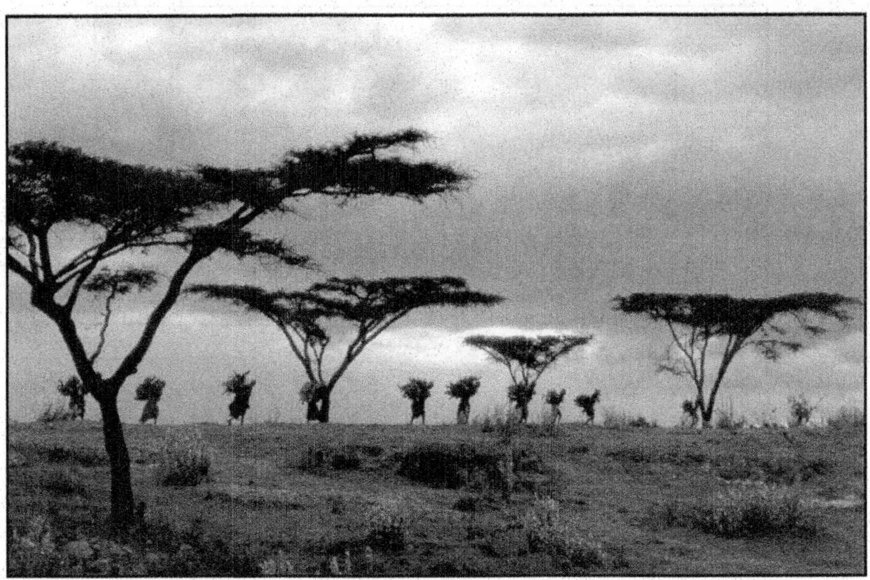

The second unit cameraman usually shoots scenes in which no stars appear—scenics, action sequences with doubles, animals, and "comin's and goin's" as my mentor, Irving Lerner, used to call them.

Elephants as far as the eye can see. They called us "The Beauty Unit".

Flamingos at Lake Bogoria in Kenya has been called one of the greatest wildlife spectacles in the world. It was here that the stunning flying scenes from Denys Finch-Hatton's (Robert Redford's) biplane in *Out of Africa* were made.

Karen Blixen (Meryl Streep) and Denys Finch-Hatton (Robert Redford). Kenya at the turn of the Century.

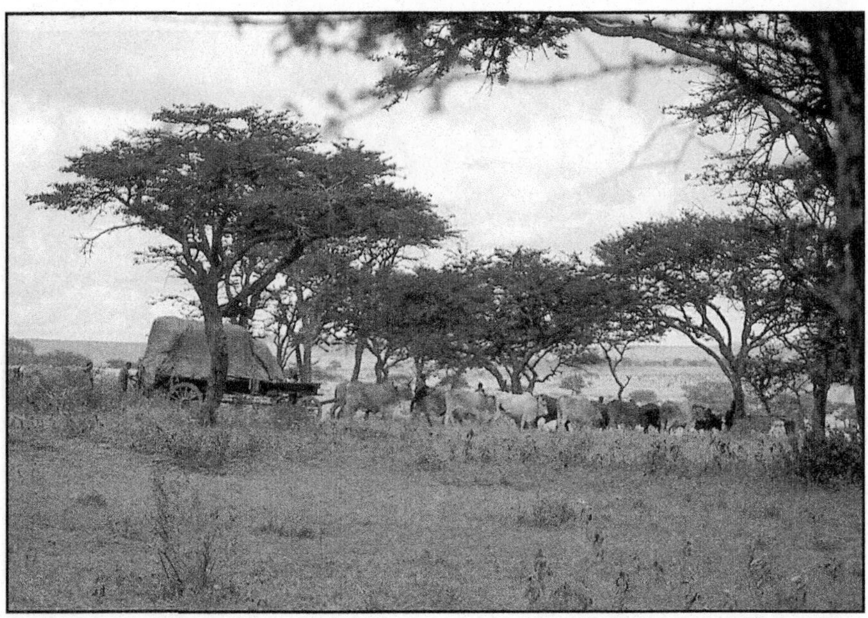

Karen Blixen's supply wagon was on the way to supply her husband's remote outpost in the bush. That night, lions attacked the resting oxen. Karen beat one big cat off a downed ox with a whip—the most exciting action moment in the film. (Photo by Hubert Wells)

The film *The Ghost and the Darkness* tells the true story of two man-eating lions that in the year 1898 held up construction of the Mombasa to Uganda railway for nine months and killed as many as 140 construction workers before the lions were finally shot. (Photo by Hubert Wells)

Robert Redford gave me a framed print of my "signature" shot for *The Milagro Beanfield War* and wrote: "It's your setup, thanks, Jack", only one of the good things he did for me. Star struck? No. But a keepsake not taken lightly.

20

Joy and Sorrow

When *Darwin* was scored and edited, I returned to America where I wrote a script treatment called *Audubon,* which Joe Strick and I thought would make a good autobiographical film with broader general interest than Darwin.

The time had come—Joan and I made our split amicably. She and Mike lived in our house and I took an apartment nearby. Grandmother's house was midway—we became an extended family in the most literal sense.

Joe stirred up enough interest in *Audubon* that I took off on a long filming trek and shot what seemed like a couple of miles of bird footage in Newfoundland, Florida, and through the west. We had the idea of a partly singing narration like Joe had used so successfully in his first film, *Muscle Beach.* John Denver liked the idea and agreed to come along if all went according to plan. But like so many other good film projects that fail to get financing, *Audubon* died. And I'd socked nearly a year into the project.

But now I had roots growing in Africa. Following Sieuwke's separation and her displacement from the large farm, she found it hard to maintain her lions. She accepted an offer from a new game park in New Jersey to adopt and care for her lion family and agreed to a publicity tour where she appeared on TV—the Jack Paar Show among others. (Paar made one of his classic witty rejoinders when one of Sieuwke's cubs peed in his lap.) Sieuwke joined me on a part of my *Audubon* jaunt, then returned to Kenya where I was soon to follow.

* * * * *

Two feature films about the experiences of George and Joy Adamson and their lions led to a *Born Free* television series and in 1974 I was again on location in Kenya with Paul Radin to attend to pre-production details. There were to be thirteen one-hour shows for the NBC network, and Screen Gems told us we'd have to turn out one show every ten days to meet network airdates which were already set. It was a challenging schedule to produce a quality series featuring animals in a faraway location.

Now we had a new couple to play the roles of Joy and George Adamson—Diana Muldour and Gary Collins—good enough actors, but still no Virginia and Bill.

I started a crew building the compound where the lions—sons and daughters of the ones we had filmed on *Living Free*—would be housed. Sieuwke was hired by the art director as his Kiswahili interpreter and local contact.

Sieuwke and I set up our tent again with its outdoor furnishings in place on Bushy Island. We had decided on the site where we would build our house, but hadn't started construction yet. It was to be during this stay in Kenya that work would begin.

While we awaited the arrival of Hubert and the lions from America, plus the crew and actors, a persistent rumor tolled an ominous knell. Joy Adamson was slow to sign her contract. Financial terms, the usual stumbling block, were not the issue, only a few "small personal guarantees" that Joy was insisting upon—but we got no further clues from Burbank (the California headquarters of production company Screen Gems) as to the specific nature of the problem.

It seemed more than a bit risky to be so deeply involved in a series based on the Adamsons' life without a contract signed by Joy—but then television production is often a game of brinkmanship. Anyway, it wasn't my problem—or so I thought.

Anxious to get ahead of what I knew would be hectic times when production began, I took off alone on a long trip to film background shots for various episodes.

After a couple days shooting along the Uaso Nyiro river, I left early one morning and drove north on an empty dirt track toward Wamba.

I was pushing my Land Rover to the limit, racing a dust cloud behind me, when a loud engine roar came out of nowhere. A plane shot past a few feet above the roof of my car, zoomed upward, circled and dipped back to buzz me again. I spun the wheel and drove into a clump of bush. *If that idiot wants to play games*, I thought, *he'll have to mow down the trees to get me.*

I leapt out in time to see the plane climb and turn again, wings wobbling a friendly greeting. On the next pass an object trailing a white rag fluttered and dropped from the pilot's window.

I ran to retrieve it. On the ground was a note tied to a screwdriver. RETURN TO SAMBURU AND MEET AT LANDING STRIP. URGENT. PAUL.

What could be so vital, or perhaps so confidential, that he couldn't send a message through the National Park radio net? Surely the warden could have located me and relayed the information. Yet I was impressed with Paul's tracking skill. Somehow he'd found me in this vast expanse of bushland. In all these hundreds of miles he'd spotted my car on the road. I'd have to compliment him for his detective work.

But at the moment my mind was racing. Why would Paul charter an airplane and set out on such a search, with a slim chance of finding me in such a remote area? Something must have happened. Perhaps an accident—maybe something serious with my family back in America? I wheeled the Land Rover around and made a dust cloud back toward where I'd come from.

When I rolled up to the airstrip in Samburu, I saw the Cessna parked under the wind sock. The pilot was sitting in the shade under a wing; Paul was pacing nervously in the sun. Thoughts of possible tragedies and awful emergencies still raced through my mind. I hoped Paul would get right to the point.

He didn't. As we walked down the taxiway, I knew Paul was deliberately leading me away from the pilot's earshot. In the meantime he was telling me about an incident that had occurred earlier in the day. Flying above the bush, Paul had spotted a Land Rover similar to mine and had pulled the same maneuver, dropping the note onto the ground. The puzzled driver had driven to Samburu airstrip. Like me, he assumed that some dreadful emergency message awaited him. When he discovered the mistake, he'd been relieved enough not to be pissed off.

"I don't quite know how to put this," Paul said at last. "It's so damned embarrassing."

"Is anybody hurt?" I asked.

"No." Now Paul was the one who was agonizing. "Look, I had to tell Sieuwke that she can't work on the picture any longer. I'm sorry. We're going to miss her."

"I don't get it."

"There's a problem with Joy's contract."

He told me that everything had been settled, cast and crew contracts were finished—but then Joy had thrown in a last-second ringer. "A blacklist," Paul explained. "Three people are not allowed to be associated with the film in any way. You'll never guess who they are."

"I guess I know who one of them is," I said with a chuckle, not yet realizing the seriousness of what Paul was saying.

"Right for number one," said Paul. "Plus Bill Travers and Tony Fitzjohn."

"That's weird," I said. "Travers has no reason to be in Africa, and Tony's the one she once twisted my arm to hire."

Paul shrugged. "Times change."

"It's none of Joy's business who the company hires," I said. "For months Sieuwke's been looking forward to working with lions again."

Paul shook his head. "I felt like a perfect bastard telling her."

"And then you come all this way just to let me know....?"

"Look," said Paul, "Sieuwke's mad as hell and I don't blame her. She understands why she's off the picture. But the problem is, she flat refuses even to talk about the next bit."

"Next bit?"

"Joy insists that Sieuwke not be allowed anywhere near the production unit. She's heard about your tent on Bushy Island. She says that Sieuwke is living next door to the lions and she won't have it."

"Sieuwke owns that piece of land. She's holed up in a tent on her own property. How can Joy think she can keep Sieuwke from living on her own property?"

"She can't," Paul said with a sigh. "But she does."

I just stared at him, absorbing the implications.

"I told the studio how ridiculous this is," Paul said. "But the word from Burbank is that Joy refuses to sign unless we agree to this final condition. Joy sees the tent on the island as our conspiracy to thwart her and hire Sieuwke in spite of her wishes."

"And she'd blow the whole deal just because Sieuwke is living next door to the lions?"

Paul nodded. "Won't budge an inch." He looked at me helplessly.

"And we've run out of time," he continued. "The lawyers say to get Sieuwke out of there now, or come home."

"And what am I supposed to do about it?"

"Talk to her," Paul said. "She won't even see me. She told her *askari* (security guard) to keep me off the property. I think she's given those damned dogs of hers special orders to go for my throat if I come anywhere near her."

"You know Sieuwke," I said. "Head hard as stone. How can I be convincing for something so weird?"

"Talk to her," Paul pleaded. "Just try."

A thought occurred to me. Sieuwke and I had built a small house on an island off the coast of Kenya called Lamu. The place still needed a lot of work, which was difficult to do from afar.

"Look," I said, "She's up to her neck with our house at the coast. She's anxious to get down there. Has to take a lot of stuff. Maybe if you'd offer her a plane ticket?"

Paul threw up his hands. "Blackmail, bribes—oh, these women!"

"Probably help to swing it if she could take her dogs. With all the other baggage, that would mean a charter."

"Anything," Paul said. "But talk to her."

* * * * *

I'd never seen Sieuwke so distraught. At first she was crying—then she hurled a glass ashtray into a tree.

It was no problem to convince her to leave, and I was thus spared that odious task—in fact, it would have been far more difficult to induce her to stay. I felt like a traitor. It seemed so weak not to take a stand against Joy's demand. Yet we knew she had the upper hand.

At last we decided that Sieuwke would disappear for a month to attend to the leaking roof at the coast. Then when the contract was signed and things had cooled down, all would be clear for her to come back and we could get on with building our house on Bushy Island.

We wondered how this whole silly situation could have come to such a point. Could it really only be the envy of a jealous woman resulting from a newspaper article printed years ago?

* * * * *

Sieuwke returned to Bushy Island and her job on the production after the contracts were signed, shooting was underway, and Joy had no further leverage. It was a hectic job turning out a one hour show every two weeks, but we finished the thirteen shows on schedule. I did second unit filming on all the segments, but my happiest time was spent shooting and directing one show that took place at remote Lake Turkana. This segment, called "A Matter of Survival," starred Susan Dey (remember *The Partridge Family*?) in the guest role.

It was a fantasy of cartoonish improbability—a young woman crashes her plane in the African wilderness and is rescued by a wandering lioness— (Elsa?). The production values of this series were superior. It was the writers who committed it to obscurity. And this unlikely segement was perhaps the most cogent of them all.

Mike, now twelve, and a neighbor chum from home, Charles Callahan, accompanied us on this safari. The boys had a ball fishing for giant Nile perch and poking around in the soil seaching for fossils (we were close to a site where the Leakey's had found the remains of early man). Near the main set, which was the crashed plane, the boys discovered their own place of archeological interest—ancient graves and bone spear points. They collected samples and photos, and reported the find to the proper authorities who later dug the site and wrote a descriptive monograph in which they credited the finders.

These were the months about which Mike and I wrote in our second collaboration: *African Summer*. Charles did the drawings—he had a knack for capturing just the moment and just the right expression for humorous caricature.

Too bad the TV series didn't reach the charm of the book.

21

Joyless

On a Sunday morning in January, 1980, ten years after I had first met Joy Adamson, who had turned out to be such a significant itch that was so hard to scratch, Sieuwke and I set out from our long-completed house on Bushy Island headed for a picnic lunch at a picturesque site on the rim of a small volcanic crater. I carried a basket with fresh-baked bread, cold roast duckling, artichokes, and a bottle of Spanish wine .

We headed west in our old Land Rover, bouncing over potholes on the dirt road. A plume of dust made a mile-long trail behind us. The powder seeped in through cracks and rotted rubber door gaskets, sifted through the floor by way of holes where screws had long ago rattled loose to fall on some other kidney-jolting track. The cloud swirled around us, settling like fine flour on everything. We looked at each other and laughed. Sieuwke's hair and eyebrows were as white as cotton wool, mine the same.

We passed the turnoff to the Djinn Palace, famous for murder and intrigue among the upper crust when this was a watering place for Kenya's so-called White Highlands and Happy Valley. Off the main road, we followed a vague track. It had been made by cattle—that is, it was maintained by cattle. It had been made by wild game a thousand years before cattle ever trod these hills.

The crater was ahead—a perfectly symmetrical cone with it's top sliced off. We stopped, grabbed our picnic basket, and climbed the slope. At the summit, we sat on barren red stone that had the texture and feel of dry bricks. When touched, it absorbed the sweat off one's fingers—as thirsty for a drink as we were.

The rim was a perfectly round bowl with a flock of pink flamingos wading in the lake at the bottom. In the tangle of jungle along the water's edge a trio of black and white colobus monkeys were picking and eating flowers in the trees.

Sieuwke fished out long-stemmed glasses from the basket, set them beside the bread, and I pulled a leg off the duck.

"You get the feeling we're the first people ever to be here," she said.

We knew there was farmhouse only a couple of miles away, yet the place did have a comfortable feeling of remoteness. I picked up a candy wrapper left by a previous visitor and tucked it out of sight into a mouse hole. I said I was sure we must be the first.

"This was one of Joy Adamson's favorite places," Sieuwke said. "She thought those colobus down there were her own."

A month before, I had been in California when I heard of Joy's death. First reports were that she had been killed by a lion while strolling near the remote camp where she had been studying leopards.

Considering the differences with Joy that both Suk and I had borne over the years, it surprised me that I should be so moved. My first reaction was shock that she died from a lion attack; it seemed so unfair. Then as the initial blow from the news subsided, my feelings became more sanguine and I realized that her end was—what was the word? Fitting? Yes, it was a fitting way for Joy to die—ironically fitting.

Maddeningly singleminded, impossibly eccentric, shamelessly egotistical, resolutely jealous, artlessly direct, Joy had also been a flamboyant, romantic, theatrical lady. Wasn't it fitting that she should die a flamboyant, romantic, theatrical death? That's what I fancied she would have wanted.

One could say that lions owed Joy Adamson a great deal—she had been an important cause for their protection. Yet, in fact, they owed her nothing. The work she had done for wildlife was as much for herself as it had been for the animals. Although every cent of her profits from writing and films beyond that required to live and carry on her work went into the fund she established for wild animal help—The Elsa Wildlife Appeal—Joy's beneficence was not entirely selfless. The work benefited Joy as much as it did the animals. She needed the notice. The gratification was as valuable to her as it was to the animals that needed the funds. Joy's foibles boosted her image and at the same time did a service to a fine cause. Of such ego trips are great works made.

But what of the guilt of the ungrateful beast that was said to have killed her? Shouldn't it be hunted down and shot as a retaliatory act in the name of justice?

Joy, of all people, was keenly aware of all lions' death-dealing nature. The danger of the beasts is a large part of their fascination, which she so romantically explored. Joy knew as well as anyone the danger of walking alone in the African bush at evening—hunting time. Even Joy, with her belief in animal-human communication through clairvoyance, and with her mystical beliefs in lion character, never ascribed to them the trait of morality. Morality is a human concept, an almost religious aspect of human character that I do not believe she perceived as an element of lion personality.

She knew that lions in the wild react to humans either as prey or as a threat; she knew that lions are killing machines, predators, flesh-eaters. If one sets out in life to associate with killers, one must accept the possibility that someday, through them, one might be killed.

Joy would have despised any notion that a lion that killed her should be shot as a renegade.

When I heard the first report of her death, it took away some of my sadness to know that it had been a lion that had fulfilled her destiny. But I wondered: given Joy Adamson's undisputed experience in the bush, how could she have allowed herself to be killed in this way?

The thought came into my mind that perhaps Joy had become tired, lonely, old; that she had completed her work, had little left to look forward to, and chose to go out in a blaze of glory. It would have been so very much like her. She had an insatiable compulsion to be noticed. How fitting that she should die under such spectacular, such noticeable, circumstances.

In those first few hours after her death, when radio, television, and newspapers announced the sad news to the world, I was moved to speculate that she might have chosen death by lion as her own dramatic finish.

Joy knew how to react when encountering a lion in the wild. She knew what to do to put off attack—she knew just as well how to provoke a charge. Even a lion that has no intention of attack can be incited by certain provocative gestures; few lions could resist a human figure falling and rolling on the ground as if injured. Even crouching and making quick, unusual arm movements, or running away, would very likely bring about a charge. I wondered if Joy could have been just mad enough, just theatrical enough, just dramatic enough, just devious enough, to have incited the lion to charge her. I thought that perhaps she could be—and I loved her for it.

Then a few days after that first report came word that police were investigating her death. It had not been a lion attack at all; Joy had been murdered.

Until then, my life's experience had not taught me that the way a person dies could be so important. The *fact* of death had seemed to me the matter of concern, not the method. Yet I found the idea of Joy's death by murder the most horrible I could imagine. The thought haunted me. I wished so much that the first report could have been true. Joy Adamson, killed by a wild lion while strolling at evening near her wilderness camp—such a fitting ending for a remarkable lady.

Sieuwke and I raised our glasses and clinked the rims. To irony. To the person who brought me here, who, despite enmity, had brought us together. "To Joy Adamson. May she rest in peace."

22 The Ugliest Rat In the World

In the early days of my stumbling career as a cameraman, long weeks often passed between job offers. I grew restless during those times. Waiting for the phone to ring was torture, so I decided to write a novel to fill the gaps. The therapy produced immediate results: I could smile again. I was a reasonable sociable human being, after all. Everyone had been having doubts about that, myself most of all.

I chose a subject based on a real-life episode from my seafaring days. A fishing boat, broken down off the California coast, had been carried on the current 1000 miles south to beach itself on the Revillagigedo Islands. The crew had died of thirst and starvation during the long drift..

My novel would use that true episode as a starting point, but I changed the cast and milieu. Instead of three salty commercial fishermen, the crew in my story consisted of a mixed lot of strangers aboard a luxury power yacht out for a midnight frolic. But the element that made my story unique came from my interest as a natural history buff.

One of the forsaken passengers aboard the yacht was a decidedly offbeat main character. On the night the yacht was lying alongside its moorings at Avalon, a huge wharf rat was tempted by the odor of cocktail snacks. The rat snuck aboard to have a bite. He was still there when the skipper started the engines to carry the party to a secluded cove for some midnight skinnydipping.

But when the yacht broke down and began to drift into the fog, the people soon learned that they were sharing bed and breakfast with a frightening creature. The idea alone was enough to terrorize the passengers, and eventually the rat indirectly caused the deaths of their personal relationships—and most of their lives.

Throughout all of the stress and death and trauma which seemed to be caused by the malevolent rat, it was only the *idea* of the rat that really made it happen. In fact, the rat was just another unfortunate passenger like the others, doing its best to survive.

Lippincott published *Swim, Rat, Swim* in 1960 and distributed it internationally. My agent was sure it would sell as a movie. It first attracted Alfred Hitchcock, who was in the market for a story with an animal character, but he decided to film *The Birds* instead. *Swim, Rat, Swim* next interested a Hollywood newcomer named Ronald Shusett, who wrote a script and tried to interest a studio. Unfortunately his efforts went nowhere. Later, after having given up on *Swim, Rat, Swim,* Shusett wrote the story for *Alien,* one of the biggest moneymaking films of all time. *Alien* was the story of a mixed lot of strangers drifting through space on a broken-down craft while being terrorized by a malevolent creature. It was *Swim, Rat, Swim* placed in a different, more popular, and timely genre—a clever bit of invention I wished I'd thought of. So much for that brush with riches.

Sixteen years passed, several options had come and gone, when my old friend Verna Fields—who'd cut her picture-editing teeth on my eagle film and now held a high executive position at Universal—talked studio president Sidney Sheinberg into taking an option on my novel.

So sure was I that it was going to be made that I staffed a kennel at Naivasha with a half-dozen giant forest rats—the size of a lean rabbit, a forest rat is the biggest, ugliest, most sagacious rat in the world. I was issued a federal permit to import these intimidating beasts into the United States, but under the strict condition that I could bring only sterilized male specimens into the country. Nobody wanted to populate America with a species of monster African rat that could clean up on even the toughest alley cat.

Sieuwke became the Rat Lady—a far cry from *Mama Simba,* Lion Lady, as she had been called—and took over their care and feeding. She tamed them and became quite attached to these specimens of *rodentia,* who carry in their fur a most unusual and repulsive-looking hitch-hiker, an arthropod that resembled a giant earwig. Its relationship to the giant forest rat seemed to be specific and commensal, but who benefits whom or how, we could never determine. The numerous giant earwigs that crawled through the rats' fur were perhaps the most decisive aspect that made a giant forest rat—even for Sieuwke—a hard animal to love.

When the powers at Universal questioned the validity of all the tricky things I claimed the rat could do, I talked my friend Hubert Wells into training the biggest, ugliest rat of the lot to do everything from tightrope walking a mooring line to playing cozy with a beautiful model. Conrad Hall and I shot a spooky demo reel showing the rat going through its paces. This bit of footage put the studio suits' doubts to rest.

Thereafter a pair of prominent writers were assigned to produce a screenplay, but their work missed the mark and in spite of the rat's impressive screen test, Universal let their option expire. But I had found a new niche—writing—and since then, whenever things got slow I kept from going stir-crazy by sitting at my typewriter.

Paramount Pictures bought the rights to another one of my novels. They paid the most money I'd ever seen in one lump sum, so I knew they really wanted to make the movie. This book featured a love story between a photographer and a young widowed mother, but what made it different was the experiences of her son, a boy discovering the natural history of Manhattan Island. The city is an unlikely field for wild animals, yet a surprisingly large variety of creatures inhabit the river banks and parks, even the window ledges of skyscrapers.

Peter Bart, who was then vice president of production at Paramount, assigned producer-director Buzz Kulik to develop the project, but my screenplay didn't jibe with Kulik's ideas. He lost interest and my story went into limbo.

By coincidence Paramount was also interested in finding a film for my friend Haskell Wexler to direct—he'd just won an Academy Award for his photography of *Who's Afraid of Virginia Woolf?*—and they turned the project over to him. The long connection between us and the evolution of my story to film was purely coincidental. Haskell liked my book, but it wasn't the story he wanted as his first dive into feature film directing.

Haskell already had his story, and it had nothing to do with a boy discovering the wild animal life of New York City. But he felt that he could justify taking the Paramount offer by extracting a few elements from my book and still make his film.

Haskell had been fed inside information that there would be disturbances during the 1968 Democratic Presidential convention in Chicago. He was there with his camera to shoot the violent riots—footage that he wanted to be at the heart of his film. All of his personal films since that time have had some strong political direction which began with *Medium*

Cool, the movie which was put into play through his contract to make a film from my novel.

The only story connection between Wexler's film and my book was that a widowed mother and her teenaged boy lived in a big city. In the movie, the extent of the boy's contact with New York City wildlife was that he raised pigeons in a loft on the roof of an apartment building in Chicago. Oh, and there was a news photographer who squired the boy's mother—another tweak from my novel.

When he had finished his film, Haskell told me what he'd done. He asked me if I'd drop any claims to screen credit, since his movie didn't resemble my story very closely. He thought I'd be angry, but I wasn't. I was happy for him to have his chance to shoot the movie he wanted to make. I agreed to drop my name from the credits, but I didn't go so far as to drop the profit participation clause in my contract.

In the end, the fiscal angle didn't matter anyway. Somehow this popular, low-budget, widely distributed movie never made a penny of profit. My piece of the Paramount net proved to have less monetary value than a piece of toast.

Medium Cool was a cult favorite with Europeans. A look at the record should convince any Paramount executive that the money they paid for my story was well-spent, because according to the corporate books the movie was produced—although in fact it wasn't made at all.

It's still your property, Paramount. You bought it and didn't make it. The dusty book sits on a shelf somewhere, and it would still make a good movie. It's called *The Concrete Wilderness,* by the way.

23

Never Cry Wolf

Although I'd found a new home in Africa, my professional life still required me to shoot in faraway places. Sieuwke often traveled with me, and as most of my film projects involved animals, she could put her skills to work and help the trainers.

There was a story I'd yearned to turn into a film for years and had gone through several options and scripts, with a couple of studio deals made and passed for all of the usual reasons. It was a book by Farley Mowat called *Never Cry Wolf.*

The story went like this: There has been pressure on the Canadian Government from hunters to explain a sudden decline in the numbers of caribou. A scholarly biologist, inept as a woodsman, is sent off by the Canadian Wildlife Service to spend a season in the Arctic studying wolves. The political bosses have already drawn their own conclusions—that wolves are the cause of the declining herds. Our hero's mission is to return with evidence of this assumption. During his studies the skeptical biologist learns to respect the lives of wolves. He doesn't find the cause for the caribou decline, but he doesn't think it's due to wolves.

In early 1982 I met with my friend Joe Strick and his Broadway and movie producer friend Lewis Allen (*Fahrenheit 451, Annie, Lord of the Flies*) in London. I hoped to work out a way to make the movie. I asked Joe and Lew to put up the money to buy out Warner Brothers, who held the present option and a script. (Warners had previously bought out Universal, the first studio I'd interested in the property.) They agreed, and *Never Cry Wolf* was back in play. I hoped Joe and Lew had the wolf's predatory instinct to grab us all a fat meal ticket.

Now that we owned the story rights, it was time to find a new studio. Our first try was at Disney. I took our idea to my friend, longtime Disney producer Winston Hibler, who conferred with the studio story department. It seemed they already knew about the story and had some interest in it. But this was in the time before Disney Studios had ever made a profit participation deal with anyone. "No profit sharing" was firm Disney policy. We wanted a piece of the action, and our policy was just as firm. We walked.

Joe and Lew tried to get things cooking again at Warners and came up empty. We received the same answer at other studios and production companies. Time passed.

We were getting nowhere with the Warners script. Joe and I had been praying since the beginning that Lew would try an obvious (to us) gambit and prevail upon his wife, scriptwriter Jay Presson Allen (*The Prime of Miss Jean Brodie, Cabaret, Funny Lady, Funny Girl*), to write a completely new screenplay. At last she read the book, thought it was wonderful, and got to work.

Jay's script was terrific. It was funny, it was sad, it was high adventure, it was topical. We thought we could go anywhere with it and make a deal.

We decided to shop a package. It was 1983.

Long before we had a production deal, I went out on a limb and spent some of Joe's and Lew's money by contracting with Hubert Wells to begin putting a cast of wolves together. We'd need a pack; we'd also need puppies in the spring, and we'd require a lead pair of handsome white Arctic wolves that could be worked without restraint in the wilds of Alaska and Canada. Hubert said he needed a year of lead time to acquire and train the wolves.

With our animal cast being assembled and attending acting school, it was time to shop for a director. Joe and Lew thought that Louis Malle (*Atlantic City, Au revoir les enfants, Lacombe Lucien*) was the man for the job. Highly regarded as a director of sophisticated drama, Malle had also paid his dues to outdoor production; he'd even worked as an underwater cameraman for Jacques Cousteau. We met with him at the old Chateau Marmont Hotel off the Sunset Strip, the traditional Hollywood hangout where possibly more movie deals have been struck than anywhere else in the world. Louis' companion, Susan Sarandon, was present. It was an imposing gathering of Tinseltown blue bloods. Malle liked the script and agreed to direct the film.

Meanwhile, Lew and Joe were still shopping for studio financing.

When Walt Disney died of lung cancer in 1966, his studio descended into a period of chaos. Speculation flowed as to who would prevail as top man. A power struggle between Walt's nephew, Roy Jr., and Walt's son-in-law, Ron Miller, was decided in favor of the more flamboyant personality—but not necessarily the craftiest or brightest of the two. Handsome ex-USC gridiron star Ron Miller traded in his football jersey for a suit and tie and now headed the studio. Under his novice management, production dragged.

Despite the the studio's recent difficulties, Lew and Joe thought Disney would give *Never Cry Wolf* the best distribution possible. It was a family film, although a bit outside the usual Disney mold: one hilarious sequence had our leading character eating mice—not Mickey, to be sure, but cute little Arctic mice nevertheless. Lew and Joe talked to Ron Miller, who as a relative newcomer at running a studio was interested in the credentials that my partners and Lewis's talented wife brought with them. It was as if they conveyed an aura of New York class into the rather bourgeois Disney atmosphere. I had the feeling that Ron wondered what in the hell I, as an old Disney wildlife guy, was doing in such illustrious company.

But when Miller found out that Disney had already passed once on *Never Cry Wolf,* he was unsure. So he hedged. And Louis Malle as director was a star in a different constellation than the galaxy Disney studios were used to, which caused Ron Miller even more uncertainty.

Lew and Joe weren't content to wait out Ron Miller's indecision. They were sure this picture would be made, if not by Disney, then by someone else. They were confident that today's expenses would be reimbursed by tomorrow's production company. Our growing pack of trained wolves was hungrily eating up dollars and howling to get moving.

Louis Malle joined me on a midwinter survey trip to the Yukon, where I thought we could make the movie. It wasn't an easy outing, helicoptering around the frozen north looking at locations. Malle soon realized that shooting this movie would be physically more challenging than he'd anticipated. When we returned to California, Malle dropped out. But he'd already given his casting approval, and Lew and Joe had signed a pay-or-play deal with a young actor named William Katt. "Pay or play" meant they'd pay the actor his fee even if the movie wasn't made, and whether or not he played the part even if it was made and somebody else had the role. Lew and Joe had made the strongest possible pledge to their conviction.

Katt was a handsome blond who'd played a role as a hunk surfer, and was the young Sundance in an as yet unreleased film, *Butch and Sundance: The Early Years,* for which expectations were running high. It was a casting decision that I didn't agree with, but Joe and Lew carried the majority with their two votes.

The next director that we partners all agreed upon was Carroll Ballard, who'd just achieved high recognition for his feature, *The Black Stallion.*

When we mentioned to Ron Miller that we were thinking of approaching Carroll Ballard, his attitude toward our project was suddenly as solid as if the contracts were already cast in concrete. Miller bubbled with enthusiasm. It turned out that Ron was furious that Disney hadn't made *The Black Stallion.* The reason for his pique wasn't clear—perhaps the property had been offered and refused. Miller thought Ballard's movie was perfect Disney fare, just what was needed to bring the studio out of the doldrums. His attitude was comically proprietary; he seemed to feel that this kind of movie could only be released by Disney, and that any poacher infringing on the territory was a crook.

Miller said that if we could get Carroll Ballard to direct our film, we had a deal. He even agreed to break precedent and for the first time ever accepted the condition that we would share a piece of the profits.

Our director showed up at Lew's hotel room in Beverly Hills in his usual rumpled attire—unlaced boots, blue jeans, and a plaid flannel woodsmen's shirt. He liked the script but wanted to make changes. Eventually Carroll hired a string of writers to polish Jay Presson Allen's script that had meant so much to floating the project. In the end, Jay declined to participate in the Writer's Guild credit arbitration.

Ballard told us right off that we'd go mad with his style of moviemaking. He said he'd drive us crazy by reshooting sequences, that he'd take forever to complete the editing, and that he didn't agree with the casting. Carroll thought that Bill Katt was too pretty and that his athletic build and bearing projected an image of competence. He wanted someone who was out of his element in the wilderness, blundering through—someone like that little comic character actor Charles Martin Smith, who'd seemed so incompetent as Toad in *American Graffiti.*

Carroll seemed intent on doing everything he could to talk us out of having him direct the movie—yet it was clear he very much wanted to do it. The one thing in the evening's discussion that I felt good about was Carroll's view on the casting. Lew and Joe were disappointed by his rejection of their star, to whom they'd already made the substantial play-or-pay commitment.

Carroll had been disarmingly upfront about his exasperating moviemaking methods. But knowing Ron Miller's feelings for Ballard, we were happy to have him under any terms; and as he was so straightforward about his annoying methods, we couldn't help but feel that he was embroidering his faults out of modesty. Nobody could really be as bad as Carroll Ballard said he was.

Lewis and Joe had the unpleasant task of telling William Katt that he was out of the picture. They paid off the $250,000 specified in his contract. Bill Katt, hardly a lofty box office name, had attended three or four brief meetings, never did a day's work on the movie, yet made a quarter of a million dollars. I had spent fifteen years of development and several months of day-to-day work on *Never Cry Wolf*, but Katt came out five times fatter. Can any business be crazier than that?

* * * * *

Crazy, yes; but look at all the fun I had.

The story of *Never Cry Wolf* encompassed all of the seasons—spring, summer, winter, and fall. I took a midwinter location scouting trip and made arrangements to set up base near Whitehorse, the capital of Canada's Yukon Territory. We would travel to other locations in the spectacularly scenic Tombstone Mountains some 600 miles to the north, and near the old 1890s Gold Rush towns of Nome and Skagway in Alaska.

If we could get into production early enough, we still had time to shoot all of the seasons in one continuous schedule. We'd start with winter, catch the spring (an essential time as it's the season when wolf cubs are born), summer, and end the picture in sequential order with autumn and the approach of winter. It was a long schedule made necessary by the seasonal birth and maturation of the wolf cubs.

In preparation for the move from sunny southern California to icy Arctic conditions, Hubert moved the wolves from his suburban Los Angeles headquarters into the Sierras near Reno, Nevada. The animals had to be acclimatized, and their coats in the cold mountains quickly grew long and dense. They looked beautiful.

One of Hubert's most challenging responsibilities was to teach one of our animal actors how to pee properly for the camera. Because of a wolf's physical similarity to a dog of the German shepherd or sled dog breeds, it's easy to think of a wolf as a sort of dog. Dogs and wolves can interbreed, thus confirming the linkage of their genes, but in many ways a wolf and dog are completely different animals. The greatest difference lies in personality and character. A dog's inbred personality comes to it naturally through thousands of years of domesticity and close relationships with humans. A wolf, on the other hand, is all wild. Unlike a dog, a wolf cannot be trained through methods of intimidation. Not that coercion is recommended when teaching a dog new tricks—a dog's reaction to browbeating can be quite damaging to character, and the reward system is the one of choice. Still, dogs have been trained through extortion. A wolf? Never. A wolf is trained only through rewards—do something right and get a treat, a bit of food, verbal or tactile praise. Attempting to strongarm a wolf only makes him a lifetime enemy. Once the method of force is used, a misguided trainer can never go back and start over with a softer method.

Another difference between wolves and dogs is that male wolves are not born with the male dog's habit of lifting a leg to have a pee. They might learn the technique in captivity by observing dogs, but most wild male wolves squat like a bitch to relieve themselves.

In *Never Cry Wolf* author Farley Mowat described an amusing interaction between himself and the wolf family he was studying. He set up his tent near the den and spent hours watching his wolves. The animals became completely habituated to his presence, but they wanted Farley to stay in his own territory and not cross the line into theirs. In return, they would respond in kind. It's the wolf's habit to recognize marked territory through the olfactory senses. Boundaries are set by peeing on objects around the perimeter, and a sniff of the urine tells the wolf a story: who did it, when, what gender—a whole letter posted in a few drops of urine.

Mowat caught on to this by watching the male wolf set out the boundary line—this side, wolf territory; that side, Mowat territory. Then Mowat replied through an orgy of tea-drinking which enabled him to respond by setting out his side of the boundary with his own line of pee.

The story was easy to tell visually. But the filmic problem was that a macho male wolf going around and marking boundaries by squatting to pee just wouldn't look right to a movie audience, however factual it might be. To make the action perfectly clear—that the wolf was going from spot to spot taking a pee—we decided to take liberty with natural history (after all, we weren't making a documentary) and have Igor, the male wolf of our family, lift his leg. That way, everyone in the audience would catch on right away.

So for six weeks, Hubert spent a few hours every day priming spots with a drop or two of bottled pee as a stimulus to induce a challenging squirt from the wolf. Then Hubert followed Igor around, timing his moves to that of the wolf, stepping in quickly and lifting Igor's leg at the right moment and giving a reward for every squirt Igor made in the raised-leg position.

Soon Igor learned to pee like a dog. He seemed to like it and eventually took to the method like the most unflagging male terrier. Igor never squatted again. Then, as an extra refinement, he learned to do it on command.

* * * * *

That inevitable moment when one's work—mistakes and gems alike (and there are sure to be both)—appears for the first time on the screen is called "viewing the rushes," also known as "dailies." Viewed by producer, director, and selected crew at the end of a long day in a small dark room—or in the local cinema when shooting in a remote location—yesterday's toil with all its blemishes unwinds in front of a nitpicking crowd of tired workers. The hairdresser is looking only at heads. If the makeup artist sees a missed bit of powder then the whole scene is a mess, never mind that it was the greatest performance since Laurence Olivier called his troops to battle in *Henry V.* The cameraman is cringing because of a misplaced light, the performer is looking only at...himself or herself, of course. Most of the people in this tense, dark room are gazing solely at that specialty at which they strive to be perfect. Only the director, editor, and producer are looking at the overall effect of the scene.

Expectations are high and the result isn't always consistent. What's right in take three is wrong in take five, but take two had a spontaneity that's missing in take ten. It's not an edited movie that's running, so there's no flow between scenes, and repeated takes of the same shot can become boring. But as professional moviemakers, everyone in the room is supposed to be used to that, and each person believes he or she can see through the weaknesses of unedited film. In fact, no one can compensate completely for the lack of polish they view in rushes. Dailies never come alive in the way these same shots can sparkle in an edited scene.

Viewing dailies is a complicated process, a ritual fraught with strange politics. Nerves are twanging like fiddle strings and everyone is ready to fend off blows. It's the second unit cameraman-director's most vulnerable time. Mixed messages hover in the room, diverse motivations crawl like slimy slugs under the chairs.

I had agreed to shoot the second unit footage on *Never Cry Wolf.* Sieuwke was with us in the north, helping Hubert's team by raising wolf pups. We had our usual happy, independent little unit that worked separately from the main unit, at different places, different times.

The second unit man's job is to shoot exciting action, visually striking establishing shots, wonderful scenics, gorgeous sunsets, beautiful thematic bridging material—all of those stunning shots that give atmosphere, texture, period and place to a film. He usually has the time to wait for the best light and the ability to go to the best places. The second unit guy gets all the breaks. That's why it's so much fun.

Thus during a dailies viewing session, after an hour of familiar takes repeated umpteen times, when a few minutes of second unit shots come on the screen, it's a welcome break. Of course it looks good. Except for the small second unit crew, no one else has seen the footage being shot and nobody knows what to expect, so everything is a refreshing surprise. It's hardly fair to compare these bright apples with the boring fruits of moments ago, but inevitably comparisons are made, and the second unit guy can come out smelling like a rose.

But inevitably, certain resentments seep forth. The main unit cameraman knows that plaudits for the second unit work will ultimately ooze off onto his credit so of course he wants it to look good. However, during those moments of exciting rushes, he may feel a bit put down, and the kudos awarded to his lesser half may seem to him like a personal slight.

It's a touchy time for a second unit guy, with all kinds of vibrations bouncing off the walls. So it's a time for him to be very, very careful.

* * * * *

We kicked off location shooting in March of 1982. As the line producer and second unit director-cameraman of our co-producing threesome, I arrived in the Yukon Territory in the middle of a blinding snowstorm. With me were Carroll Ballard, actor Charles Martin Smith, a small production crew, a second unit assistant cameraman, Sieuwke, wolves, Hubie and two other trainers. Winter, with its frozen lakes and snowy mountains, was all around us.

We settled in. With the second unit I shot some footage of the wolves stalking through a snowy forest in what was to be a nightmare sequence—Mowat's dream of being chased and chewed up by wolves.

Carroll decided that in order to get into the feel of the country and the animals, he wanted to ease into production by doing some filming of the wolves himself. First unit cinematographer, Hiro Narita, agreed.

Carroll's shooting style seemed to be, "if it moves, shoot it." His hope was that out of a mile of footage, a single foot-long gem might shine through. He wasn't selective in what he shot. He wasn't tuned to economy, and his rushes revealed an off-the-cuff attitude as if saying to himself, "Well, if I keep the camera running long enough, maybe one of these wolves will do something interesting." No one could say he didn't warn us that his methods would be irksome. And of course, the jewels do sometimes occur.

My school has always been that a cameraman's reputation is made in the dailies viewing room. I learned early on, while sitting beside half-interested producers in a projection room watching hours of boring footage peppered with technical imperfections, that the seats can get very hard. Before I push the camera start button, I always ask myself, "Does this shot have a chance of getting into the movie?" If it doesn't, or if I'm not fairly sure that what I see in the viewfinder is going to make the sleepy eyes in the projection room open up, I don't shoot. And on long assignments to faraway places where there was no chance of getting more film when I used up what I had with me, I learned the ethic of frugality.

Some directors don't allow crew members other than the camera team and special invitees to look at rushes. Other directors, like Carroll, invite everyone with the idea that seeing their work paves the way to improvement. There's good argument for either point of view.

On the night the first rushes were shown at the cinema in Whitehorse, I soon felt an ominous foreboding that Carroll and I were in for trouble. All of the crew and assorted outsiders were present in the theater for this first peek at the footage for *Never Cry Wolf.* Carroll's hourlong clip of wolves wandering around aimlessly, brought a lot of seat shuffling, coughs, and sighs.

Unfortunately, my ten minutes of footage contrasted with Carroll's in every way. Halfway into my reel I saw the way the audience was responding, and before the lights came on I tried to duck out of the theater. But I didn't make it in time and was stopped by praise and congratulations that I didn't want to hear. I glanced at Carroll as he slouched out, and saw that he was fuming. It wasn't the way things ought to be, but on this first night of dailies, I'd made an adversary of Carroll Ballard.

From this time on, a uneasy relationship existed between Carroll and me. I considered this enigmatic man to be one of the most talented filmmakers in America. No one has a better eye for a shot. It might take him a long time to get there, but his films are told in a striking visual language. In that respect, Carroll could be a disciple of my old mentor Slavko Vorkapich. Ballard's films achieve acclaim for their visual style, and a few—*Never Cry Wolf* among them—have had a large audience. But Carroll has only made a handful of films. I believe Carroll Ballard is worth whatever problems he creates for himself and his producers.

After that first screening of dailies, on the pretext that I was of the school that don't like to have my rushes shown to the crew, I viewed my work alone on the Moviola.

* * * * *

Zane Palmer was one of the most celebrated of the exalted breed of Arctic bush pilots. A seat-of-the-pants flyer, Zane piloted a classic single-engined Otter that served as the plane in which Mowat flies into the snowy skies and is dropped off in the heart of wolf country to face the elements alone in the wilderness. Zane's old plane was also my wings to visit out-of-the-way locations.

In setting up the shoot for a sequence in which Mowat first encounters a herd of caribou, Zane flew me from Whitehorse north to Aklavik and Inuvik, Eskimo villages at the mouth of the MacKenzie River in the delta of the Beaufort Sea. Here I'd been led to believe that I could find Eskimos who owned herds of reindeer—domesticated versions of the wild caribou—which we might be able to use for our shoot.

Another reason for the flight was to shoot aerial footage of the frozen mountains and glaciers.

Our journey was a springtime flight of 600 miles over high snowy mountains, tundra, and frozen lakes. We could expect to encounter sudden changes in weather. Zane carried a kit of sleeping bags and food in the event of an emergency landing, and the plane was equipped with skis rather than wheels or the summertime floats used in this watery country for landings.

It was a flight of wonder and adventure for me. From the air we saw the famous Porcupine Herd of caribou, mile after mile of long dark strings of animals against the snow; we saw wolves in the valleys and Dall sheep on the mountains and countless acres of wild empty country. We saw not a single living person—no house, shack, curl of smoke, or road—in 600 miles.

On the way, Zane told me that late in the winter a couple of years past he'd landed on a remote frozen lake—not quite frozen enough—and the plane had dropped through the ice into water of considerable depth. Because of transportation difficulties in this roadless land, it was impossible to bring in salvage equipment by land. Zane's aircraft remained submerged through the spring, summer, and half the next winter. But at Christmas when the lake's surface was hard and thick, he flew in retrieval gear, chopped a great hole in the ice above the plane, lifted it, dried it, relubricated the engines, and flew it out.

In that same plane, still smelling a bit of moss and mildew, Zane flew me across this endless wilderness with no aids to navigation other than a chart, a radio, and a compass. A couple of hundred miles south of our destination we ran into low clouds. From there, Zane's method of navigation was simple. He found the frozen MacKenzie River, dropped down to an altitude of a hundred feet and followed the twisting path of ice.

When we finally landed at Aklavic, I rode out with a guide on a snowmobile to meet the reindeer herders.

The reindeer—which had originally been domesticated for their milk, meat, and hides—now presented a new source of income for the Eskimos. Reindeer and caribou shed their huge horns and grow new ones every year. At the time the horns have reached their peak and are still covered with the soft velvety skin that will soon rub off, the animals are caught, dehorned, and the horn is sold at auction to Chinese and Taiwanese bidders who then ship it home for medicinal and aphrodisiac use. The use of reindeer horn has helped to lessen the pressure on rhino horn, the most desirable, expensive—and scarce—commodity for the purpose.

Our filming schedule wasn't compatible with that of the Canadian herdsmen. By the time we wanted to shoot, the reindeer roundup would be over and the animals would be dehorned. But I'd hoped that we could "buy" a fully-horned herd for filming. Now I learned from the Aklavic herdsmen that all of their horn had been contracted for by Chinese buyers. Fortunately, I'd already met with a Nome herdsman who had agreed to forego the dehorning. I knew I could strike a deal with him which would fit our schedule.

But we were in Canada and Nome is in the United States. We'd had no trouble bringing our wolves from California to the Yukon, but bureaucratic troubles popped up when I applied for permits to shift our pack back across the boundary. I'd anticipated this problem—that's why I'd been looking for a Canadian carabou location. In a strange paradox, the wolf was considered as vermin in Canada, to be shot for bounty, and an endangered species in the USA, illegal to move across international borders. The red tape involved in moving the wolves had become more complicated than I expected.

I finally managed to obtain the necessary permits by certifying that our pack were hybrid wolf-dogs, thus exempt from the Endangered Species Act. I wasn't lying—their bloodline was a difficult distinction to be proved one way or the other as our animals came from several generations of captivity. I believe they did have some domestic blood infused into their veins by a randy German shepherd at some time in the past.

When my Eskimo snowmobile driver brought me back from the reindeer folks to civilization (such as it was) on the edge of the Arctic Ocean, I found Zane looking sad. The weather we had encountered on the way up had dropped the altitude ceiling to zero. Without instruments, Zane couldn't fly his Otter out. The plane was stuck here until the sky lifted.

I waited with my pilot for two anxious days, then gave up and caught a commercial flight south. This change of planes turned out to be more dangerous than winging it in the submarine, as we'd dubbed Zane's diving Otter. On landing at the airport in the Eskimo town of Old Crow the twin-engined commercial jet hit the runway so hard that it bounced high into the air, returned for a couple more jarring collisions with the ice, blew a tire, and skidded to a halt in the snow. I sat out a couple of days in Old Crow—no one's idea of a vacation spot—while spares were flown in and repairs made.

When Zane eventually returned to Whitehorse, our art director, Graeme Murray, had a go at his plane. To make the old Otter even more distressed-looking than she was, Murray muddied up the fuselage, replaced the functional pilot's side door with an unpainted slab of plywood, added some rusty bailing wire struts, and lashed a beat-up canoe under the belly. Now we had the tin-Lizzie airplane that would carry Farley Mowat into the frozen north where it would leave him alone and afraid, stranded in the middle of nowhere.

To shoot footage of the rattle-trap plane in the air, I sat in the doorway of a helicopter with my feet on the struts. I wore a huge fur-lined World War II surplus flight coverall, long johns, mittens, fur-lined boots, and watchcap and filmed Zane flying his seedy-looking "Otter" airplane over the glaciers and between the snowy peaks of the St. Elias Mountains—19,850 feet tall with their feet in the sea. The temperature at that height, with the wind chill, was far colder than anything I'd experienced in Antarctica where I'd shot a Disney documentary.

Later, when the plane was on the ground, Carroll would film the cockpit scenes with Charles Martin Smith and Brian Dennehy manning the controls while a grip jiggled a wing.

* * * * *

Never Cry Wolf was my third experience living with wolves and working closely with the pack for months at a time. I had learned their ways, learned to love them and to respect them individually and as a group. Both *The Legend of Lobo* and especially *Never Cry Wolf* made strong statements for wolf protection. But these films were not impartial documentaries. They were romanticized stories that expressed a fairy-tale point of view. Perhaps they helped to set an attitude and served as ammunition for the great movement to protect wolves that sprung up and gained so much momentum in the 2000s. Both wolves and many humans rode on that bandwagon.

All of the wolves I have worked with—and there have been more than two dozen—were as fixed in their nature as, say, different breeds of dogs. The habits of working dogs like border collies, dobermans, terriers, pointers, setters, huskies, and Labradors are as predictable as the rising sun. They have been bred through many years and countless generations to perform the work intended for them and they do it very well.

Wolves are dogs' closest kin. In the distant past, individual wolves were changed in shape and nature to become different, and dog varieties were made. But no human has interfered with the genes and shaped the instincts of the wild wolf. They are what they have always been—top of the line predators.

The purebred wolves that comprised the pack in T*he Legend of Lobo* were called upon in the script to attack a herd of cattle. These were "trained" wolves, but their training consisted of little more than coming when called and not running away (and they were hardly consistent even in those basic commands). They were zoo wolves, generations removed from their wild ancestors, yet their instincts remained in their blood as conspicuously as their shape and color.

When introduced into our herd of Mexican longhorn cattle they behaved exactly as if they had read the script. It was in their nature. They knew what to do. Their genes told them that the cow was prey and they acted accordingly. No surprise. My job was to get the shots, complicated at the same time by protecting our valuable longhorns.

My years of living with wolves taught me to see both sides of the wolf issue, and I learned that wolves do have their place in the modern world. I love wolves. I enjoyed knowing and working with them. At the same time my warm feelings are mixed with paradox. I believe that the welcome matt for wolves is correctly placed within the National Parks and remote wild places where natural prey species roam free and wild. Rather sadly, my experience also leads me to take an unhip position. I can understand why the welcome matt is not properly laid on the doorstep of a sheep herder or cattleman.

* * * * *

One of the most useful lessons I learned from Carroll Ballard was the importance of holding preview screenings in front of a "real" audience—that is, non-movie-folks, people off the street. Prior to *Never Cry Wolf* I'd never been a part of this eye-opening exercise, which can be so important in bringing forth unexpected results. As the movie came together in editing, we held three public screenings. At each one the audience filled out preview cards, telling us what they liked and what they didn't. After each screening Carroll made adjustments suggested by the preview cards. He chose to ignore a couple of audience criticisms.

Among the several hundred questionnaires, a few objected strongly to the "nudity" in the film. It had never occurred to me that there was any nudity at all, and the complaint puzzled me. Then I realized what the cards were referring to.

On a summer day while Mowat is out searching for wolves, the camera finds him lying on the tundra, asleep on the soft moss, letting the warm sun soak his bare backside. A strange sound penetrates the Arctic stillness, bringing Farley awake. It grows louder, and suddenly Farley and the audience realize that it's caused by the approach of a stampeding herd of caribou—the first he's met—being pursued by a wolfpack. Mowat leaps to his feet, jerks on his boots, and runs with the herd, exhilarated that at last he's seeing what he came so far to find.

As for nudity, the camera glimpses his white butt a few times, but nothing more. There's nothing even faintly erotic or immodest, and most of the time Farley's derriere is hidden in the midst of running animals. I believe the reason that Carroll shot the scene with Mowat in the buff was that he wanted to suggest a feeling of primitive man in touch with nature: Farley is changing; he's becoming a part of the wilderness. At least that's what I got out of it. That anyone could find this scene objectionable blew us all away. We supported Carroll's decision to let it stand.

The other scene which proves you can't please everyone was one my favorites, but many in the audiences who had filled out preview cards found it repulsive. At a point where Farley discovers his wolf family is sustaining itself on a diet of mice, not caribou, he decides to sample the rodent diet himself. In a scene inspired by the classic Charles Chaplin pantomime of eating his shoes in *The Gold Rush,* Farley is watched by some resident mice who escaped the pot, while he apologetically carves and greedily puts away the carcasses of their stewed brothers.

Some of our preview audiences were so turned off by the idea that they couldn't watch this scene. We thought it was a funny highlight. Again I voted with Carroll to let it stand.

At the time the scene was filmed, Charles Martin Smith thought he was going to be eating some tasty article put together by the prop man—something that looked like a cooked skinned mouse but tasted like a chicken croquette. But the prop man was stumped in coming up with a concoction that would fit the bill. I told him that when I'd been a student on museum collecting trips, I'd often eaten mouse. Kangaroo rat stew and Peromyscus pie were favorites of my biologist mentor. At the end of a good trapline, after we'd skinned and stuffed a mixed bag of a dozen mice of various species, we never wasted the carcasses but had them for lunch or dinner. After all, they're not much different from miniature rabbits.

It fell into my lap to prepare mouse in several recipes to see which one fit the bill by appealing to Charles' appetite while still retaining the general appearance of a small rodent. The one that I favored was deep-fried mouse. In this recipe the head was tossed away, but the legs stuck out like those of a piglet done on a spit, and the skinned tail remained attached and intact as a handle. The mice were small and when fried to bacon crispness had the texture of a well-cooked whitebait. As with those small fish, the crunch of the bones when you chewed added to the pleasure of the meal.

Charles Martin Smith played the game admirably. He not only *looked* as if he savored my concoction, he smacked his lips with real gusto.

* * * * *

And what of Disney's first dive into the mysterious world of sharing profits with their producers? As the last holdouts against the profit-sharing system, they became quick learners. Of course they had a lot of places to go for advice; all of the other studios had already taken the plunge. The answer was simple: okay, give a share in the net, but not the gross. It looks good on the contract, but through creative accounting—sometimes called "Hollywood math"—it's easy to make sure there are no net profits to distribute in the end.

Never Cry Wolf played long and wide, enjoyed wonderful reviews and pleased audiences all over the world. It sold well to television and the home video market. Yet it never made a penny of net profit.

Isn't it strange how the studios can keep turning out successful movies that lose money? Truly, Disney *is* The Magic Kingdom.

24 The Queen of the Jungle

I have always tried to focus on people's agreeable traits. But at the same time I'm vividly aware that it's the rogues, wags, and rascals, who make the most interesting folks to read about—or to write about. One of these interesting people was my friend John Guillermin.

Guillermin was the director of *Sheena, Queen of the Jungle*, a silly 1984 film based on a popular comic book. John had made some exciting action movies—*The Blue Max, Towering Inferno,* a *King Kong* remake, *Death on the Nile*—but it was probably his experience directing one of the Tarzan flicks that got him the *Sheena* assignment.

It was impossible to take this movie seriously, but having accepted the assignment, I took pride in doing the best job I could. My second unit work on *Sheena* was fun because the animal action in its cartoon-like conception was unusually challenging, and because of the unusual frame of mind of its director.

Guillermin seemed to believe that nothing was worth doing if it wasn't difficult. If there was an easy way, John racked his brain to come up with an arduous alternative. He seemed to choose locations not by their scenic value or practicality, but by the degree of stress or potential trauma they presented. The rougher the road to a shooting area, the worse the weather, the more challenging the dust, heat, or cold, the better John liked it.

If there was a stunt to be done, John wanted to be the first to do it. In this flick there were a lot of planes crashing, cars blown to smithereens, perilous cliff-climbing, fights with dangerous animals, and all the other wild stuff of adventure comics. John knew better how to ride a horse than the wranglers, to fly a plane better than the pilots, to throw a spear better than a Maasai, to shoot an arrow straighter than a Waliangulu. About the only things of which Guillermin didn't claim mastery were how to wrestle a lion or outrun a rhino the—stunts which we in the "animal unit" hoped that John would try.

Sheena was the only movie I ever worked on where money seemed to mean nothing. The budget was wide open. Coca-Cola owned Columbia Pictures at the time, and Coke had a bottling plant in Kenya. Next to Tusker beer, Coke was the most popular bottled drink in the country, and the Coca-Cola Company had billions of shillings tied up that it couldn't get out in spendable money because of currency restrictions. What better way to turn shillings into dollars than spend it on a movie?

The money flowed so freely that Hubert Wells was allowed to charter a 747 and fly an elephant, a rhino, a few lions, chimps, monkeys, and horses from California to Africa.

In keeping with his first principle of film production—doing things the hard way—John Guillermin scheduled his shoot to coincide with the weather at its most extreme. Against all local advice, we shot in the desert during its hottest season. After surviving that, we headed for the mountaintops as the first black clouds that foretold the coming of the rainy season swirled over the summits.

A sexy-looking and athletic actress from the Bronx, Tanya Roberts, played the part of the gorgeous Sheena. Orphaned in the story at age six, Sheena grew up with wild animals under the tutelage of an African woman shaman. Just where beautiful Sheena picked up her accent was never explained, but a Bronx twang was evident in her every word. Never mind that Roberts wore but one costume throughout the entire film—a tiny ragged leather bikini.

In standard cartoon gimmickry, Sheena could communicate with wild animals. She did it through extrasensory perception, a little trick taught to her by her foster mother, the African shaman.

The part of the shaman was played by a real-life Princess. Elizabeth, Princess of Toro, was royalty from a Ugandan enclave once known as the Kingdom of Buganda. The kingdom had been made obsolete by the changes brought about by democracy, but Elizabeth was still a Princess—and very much looked and behaved like one. She spoke English with an accent that reflected her education in England, and she broadcast an aura that confirmed a childhood as the darling of a distinguished royal family.

Thus the cultural differences between this common girl of the Bronx and the cultured woman of the jungle were as much in contrast as the differences in the colors of their skin. Both of them radiated great beauty—but only one of them shone with charm, dignity, and social grace. And because of their differences in background, a palpable tension hung over the set whenever the two women appeared in a scene together.

Tanya was athletic and good at riding a horse. But in the script, Sheena's mount was a zebra—which is not the same. The first time Tanya climbed aboard a trained zebra and went for a trot, Guillermin shouted, "No! No! No! This will never do."

In spite of its superficial resemblance to a striped horse, a zebra isn't a horse at all. With its short legs and chunky back, it's what equestrians call short-gaited. No champion rider in the world could sit a zebra gracefully. In countries where people ride short-gaited donkeys, they don't sit in the middle of the animal's back—they perch way back on its rump. That posture looks funny—not the stuff of graceful Sheena—but if you sit on a donkey or a zebra in the way you'd sit on a horse, you bounce up and down in a most inelegant manner. There was just no way Guillermin could have beautiful Sheena, with her swanlike poise, bouncing around like a clown on a short-gaited zebra.

So white Arabian horses were brought to Kenya and painted with black stripes. All that could be said of the newly-invented breed was that it was graceful. But there's no way you could pass off a painted horse as a zebra. Guillermin's answer to this anomaly was, "It's not supposed to be a horse; it's not supposed to be a zebra. It's a mythical beast. The whole story's a fucking myth, anyway."

Problem was, the animal looked exactly like what it was—a painted horse. Early in the movie we saw Sheena, costumed in her brief bikini, ride this curious animal in a long tracking shot. In spite of the wonderful slow-motion bouncing of Tanya's elegant body, the painted horse was the first thing about the movie to put you off. And then just as you got settled into the story and accepted all the other silliness, along came Sheena mounted on her painted horse—and again all feeling of belief flew out the window.

Working with John Guillermin was my first and only experience with a director who was a real-life caricature of the wild, shouting, movie director tyrant that one hears about but seldom sees. In the belief that Guillermin's language was too spicy for young ears, the producer banned child visitors from the set and carefully screened and warned adult guests that the words they might hear could offend them. It was the only time in my filmmaking career that I came across such reason for restriction.

Guillermin was hardly built like Tarzan. He was wiry and slight, but his bravado exceeded that of the Ape Man. He loved to swing on vines, and he took a trial swing on nearly every new setup—while the whole crew hoped that the rope would break. I learned a great deal from Guillermin about swinging on vines, although I never grabbed ahold of one and took a leap. After all, my philosophy is, "Why ask for trouble?"

A real vine in a tree has a single point of attachment; thus a swing has an arc limited to the length of the vine. With such a short trajectory, you can't actually go very far through the jungle swinging from vine to vine. But when Tarzan—or Sheena—swings through the treetops, they cover a lot of ground. Their swings are long and graceful—long enough in Tarzan's case to cover an extended yodel. It looks natural, but in fact it's been rigged by a team of vine-swing-rigging experts who have spent the previous day stretching a long steel cable tightly between widely-spaced trees. A wheeled block to which the vine is attached runs on this cable (which is concealed in treetop foliage), and thus Sheena sails through the air on a much longer trajectory than would be possible under natural conditions. It's not an arc at all; it's a beeline glide through the trees on a slightly descending gradient.

It was a rare day when Guillerman didn't stalk off the set in a huff after a profane tirade against some member of the crew. Then after an hour of solitary cooling off with a bottle of Tusker beer, he came back from his tent and solved whatever had been bothering him by firing the offending crew member.

It appeared that Guillermin had a deep personal fascination with his star's creamy smooth skin. Because of this interest, Guillerman took every camera setup as the opportunity to touch Tanya wherever she wasn't covered by leather, which was just about everywhere. Inevitably he sidled in before his last-minute command to "roll camera" and adjusted his star, as if fine-tuning a manikin in a shop window. He changed her pose by hand, altered the drape of her floppy costume—just a bit of a lift to the shoulder here, a turn of the hips there, a tweak of the bikini top to show a bit more boob in this place or that.

Guillermin loved low angles. His favorite placement of the camera had it shooting up into her buckskin panties where you could almost—

but not quite—see into the shadowed area. He teased his audience with this angle by having Tanya climb trees, scale cliffs, hang from helicopters, and swing from vines.

Tanya's husband-manager must have seen a spark in the director's eye when they set her deal back in California. Her contract included his travel and location expenses, and he was present during nearly every scene.

* * * * *

It seemed that Guillermin chose a new victim from the crew to harass every day—a quirk of his nature that everyone soon caught on to. One of the stunt gang was the usual victim. Guillermin fired his vine-riggers (and later re-hired them) at least once a week; props, costume, and makeup departments inflamed Guillermin's temper nearly as often. It got so bad that the crew had a betting pool going: who is going to be Guillermin's victim today?

Lorenzo Ricciardi, a colorful local, took a minor part playing the role of a mercenary, one of the heavies of the story. As driver of a vehicle in a line of armored personnel carriers, Lorenzo appeared frequently in the movie.

On the day that Ricciardi became Guillermin's target we were shooting a long tracking shot. The truck column was to drive through the jungle to a certain spot and stop on the mark. Then everyone would disembark, AK-47s at the ready.

On the first take, Lorenzo overshot the mark by a couple of inches—an inconsequential margin of error.

Guillermin shouted angrily, "Again! Lorenzo, try to get the damn wheel on the god-damned mark next time, will you?"

Take two: again Lorenzo was off by a couple of inches, or so the director proclaimed. The camera operator said the shot was good, but it was Guillermin's day to play monkey on Lorenzo's back, and he didn't want to hear any backtalk from the crew.

"Lorenzo," Guillermin hissed, "put the god-damned wheel on the goddamned fucking mark next time."

Take three: off by an inch. Again the camera operator reported a usable take, but Guillermin wouldn't hear it. He wanted to push Lorenzo's buttons.

"Lorenzo, this time put the goddamned fucking wheel beside the mother fucking mark, will you!"

Lorenzo smiled calmly and spoke so all could hear. "Sorry, John. But I'm a bit confused. Just where do you want the fucking wheel? Beside the goddamned fucking mark? Or do you want the fucking wheel beside the goddamned mother fucking mark?"

Guillermin promptly sacked Lorenzo for insubordination, but as he was by now well-established on film as a vehicle driver, Guillermin had to reinstate him the next time the mercenaries had a scene to shoot.

* * * * *

Somehow, we in the second unit escaped Guillermin's wrath. I don't know what it says for us, but he treated us well. We had a lot of work to do on the picture, mostly stunts with animals. I also shot the long prologue sequence of Sheena growing up. As a child, first at age seven and then at twelve, the adorable orphaned blonde girl was seen under the tutelage of her mentor, The Shaman, who taught her the mystique of the jungle.

The second unit also shot stunts of grownup Sheena riding her painted horse through herds of wildebeest and giraffe, trekking through the wilderness, and calling her wildlife friends to war through the amazing telepathic trick of placing her fingers on her forehead and looking oddly skyward through her beautiful eyes, half-lidded and fluttering strangely.

One of Guillermin's most dazzling excesses was his insistence on using an especially picturesque species of tree for an action scene. We find the mercenary column winding its way up the bottom of a narrow gorge on its way to a sneak attack on Sheena's warriors. But through her powers of extrasensory communication, Sheena summons her elephant friend, who pushes over a huge tree in front of the lead armored vehicle, blocking the gorge and thwarting the advance of the mercenaries.

The famous upside-down tree of Africa, the baobab, was the only species of tree Guillermin considered to be appropriate for this scene. Baobabs, however, don't grow anywhere near the gorge where we were filming. The closest living baobab was a hundred miles away.

One of these massive trees, with a trunk fifteen feet in circumference, and a wide array of thick branches, was cut up into pieces and carried in a column of trucks to the gorge. There the numbered parts were reassembled on site for the scene.

On the day of the shoot, my second unit was called in from the field to provide an extra camera to give the widest coverage to this expensive, one-time-only event. The tree had been rigged to fall in the desired direction by setting it up with a slight lean; a cable with a slip-hook was attached to the top to keep it from toppling prematurely. The hook would be pulled by an invisible wire at the moment of action. Hubert's elephant, Tembo, would pretend to push on cue, then the tree would fall from its own weight.

Preparation for the shot, from the time the tree was found, taken apart, transported to the remote location site, and reassembled, took two weeks. Twenty men, aided by heavy construction equipment, were involved. So much depended upon getting it right the first time. Tension was high.

Hubert led Tembo down a narrow pathway that had been laboriously carved into the side of the ravine to give her access—another labor of a dozen men for a week.

Tembo stood near the tree, awaiting her trainer's cue.

As the mercenary column approached, all cameras were rolling. I had the best angle—the master shot where my camera could see all of the action. In the lead vehicle, Lorenzo drove up the gorge, watching in his peripheral vision for Guillermin's signal for everything to happen—the silent lowering of his raised arm.

As Lorenzo reached the designated point, Guillermin's arm dropped. Hubert's arm dropped.

Tembo took her cue, stepped up to the tree and gave a mighty shove. The sliphook slipped, and just as the leading armored vehicle reached the critical spot the huge baobab crashed down.

This time, Lorenzo had gotten it just right. The timing had been perfect; the tree hit the bottom of the gorge a few feet in front of the lead car's bumper. There was a huge crash as the tree exploded and splinters of broken trunk and limbs flew far and wide.

Tembo hadn't expected such a momentous chain reaction from her shove. She took off like a scared rabbit. Her exit was a bonus I'd caught perfectly from my angle. It all looked great to me, but Guillermin had a long face.

"How'd it look?" he asked me.

"Great," I said. "Congratulations. That's a big one in the can."

"Are you sure?"

"Positive," I said. "It was perfect."

"Hmmm," Guillerman said. "I'm not so sure. Did you see that little puff of dust at the roots? The explosive breakaway that cut the base anchors?"

"I didn't notice any puff of dust," I said.

"It looked fake to me," Guillermin grumbled.

He turned to his beaming crew of art directors, prop men, and their gang of workers, who were delighted that their weeks of work had paid off so brilliantly.

"Clean up the mess and get another baobab tree," Guillermin said. "We'll make another take when I get back."

* * * * *

Nobody knew what he meant by that. Get back from where?

With the end of the shoot in sight, Guillermin had just received shocking news. His son, who had come out with his father and had been working with the crew through the first few weeks of production, an aggreeable young man who had been everyone's friend, had grown unhappy with movie work and returned to California.

Guillermin had just received word that his son had been killed on an icy road near Lake Tahoe, the recreation area on the California-Nevada border.

Only a few of us on the crew could talk with Guillermin on a personal level. I joined him as we walked away from the fallen tree and into the world of deep personal grief I knew he was feeling. I tried my best to say the right things. Under the most difficult situation imaginable, I felt nothing but the deepest sympathy for him. I knew the situation was doubly hard for John—that he was feeling guilt because of differences he'd had with his son, differences he thought might have caused the boy to leave the production. If it hadn't been for these troubles, his son might still be here in Africa, he reflected, and not at Tahoe.

Guillermin left that night for America with the promise that he would return in a couple of weeks. In the meantime the crew would be kept busy doing action sequences that didn't require the director's presence.

Columbia sent out stunt coordinator Max Kleven to supervise the various car crashes, helicopter crashes, explosions, and other dangerous-looking tricks at which he specialized. The idea was to keep the production alive and the crew busy shooting necessary material until Guillermin's return.

With my crew we happily joined his team to shoot the animal attack stunts.

One of the big sequences on which Kleven and I were to collaborate involved the climactic battle between the mercenary column and Sheena's adopted tribe who were aided by the host of animals she summoned to the assault. I did the animal attacks: chimps rolling boulders onto the mercenaries who were pinned down by Sheena's warriors in the bottom of a jungle canyon. I staged dangerous-looking scenes of rhinos chasing mercenaries, elephants throwing mercenaries, lions mauling mercenaries, and Sheena's double charging around through the fray mounted on her painted horse, shouting orders and encouraging her human and animal troops to slay the mercenaries one and all.

Max and his camerman Don Burgess (who would go on to greater things—*Forrest Gump, Castaway, Spider-Man)* were in charge of the human participants in this battle of primitive versus modern.

Some of the scenes we filmed were nearly as dangerous as they looked. Hubert had brought a cantankerous rhino from California in the 747 with Tembo. The rhino's job was to chase mercenaries, who were played by members of Hubert's team. There was no training necessary—the rhino was of a temperament to chase anybody who came near, mercenary or civilian. But it took skill and knowledge of the ways of animals to stage those shots where a running mercenary was almost—but not quite—caught by a mad rhino chasing flat out behind him.

All of this took place within an outdoor filming corral, hidden by foliage, 200 feet in diameter and built of strong logs eight feet high. During one take, Hubert, dressed in mercenary uniform, lost his lead on the rhino. In his mad scramble to get over the log barrier just in time his belt caught on a nail. He hung over the top with his head on one side, legs on the other, with the rhino's horn jabbing furiously between his feet. Then the nail fell out and Hubie dropped on his head outside the barrier. He was lucky to suffer only a bump and be the brunt of a joke.

As opposition to the mercenaries, we had a small army of young Maasai tribesmen whom played the parts of Sheena's warriors.

Max Kleven had never worked in Africa before and had no appreciation of the rather idiosyncratic character of Maasai warriors. I wouldn't say that these were unsophisticated young men—certainly they knew more than we would never know about many things. But their awareness was about different matters such as cattle husbandry, and had nothing at all to do with filmmaking.

Always known as fierce warriors, the Maasai pride themselves in fighting skill. One of the favorite games of Maasai teenagers involves warfare practice. Two teams use the hard, swordlike leaves of a yucca-type plant as weapons. They throw these dangerous missiles at each other, and the trick is to fend off the flying projectiles with buffalo-hide shields. They usually succeed in blocking them, but a hit results in a painful impact.

It's Maasai tradition for a young man to kill lions with spears. Every Maasai warrior grows up with a spear in his hand, so they know a thing or two about spear warfare. When Max issued each Maasai warrior a handful of rubber-tipped spears from a stack and told them through an interpreter that this was war and that he wanted them to throw the spears at the white men at the bottom of the canyon—and he wanted them to make it look real—they got the idea right away.

Kleven shouted "Action!" and the guys at the bottom of the canyon began firing rifles and machine guns that were spitting smoke but not bullets—but it looked very real to the Maasai on the canyonside above them. The tribesmen happily returned fire with a volley of spears. To the young Maasai *moran* this was a game of the most joyful kind—throwing spears at helpless *mzungus* (white people)—downhill all the way—and they were getting paid for it! They couldn't have been more cooperative.

Even with a rubber point, a prop spear can be a dangerous weapon. A rubber-tipped spear thrown by a Maasai who's just been told he'll be paid to "kill" the white guys down there like sitting ducks in the bottom of a canyon, is an invitation to disaster.

When the first flight of spears hit the mercenaries, all fire from below ceased and shouts of pain and surprise echoed in the canyon. The mercenaries dove for cover. Seeing that they had achieved such a quick victory, the Maasai charged down on their cringing "enemies." Triumphant cries echoed in the canyon as Max waved his arms and bellowed: "No! No! Stop! Cut! Cut!"

It was the end of shooting for the day. Wounded mercenaries were treated, bandages applied to spear holes, victorious warriors were given iced drinks to cool them down while it was explained to them that they weren't really required to kill anyone and those shots being fired at them were only "play" guns with blank bullets.

Hereafter there would be no more massed army-against-army scenes. Everything was broken up into short takes of individual actions. It had all been too real, even for Max Kleven.

* * * * *

John Guillerman returned, itching to get back to work to clear his head of sorrow.

High in the mountains our cozy cluster of second-unit tents was nestled comfortably under the trees half a mile from the main unit. Sieuwke was with us, helping the animal trainers with everyday chores.

On the other side of the valley a hundred tents were arranged in straight rows in the sun, looking like an army bivouac. Vehicles parked in lines, water bowsers, a huge circus-like mess tent, latrine and shower tents. Smoke from cooking and water-heating fires hung over the camp—all of it added to the effect of military order. The appearance of efficiency was misleading. Only the camp management was proficient; the production itself was a shambles.

We'd separated ourselves from the main unit for several reasons: we could always find more comfortable sites for our tents; we wanted to keep our animals from being bothered by visitors (the animal trainers always camped with the second unit); we had our own separate safari staff including cook, laundry, and camp management; and as we were usually made to feel separate anyway, we preferred to be detached. Not that we were outcasts—not at all. Our squad was the envy of everyone in this army, and a dinner invitation to the second-unit camp was the supreme gift for any member of the main unit.

In defiance of local advice, we were up here at 10,000 feet near the summit of the Aberdare Range during the rainy season—the time we should have been shooting in the desert.

Our first problem had nothing to do with the weather. The first few days on the mountain were clear and fair. Hubert's lions lived in portable cages surrounded by a chain-link perimeter fence. In addition to the lions, an elephant, three horse-cum-zebras, a rhino, and a couple of chimps were housed within the perimeter fence. Its purpose was to keep people or wild creatures—most particularly wild lions—away from the trained animals.

Kibor, Hubert's big male lion, was unused to sharing a territory with wild brothers. He had been reared in California, where he'd learned to roar his macho statement of property rights to all and sundry every evening without thought of an answer from any of his kind. What he said in lion language was the same in either California or in Africa. The sounds that a lion makes when it roars have been interpreted to mean, "This land is mine, mine, mine." (In Swahili, it's different words but with the same meaning and rhythm: "*Inchi hii, yango, yango, yango*".) Kibor's habit had never landed him in trouble and gave his owner immense pleasure. To Hubert, a lion roaring every night in his backyard was the next best thing to living in Africa, which was the next best thing to living in Heaven.

It turned out that our camp in the Aberdares was smack in the middle of the established territory of a large lion pride. The nightly roars of our male invader into his domain caused the local Don much embarrassment. His many wives didn't understand why he put up with such an impudent intruder. To roar in someone else's territory was not only a gross social infraction, it was a challenge to war, plus that weird California accent would grate on any real African lion's nerves.

We all knew that there'd be hell to pay if Kibor didn't shut up. But for some reason the residents didn't come close right away. They gave this stranger the chance to clear out before they came investigating—but of course Kibor couldn't leave if he wanted to.

Then three nights after setting up camp and enduring the mistake that we all knew Kibor was making, we were lying in our tents, just beginning to nod off, when from far away we heard the wild lions coming.

"Huh! Huh! Huh!" they said to let us know they were on their way.

We lay shivering in our tents, praying that Kibor would be smart enough to keep his mouth shut.

Again we heard "Huh! Huh! Huh!"—closer this time, but still half a mile away.

And of course Kibor roared back.

For the next three nights the wild lions came a bit nearer each time they visited. Although they always stayed out in the darkness while they swapped roars with Kibor, their answering roars were closer and louder each night.

The first night that The Lord of the Aberdares came into our camp to see who had such effrontery, he strolled around between our tents, gnawed at the chain-link fence that surrounded the animal enclosure, and matched each of Kibor's roars with one of his own. As the nobleman was so close and a lion's roar has something of a ventriloquistic nature, it seemed as if each loud roar burst forth from right under our beds. This went on most of the night and made things uncomfortable for us, huddled under our blankets with only a thin wall of canvas between our bodies and a large irate lion.

On the next night, The Lord brought his family. The pride couldn't seem to fathom the effrontery of a strange lion with the guts to set up housekeeping in their territory. Lions strolled everywhere through our camp, roaring, tugging at tent ropes, knocking over wash basins and chairs. Young lions played between the guy ropes and rubbed at the tents' walls. I expected to see claws rip through the canvas.

It was definitely too much. Hubert and his trainers, Sled and Julian, got into their Land Rovers and drove around between the tents, hooting horns and throwing rocks at the lions until they ran back into the forest.

Nothing new happened early the next evening. Perhaps the attack of the Land Rovers had made an impression. Kibor resumed his solo baritone, singing *Born Free* to the moon.

Hubert's assistant, Julian Sylvester, who was assigned night duty while we were camping in the mountains, had his tent set up nearer to the high fence that surrounded the animal compound than the rest of us.

Kibor began his usual song.

"Shut up, you stupid jerk!" I heard Julian shout from his tent.

This evening Kibor seemed to have gained some sense and was replying to the wild lion at only about half the previous night's volume. When the wild lion was really close and our tents shook with his roar, Kibor barely made a muffled answering yowl. He was getting the message, but it was too late.

Kibor had respectfully tuned down the volume of his replies, but we knew that any answer at all was enough to really piss off this wild lion who was strolling around between our tents as if he owned the place. I pulled back the canvas window flap and peeked out through the flimsy mosquito netting. I saw Julian slink out of his tent and head through the moonlight toward Kibor's cage. He was going to try to talk some sense into him. Julian carried a flashlight, a wooden cane, and a fire extinguisher—not for fires but for the frightening blast of foam and noise it makes when it's been set off.

I could barely see Julian in the shadows half way to Kibor's cage. A few more steps and he was lost in the blackness of bushes.

Then the King of the Aberdares let off a really loud roar from very close by.

There was no movement from the dark bushes. I knew that Julian was frozen and holding his breath where he was. It was dead quiet for a long time. Julian waited, not twitching a finger. Finally he relaxed.

"And then," as Julian told us in the morning, "the lion must have crept close with absolute stealth—and thinking about it later I can almost hear the old boy saying to himself, 'Now just watch this....' Just as I was breathing comfortably again, out comes this deafening bellow from the darkness. It seemed to be right beside me."

Then the wild male charged the fence. He ran up the side and when it sagged, he came down on the top overhang. His weight of 600 or 700 pounds flattened the wall of wire between the poles, and he walked stiff-legged into the compound.

In a moment, there he was, nose to nose and eyeball to eyeball with Kibor—Kibor inside his cage and the big wild male outside. In seconds they were growling, snarling, and tearing at the wire with their teeth and claws, trying to get at each other.

Julian ran over the flattened wire and into the compound. He pointed his fire extinguisher at the big lion. There was a loud hissing shush, and an explosion of white foam shot out in a cloud that totally obscured the lions.

A CO_2 fire extinguisher is an animal trainer's best defense. It harmlessly scares the fight out of beasts of any size or temperament. Julian thought the blast of foam and noise would send the pushy lion high-tailing it back where he'd come from.

But instead of turning tail, the lion charged right at Julian. Julian threw the cane and it bounced off the lion's head. Then he threw the fire extinguisher and ran.

Julian could hear the lion charging behind him—or that's what he thought he heard. The faster he ran the more leaves he kicked up behind. It sounded like the lion was right on his heels.

But the lion wasn't chasing Julian. It was trying to get out of the enclosure. Being a wild lion and not knowing anything about fences, he ran with his shoulder against the wire. The fence was nailed to the outside, and every ten feet there was a post on the inside. And every ten feet the lion smacked his head into the next post.

Then Julian plowed into a tree. When he picked himself up and turned around, the lion was headed in the opposite direction toward and then over the flattened section of fence.

Julian was lucky. And the Lord of the Aberdares never came back.

* * * * *

Hubert's first assistant on the *Sheena* shoot was a trainer named Sled Reynolds. Sled's father had been one of the most famous wranglers in Hollywood, and Sled had learned all about horses from him. Then he went to work for Hubie and learned about other types of animal training.

There were two things that never changed about Sled: he always wore a cowboy hat, and he always had a rope in his hand. He could do magic with that rope—flip it out and lasso a post, a foot, a hand, anything. It wasn't safe being anywhere near Sled because you never knew when you'd find yourself with a rope around your neck or a loop on your foot.

The night before Julian's experience with the lion and the fire extinguisher, the angry lions had come visiting. Sled got Julian to drive him around the compound while he stood waist-high in the open roof hatch of the Land Rover, twirling his lariat. "I always wanted to rope me a wild lion," he said. "I'll never have a better chance."

"He nailed a lion on his first throw," Julian said. "A most godawful roar erupted that made my fire extinguisher sound like a sneeze. The lion took off with the rope, and Sled was unable to find it that night or the next morning. He'd still be looking for his best lasso if he hadn't gotten distracted."

Because he was a California boy on his first African safari, Sled didn't know the rules of safari life, where one has camp staff jumping to one's every wish or whim. If you want a hot shower, yell "Hot shower!" and a couple of staff run to fill the bucket in the outdoor shower stall. You want a towel, shout "Towel!" and it's in your hand. If you crave ice for a drink, shout "Ice!" and it appears as if by magic.

Some things on safari aren't even asked for in words. They are taken for granted—laundry, for example. Everyone knows that when you walk out of your tent, anything you leave on the floor is meant to be washed.

So Sled went to the shower and left his hat on the floor. He'll never forgive the tent boy who scrubbed his white Stetson and hung it in a tree to dry. A while later, a Maasai came strolling by with Sled's rope in his hand. He said he'd found it snagged on a thorn bush a couple of miles away.

* * * * *

The next day it began to rain. The predicted wet season had begun; it would probably last for a month. John Guillermin said a little rain wouldn't stop him. It was just another of his cherished production adversities to be surmounted. We worked under umbrellas for a couple of days as the mud deepened.

One soggy afternoon a radio call from the production tent reported that several four-wheel-drive trucks from the bottom of the mountains were bogged down in mud and couldn't get up the roads to resupply our camp.

"Good," Guillermin snorted. "This will separate the men from the boys."

A day of fair weather finally broke the constant downpour. Then Hubert's rhino broke out of its log enclosure. We spent all day with our four-wheel drive vehicles trying to herd it back. We were five miles from camp with darkness approaching when Hubert finally immobilized the rhino with a tranquilizing dart. We brought it back in the bed of a huge all-wheel-drive lorry, which was towed through the mud by another huge all-wheel-drive lorry.

The rain resumed its relentless pounding. Our army of vehicles had churned all of the roads into slippery oceans of mud. Another day of this and any ordinary vehicle would be stuck on the mountain until the rainy season was over and the roads dried out.

Hubert and I discussed the impending situation. It was one thing for an army of people and their cars to be stuck on the mountain—they could be evacuated by helicopter and the cars could sit it out or be towed down the mountain by tractors. But animals were a different story. They were required for production, they needed food, and the constant wetness was unhealthy. We had to get the animals off the mountain before all of us became hopelessly stuck. We who had worked in Africa before, we who had spent months in the bush with no support other than ourselves, knew the situation was growing precarious. Our local advisors told the production brass that the conditions could quickly get desperate and advised immediate evacuation to low ground.

In spite of this advice, nothing happened. Day after day we sat in our tents listening to the rain beat against the canvas.

Hubert and I were desperate. We knew what we had to do—but to pull out now, against orders, amounted to desertion. How the production manager and his assistant, Udi, could persist in trying to satisfy imprudent edicts from above was nothing short of nutty.

I called Udi on the radio in the evening and told him that we had to get the animals off the mountain and had decided to pull out at first light. The wheel chains I'd requested a month ago for our only two-wheel-drive vehicle—the camera truck with its load of equipment—had never appeared. We'd be lucky if we could get the elephant, rhino, and horse trucks down the mountain by towing them. If necessary, we'd abandon the trucks in the mud and walk the animals down.

Our rhino, on the other hand, had to be moved by truck. We couldn't lead him on leash, and we would concentrate all of our resources on the rhino truck if the situation came to it. Even if we had to hitch up the elephant to help tow the rhino truck, we'd get him off the mountain.

I told Udi that we'd leave the camera van where it was, locked up securely, and explained to him where the keys would be hidden. Everything in our camp, along with the camera truck, would have to be brought down the mountain by the support team, pulled through the mud by tractor if necessary.

Udi told us to wait it out. But we couldn't wait any longer. We were out of animal food. The clouds stuck to the mountains like frosting on a cake and the rain poured down; the mud only grew deeper in the puddled tracks.

Hubert and I were already packed up and in the process of moving out—the elephant and rhino were on the road—when at last a full-scale emergency evacuation was declared.

There were three routes down the mountain. Udi told us which track to take—the same as the others so everyone would have support. I told him that we'd already made our choice—a different, longer track, but one which hadn't been in use by the film company and therefore wouldn't be churned to mush by the passage of so many wheels.

Udi said no; we'd have no support on the route we'd chosen. I told him we'd rather be responsible for ourselves. Besides, half of our unit had left before dawn and was already traveling that route. Udi was furious. How could we have started before the official command to move out? I was happy that we'd gone out on a limb and were well into our march before the others had begun.

The evacuation took all day, with constant shuttling of towing vehicles back and forth to help the large horse, elephant, lion, and rhino lorries through the worst mudholes. But we got to the bottom under our own steam.

The main unit took three days to get down; roads were blocked by stuck vehicles, lorries had slipped crossways across the ruts, cars had slid into ditches. It was the chaotic mess of an army in the mad scramble of retreat.

Guillermin had succeeded beyond his wildest dreams. He'd created this bungle—a contest against nature that must have satiated his unrealistic spirit of adventure.

* * * * *

One of the actors in *Sheena* had become a good friend of the animal and second unit teams. Of the privileged few who were welcome at our camp, Donovan Scott was a happy soul and always full of fun. The part he played in the movie was as a television cameraman, side-kick of the news reporter assigned to find the Queen of the Jungle for a TV station. When Donovan wasn't wasn't acting, his own videocorder was always on a strap over his shoulder, ready to record off-the-cuff remembrances of his African safari.

Like his character in the movie, Donovan had a sense for when and where to be with his camera to catch the action. He was there for the big Aberdare Mountains evacuation, he was on hand for the wild chase after the escaped rhino, and he was present for the Maasai attack on the mercenaries. He captured Lorenzo's provocative retort to Guillermin's profanity—all recorded in gutsy non-censored authenticity.

When we all returned to California, where Donovan Scott premiered his edited video before an audience of selected crew and cast. We unanimously agreed that *Behind the Scenes in the Making of "Sheena Queen of the Jungle,"* in spite of some minor technical shortcomings, excelled in every other way over its more extravagant rival production.

By the way, *Sheena, Queen of the Jungle* received 5 nominations for "Razzie" awards in 1984—which disproves again the Hollywood adage that money equals value.

25 The Seven Dinosaurs

Sieuwke and I were at the thinking stage of expanding our house on Bushy Island—I hadn't even sharpened the corner stakes to pound into the ground—when an old friend said he'd like to take us up on an invitation and pay a visit.

Herbert Ryman at the age of 76 was one of the Disney Dinosaurs, the group who had been among Walt's first employees and had initiated their "club" when their number was nine. After awhile their membership dropped to seven, then stood steady for a few years until one dinosaur after another joined the fossil record.

Herbie was among the finest artists at the studio. His landscape and portrait paintings were exhibited at galleries around the world. Ryman's specialty at Disney was creating concept renderings for films and theme parks.

Herbie came to us to spend a week—and stayed two months—a joy for us all. Sieuwke soon learned why I so much enjoyed Herbie's invitations to the Dinosaurs' luncheons in California. I'd told her of those weekly get-togethers, which were mainly reminicenses by the old-timers about early days at Disney. Often the talk drifted to reflections on how they'd one-upped the boss—or how he'd one-upped them.

One story Herb told was of a trip in the early 1940s made by Walt Disney and a group of animators, writers, and directors to South America to gather impressions for a film on the drawing board called *Saludos Amigos*. During a warm evening as they all sat around a table in Rio, laughing and swapping yarns over drinks, Walt put a cigarette to his lips and began searching his pockets for a light.

My other friend among the seven, Ken Anderson, pulled out his Zippo, held it under Walt's chin, and struck the spark. A flame leapt up higher than expected and caught Walt's moustache on fire. The moustache burned to the roots before Herbie had the presence of mind to throw a glassful of water in Walt's face. As Herbie put it, "Walt never forgave me for saving his life."

Herbie always spoke his mind, even to the boss. Prior to the water-dousing episode, Ryman had been alternately fired and rehired a half-dozen times for his unforgivable outspokenness. It was during one of those forced retirements, that Herbie got a call from Walt, who apologized for having sacked him the week before, and told him he needed his help this week.

Walt told Herbie that he'd gone off to New York on a business trip and came back with more than he'd bargained for. As Herbie told it, the idea for an entertainment theme park had been hanging around in Walt's head for a long time, but he had no solid details as to its design or implementation. At a meeting of New York businessmen, on the spur of the moment, Walt felt a sudden inspiration and pitched his theme park idea. To his surprise he sold the concept. He'd made some strong commitments, underwriting everything with an exaggerated account as to the advanced state of development of his brainchild, which at the time was really only the germ of an idea.

Now all Walt needed to clinch the deal with the financiers and put the project into play was the detailed layout plan for the theme park—the plan he'd claimed already existed. And he needed the drawings for the big meeting on Monday. It was already Friday.

"I'll work with you, Herbie," Walt said. "Just call me when you've got a problem. Then Sunday night I'll catch the red-eye to New York and make the presentation on Monday morning."

Herbie agreed to work on a plan for the new park, but on one condition: that Walt sit beside him through the weekend. Walt reluctantly agreed. They started on Friday and together, through Friday night, Saturday, Saturday night, and Sunday—in one marathon weekend—they laid out the themes, design, and geography for what would become Disneyland Park.

* * * * *

From the day bulldozers began ripping out orange groves in Anaheim, California, whoever was available from among the Disney stable of 16mm cameramen made periodic trips to record the various stages of the park's development. I shot a few different phases and others did the same. One cameraman, Howard Diamond, was assigned the task of shooting a long-term view—the area as a whole as it changed from orange grove to finished theme park, with various stages in between. The idea was that these scenes, shot from a helicopter hovering over a certain spot, could be dissolved from one to another to illustrate a year's growth in just a few seconds.

The cameraman tasked with the job had a specialty of time-lapse photography. Under the watchful eye of Howard's camera, flower buds that normally took a week to mature would unfold into beautiful full-blown blossoms in a short ten seconds. These scenes were classics of the day. You saw time-lapse flower shots in so many Disney nature movies that they became clichés of the genre.

Ordinarily this photography was done under tightly controlled conditions in Howard's studio where everything including temperature and humidity was regulated. Shooting off-the-cuff from a helicopter made him very nervous. He didn't trust these rickety-looking, noisy machines; and even worse, to get the shot he would have to sit in the open door, feet on the skid, with his body as much outside as inside.

"What if the motor conks out?" Howard asked the pilot. "An airplane has wings. You can glide back to earth. This damned grasshopper will fall like a stone!"

"Not to worry," the pilot said. "If the engine quits, I let it windmill down. The rotor turns from the pressure of falling, slowing the descent. Then, just before we come to ground, I throw it into reverse torque, and we touch down as easy as a feather. If anything happens, just sit tight; you won't feel a thing. Eggs wouldn't break."

Howard understood the principle of slowing the descent by windmilling the rotor blades, but a cushioned stop made no sense to him. "Like hell!" he thought. "This double-talk is only soft soap to put me at ease." So he decided that if ever an emergency occurred while he was in the air, he'd put his own method of survival into play.

On that inevitable day when high above Disneyland the engine did stop and the chopper began to drop, the pilot calmly glanced at Howard, smiled and gave a reassuring nod. Everything went as if rehearsed: the craft dropped slowly, held back by blades turning in the self-made wind of descent. Twenty feet above the ground—a couple of seconds before the pilot engaged the counter-rotation which would cushion the fall—Howard put the plan he'd thought about on every takeoff into play. He jumped out of the helicopter.

The chopper settled softly beside him on the ground. As the pilot had promised, even eggs wouldn't have broken. But Howard Diamond's landing had broken both of his legs.

* * * * *

We put Herbie into the old tent we'd lived in before we built our stone bedroom, down under the trees where the hippos cruised by at night. We told Herbie to be sure and shine his flashlight around a bit before stepping outside into the dark. We weren't sure how Herbie—who had never slept in a tent in the wilderness before—would adapt to this new experience. But he loved it. Living in the wild was the adventure of a lifetime for this man of big-city sophistication—except for the night when a few battalions of *siafu* (army ants) invaded his tent and crawled into his bed. Herbie awoke with a hundred big black insects painfully clamping their jaws into his skin. I was awakened by cries of distress and raced into the darkness with a flashlight expecting anything.

I gave him a Doom insecticide spray-down, made up a mattress on the floor of our *banda*, and Herbie had yet another story to tell at the Dinosaurs' luncheons back in California.

26 The Heartbeat of Africa

When Walt Disney Studios decided to build an Africa pavilion during the planning phase for EPCOT Center in Florida, I was one of the first to be called.

The World Showcase section of the park was to be a collection of buildings typical of the traditional architecture of the countries represented. The various cultures, arts, and histories would be presented as entertainments. Disney's theme park subsidiary, WED Enterprises, would design and construct the buildings—enclaves called "pavilions"—and create the shows for each participating country. Each pavilion was to be paid for by the nation it represented.

When Disney originally proposed the EPCOT park, several governments had quickly signed up: China, France, Canada, Mexico, and England. As EPCOT's theme of "World Showcase" assumed worldwide participation, all continents should be represented. But Africa true to its lore, had remained remote.

The suits at Disney soon realized that few of the nations within the African continent would be able to foot the bill for an expensive pavilion. Morocco took part, but as a northern territory it didn't show Africa as Disney imagined the public perception of the continent to be. South Africa had the money, but the country was then in the midst of the apartheid years and was therefore a political minefield that Disney chose not to step into.

A team of Disney sales folk toured the continent to enlist support, but they had no experience dealing with Africans and their sometimes quirky ways and came home to Burbank little wiser and with no contracts for pavilions. As a result of this fruitless probe, the decision was made to proceed as planned with a pavilion, but without African financial participation. That is, because the World Showcase would be incomplete without Africa, Disney would pay for an in-house project that would represent not a single country but the continent as a whole. The area to be covered would be a swath across the equatorial middle—Tarzan's Africa—the Africa of jungles, animals, and mysterious peoples and customs.

Months had gone by as Disney unsuccessfully attempted to enlist financial support. So when the go-ahead was finally given, it was with the understanding that the venue would not be ready for opening day on October 1, 1982. Instead, one year after the park's launch, Africa would join the world with a grand inaugural celebration of its own.

One of the studio "Dinosaurs," animation director Ken Anderson, who had been responsible for portions of *Snow White, Puff the Magic Dragon, Fantasia*, and other classic Disney shows, was given the reins as head designer. He enlisted another of the prehistoric reptile gang—our friend Herb Ryman—to come up with concept renderings. As a relative youngster, I was not one of this elite group, but was hired to create the shows.

The first requirement for a World Showcase show was that it would be presented in a way that set it apart from an ordinary movie or from any other World Showcase exhibit. By the time the belated Africa Pavilion was approved, several shows about other nations had a head start on us. A couple were already being shot in the widescreen IMAX process, and one show would be in 3-D. It fell into my lap to come up with something new.

I imagined a show even grander than IMAX: three IMAX-sized screens, side-by-side, each with an image of the same action but shot from different points of view.

Three huge screens, each with different images, all running simultaneously, might seem difficult for an audience to absorb. One can't see everything at once on so large a scale, just as one doesn't see a lot peripherally in real life. But one's eyes tend to rove—or be directed—and it's easy to gather an impressionistic feeling of all that's happening.

The main center of action was the middle screen, but the eye could be randomly directed, (remember Vorkapich's "dot in motion" principle?) shifting from middle to one side screen or the other. With this dazzle of imaging, editing, and sound, the format alone—the three huge screens—would be exciting.

The subject of my show, *The Heartbeat of Africa*, would be the influence of African rhythm on modern Western music.

Music plays a vital role in traditional African social life. Musical accompaniment goes along with many everyday events—boat paddling and sailing, sowing, and harvesting. Athletic teams are urged on by competing musicians; wrestlers are supported by rival teams of drummers. Births, weddings, funerals—all are celebrated with music and dance, and every religious event has its extra musical fillip.

To see first-hand which events I'd select for the film, I traveled across equatorial Africa by airplane, then struck out by vehicle from city hubs into the hinterlands where traditional life had been unchanged for centuries. Because I'd be in many French-speaking countries, and my grasp of the language was nil, Sieuwke was my interpreter wherever I went.

I'd heard about Senegal's drummer, Dudu Rose Ndiaye, whose entourage consisted of his nine sons. We made arrangements to listen to Dudu's drums at his home in downtown Dakar, one the biggest cities in West Africa.

The court of this famous musician was large, his wives plentiful, and his children many. A dozen spectacularly beautiful women flitted garrulously around the U-shaped compound. I was to learn that all were family, and that nothing could be assumed from their apparent age—the younger could be a wife, the older a daughter. The women shared several attributes: all were lovely, all were dressed immaculately, all wore plentiful gold jewelry, and all seemed happy and congenial.

Soon after our arrival and introductions, Dudu's sons began carrying folding metal chairs out of the compound and setting them up on the sidewalk alongside the busy downtown street. Sieuwke and I were given chairs among the wives and daughters. I was surprised about being out in the street because there seemed to be ample room for our audition in the private central courtyard. But I was soon to learn why the move was necessary.

Presently, several boys, young men, and Dudu, who was in his mid 40s, each carrying an hourglass-shaped drum with rawhide heads and lacings, made their appearance. Some of the drums had bits of dangling metal that clattered as the instruments were moved. Each drummer carried a handful of sticks. The performers walked in a line out the gate and across the sidewalk to the middle of the road. The nine sons took positions in a semicircle, crouching over their instruments or sitting on stools with the drums between their knees.

Automobiles couldn't get past the drummers, and one or two cars backed away. Most just shut off their engines and stopped where they were. A gap of empty pavement lay between the nearest cars and the musicians.

Moments passed as everyone got settled.

No words were spoken. Dudu held up a drumstick like a baton. It poised aloft. Dead quiet. Then he let his arm fall. A slow mechanical beat began to echo between the buildings. As the sound continued it passed like a signal down the street; the steady beat became dominant over the traffic noise.

People began to emerge from doorways. Windows of the multi-story buildings that lined the avenue opened and heads poked out. People trotted toward us on the sidewalk. It was apparent that Dudu's concerts were salubrious events. Everyone within earshot—and those further away who heard by word-of-mouth—moved in a flood toward the scene. I was impressed both by the sudden accrual of the audience and by the unofficial and uncontested shutting off of a busy city street.

As the drumming grew in volume and intensity, more and more people came. The infectious sound drew the young and old, male and female, from near and far. Soon the street was jammed with people. The air was electric with anticipation.

Everyone listened, a few heads bobbed to the rhythm, some fingers snapped in time. All were smiling, happy.

Then Dudu raised a drumstick over his head, held it theatrically for a moment, high and still, and looked around. The drumming stopped.

A sigh came from the crowd as everyone took in a breath and held it.

Then Dudu let his arm drop. The stick hit sharply on his drum. The loud rim-shot was electrifying; immediately his boys changed their mood.

All at once, a tremendous roar of drums erupted. This was the moment the people had been waiting for. A cheer echoed between the buildings. A wild rhythm took control.

Dudu's wives and daughters, until now demure and chattering where they sat, leapt from their chairs and into the street. Suddenly they were transformed by the music, dancing as I had never seen anyone dance before. Others joined and the street came alive. There were no couples; everyone was doing his or her own thing, alone, oblivious to each other, cognizant only of this incredible, hypnotic sound.

I realized that I'd never find anything more exciting in African music. I imagined Dudu and his boys as a part of the conclusion of my film—Dudu as one side in a contest, pitted against another in the way of John Boorman's wonderful piece of cinema, the Dueling Banjos sequence, in the film *Deliverance.* Our duel would be between the traditional music of Dudu Rose and modern African jazz, as played by the band I was yet to find.

It was this concept, discovered on the first stop of our research, that I would develop as we crossed Africa.

* * * * *

Sieuwke and I made three separate trips across the continent for *The Heartbeat of Africa.* The first was reconnaissance; the second, in the company of production manager Eva Monley, was to make arrangements and set the schedule for the third trip, during which we'd do the filming.

Eva Monley had grown up in Kenya, where her first job had been as an assistant for director Andrew Marton. That was in 1949, the same year I was attending film school at USC learning the directing craft under Andrew's teaching. Since then Eva had amassed a stunning list of credits: *Lawrence of Arabia*, *Exodus*, and *The African Queen,* for starters. I felt lucky to have such a person behind me for the projects we'd already done together—*Living Free, The Darwin Adventure, Born Free* TV.

Eva told me about a trip she'd made to Zaire (then called the Belgian Congo, now called the Democratic Republic of Congo), when John Ford was filming *Mogambo.* They'd traveled to the spectacular rapids of the Congo River, the place near Kisangani that blocked further upriver travel for large ships. Here crews of thirty men standing at tall paddles drove forty-foot-long canoes through the rapids, all to the rhythm of a drummer and chanting of the crew. It sounded like perfect material for my film, and I had to see it—if it still existed.

When Sieuwke, Eva, and I arrived in Kisangani, it was a totally disabled city, a decrepit shipwreck stranded in the jungle. A row of tall rusty loading cranes stood along a deserted quay, angled against the sky like storks with broken legs. They were canted at crazy angles and falling apart. There hadn't been a can of paint opened in this ghost town in years. Every building was green with accretions of moss, algae, and lichen. A few shops were open. Why? Their shelves were empty. Somehow

Eva found someone who would send word upriver that we wanted to see the canoes. A time was set.

The next morning we stood on the river bank at the appointed spot watching three huge canoes approach us through the whitewater. Onboard the canoes, drums were beating, paddle strokes in time, the chant sounding above the rush of the waves. It was spectacular, just as Eva had said it had been fifteen years ago.

Eva stood apart from us, her tiny frame capped by white hair, alone on a rock at the edge of the great river rapids. As the lead canoe drew close, the drumming and chanting ceased and the canoe came on in near silence with only the muffled splashes of dipping paddles. Then a voice called from the lead canoe. I couldn't believe the words—was I hearing right?

Yes, the voice sounded again clearly.

The leader of this band of wild canoemen, here at the farthest reaches of nowhere, had been one of the crew from *Mogambo* fifteen years before. He recognized the little white-haired lady on the shore and greeted her.

"Hubba, hubba, hubba!" he shouted, his voice closing the gap across the water.

It was John Ford's familiar bellow, sounded loud and clear whenever he wanted his crew to get a move on.

* * * * *

We traveled on across the midriff of Africa. My film crew consisted of Sieuwke and Eva, interpreter (French is the language of West Africa) and production manager respectively, camera operator and Steadicam specialist Steve St. John, gaffer Larry Prinz, soundman Michael Evje, accountant Mac Meltzer, and two production assistants—Michael Fields and my son Mike, then nineteen.

We drove across Senegal from the Atlantic coast, through Mali, touched Burkina Fasso, and moved down through Ivory Coast, passing through towns and villages with names like Segou, Ferkéssédougou, Bobo-Dioulasso, and Korhogo. We traveled in three vehicles, two minibuses, and a small panel truck for the equipment, all driven by locals. We never saw an inch of pavement and the dust was always in our faces. In spite of my constant cajoling I could never get our drivers to follow at the end of the preceding car's dust. No, we were always riding the bumper of the car ahead, right in the densest part of the cloud. It drove me crazy.

One of our dust-cloud-loving drivers wanted to learn English, so Larry taught him a phrase which this driver thereafter spoke with perfect elocution to everyone he met: "I'm a wanker!"

In Mali we spent a day at the town of Djenne, where we planned to film at the largest mosque in the world constructed entirely of mud—a colossal structure of splendid architectural style. The leading character in our film was a well-known Senegalese actor named Douta Sek. His part was that of a west African griot, that influential caste of storyteller and agent of black magic. A jangle of mysterious juju charms hung from the griot's shirt. The imam at the mosque of Djenne was horrified at the thought of our filming such an iconoclastic sight in connection with his mosque. Eventually Douta brought his actor's seductive powers to bear and we were permitted to make a few shots of the griot close to the mosque—but the camera was never allowed a squint inside.

We drove east from the bustling port of Mopti on the Niger River and across plains dimpled by cities of knee-high termite nests that were shaped like huge mushrooms. I fancied that they could have been the houses of elves—or maybe the hobbit Bilbo Baggins had built them. We moved on through groves of thick-trunked baobabs, past Bambara villages made of mud, into hills and up toward the Dogon villages. This was an Africa I'd never seen before, with people living in villages exactly as they had for centuries, a land tilled with agriculture and domestic stock and virtually without wild animals or birds—they'd all been killed off long ago. It was no place for a natural history buff like me; but fascinating for its cultural variety and purity.

After a long climb up a rocky track we left our cars at the edge of a high escarpment at the end of the road. Because of the remoteness, I'd chosen the location on the basis of a photograph. The village I saw in the picture was nestled into the scree and rockfall at the foot of a sheer escarpment. It was called Amani and was typical Dogon, an elegant arrangement of picturesque huts of many shapes and angles. Our filming schedule was tight; Amadou, my Dogon contact, knew the village and had made all arrangements for us to film on the day following our arrival at the clifftop.

Amadou said it was only an hour's walk from Sangha, where we'd parked the cars, down to the village. I wanted to have a look at the place. Steve, Mike, Larry, Amadou, and I started down the trail after a quick lunch of baguettes and canned sardines. The footpath chiseled into the rock clung to the sheer wall. In many places the pounding of bare feet over the centuries had eroded the hard sandstone into deep grooves. We met a few Dogon people coming up and they greeted us cheerfully; some of the nimble-footed locals passed us going down. Here and there along the trail, niches and caves in the cliff were stuffed with the mummified bodies of Dogon ancestors. High above, in nooks in the cliff, one could make out the graves of more ancestors. How they flew up there was anyone's guess.

The flatlands that stretched to the horizon went so far that we could see the earth's curve. It was tough travel. An hour later, when we reached the bottom of the cliff and began our trek along its base, I was puffing.

We passed many small terraced fields. Onions, which were dried and sold in bundles, were the main cash crop of the Dogon, and they tended them with an efficiency and diligence I'd never seen before in an African culture. On the hard sandstone highlands at the tops of the escarpments, each little stone-walled onion field was cultivated on thin layers of soil that had been carried to the plot in baskets and then watered in the same way. The villages were immaculately clean. Everything about the Dogon spoke to me of the most fastidious and hardworking traditional culture I'd ever seen.

Amadou's one hour's walk became a three-hour hike. But at last we reached the village. In a way this country and its people reminded me of my days among the Arizona Hopi pueblos—the way Walpi might have looked a hundred years ago (and in many ways still looks today).

I saw right away the locations where I wished the dance to take place. Because of the longer than expected time it took to get there, it was already past time for us to start back. I realized that dawn, when the rising sun would strike the village at a raking angle, was the time this sequence had to be filmed. The idea of racing back up that steep trail only to get a meal and a night's rest before making a quick turnaround was too much for me. I told my younger, more energetic crew to head on back without me. I'd meet them when they returned with the equipment at dawn.

The village chief offered me a room for the night. I declined politely and asked only for a blanket. I'd already picked a big tree out in the flats with a sandy place beneath where I'd make my bed.

Before dusk the chief appeared beside my tree with a live chicken under his arm. He managed to convey the message that it was a gift. I responded in crude sign language that I was delighted—but could it be cooked?

Later, a dozen children crowded around the edge of my firelight watching this strange-looking person, the likes of which they'd never seen before, tear apart and devour the bird. The children probably would have stayed all night, but to my relief, the chief came back and shooed my audience away.

Sometime during the night I awoke to the sound of hooves hammering against the earth. Eight riders were passing by. In the moonlight I saw that they were Fulani, those wild masters of horsemanship from the arid Sahel. I could see the ornate leather and bangles of the saddles and tack and the silhouettes of rifles against the sky. My fire had died to black ashes, so they didn't see me. I wondered what these men were doing, riding at night through country far from their usual turf. I was quite happy that they hadn't seen me lying under my blanket and watching them ghosting past.

Later I heard the sound of voices. It took a moment to clear my head; then I peeked out from underneath my blanket and saw daylight. The voices belonged to my crew, who were arriving for the morning's shoot.

We had come to Amani to film the Dogon tall mask ceremony. A long line of masks was already making its way down the cliff. Amadou told us that this was the largest gathering of tall masks since a grand celebration had been held thirty years ago. I couldn't see how these twelve-foot-long masks were supported—but then I couldn't fathom the skill of the stilt dancers who accompanied them either. Drums, chanting, and a long line of other participants followed the parade of tall masks to the open space where the ritual was to be held. We set up our equipment and began filming.

It was a thrill to know that we had recorded an event on a scale that had probably never been filmed—and possibly never would be again.

* * * * *

We continued on across the African midriff and filmed the improbable Burundi drummers, who walked in long single file balancing huge drums on their heads as they played. We were in the land of the tall Watutsi, those dancing stick figures with fluid limbs and headdresses of high white plumes. I wonder where those magnificent men are now after the genocide of that country, and if they will ever dance so wildly and carefree again.

A troop of Hutu dancers showed up to present a traditional cotillion. They wore western knee-length shorts of assorted colors and tall socks with dusty street shoes. On top of their attire of modern western clothes, the men tied traditional grass skirts around their waists. For a film of a different kind, the scene would have been amusingly (or sadly) ironic.

I was touched, if exasperated: these simple men felt honored to be photographed by the famous Walt Disney, and despite using all the persuasion I could muster, I couldn't convince them that they'd look better for the film in bare feet and their usual grass skirts. But in the minds of these people, to appear in traditional apparel was too unsophisticated. It embarrassed this proud but uneducated elite. Rather than portray a pure and ancient culture with historical honesty, they feared that they would present a picture to the world of primitive wretchedness. Frustrated, I packed up the camera and made ready to leave. Only then, given the choice of my way or not at all, did they consent to wearing their traditional garb.

Later, when the dancers got into it, I couldn't imagine their wildly exuberant performance any other way. Clearly they were more agile and comfortable without shorts and shoes. If I'd shot the sequence as they'd originally wished, it would have appeared to be a cruel joke.

Later, lost on one side or the other of the border between Liberia and The Ivory Coast, we filmed the tall stilt dance. During this ceremony, masked men atop ten-foot-high stilts grappled and tried to knock one another down. It would seem they'd be ungainly way up there, but in fact the stilt men were incredibly agile, and with great strides on long legs they covered the ground at surprising speed.

Another part of the ceremony, the knife dance, was a heart-stopper. One man lifted a small boy on a tall forked pole then threw him over the head of his partner. The catcher stood below, aiming a long dagger toward the falling child. The child fell and fell, closer and closer to the blade which didn't waver. The sharp tip held steady on its target. The child seemed sure to be impaled—until at the last possible moment the knife disappeared and the man caught the falling boy in his arms.

I never understood the significance of the dance, which was commonly held in this part of the world. Perhaps it was merely a performance of agility and magic. Whatever the reason, it was an unforgettable show of trust.

In this village, far off the beaten track, beneath an arbor made for the occasion from woven palm leaves and flowers, I was made an honorary chief and presented with a handwoven embroidered caftan. But there were strings attached: I was expected to make an acceptance speech (which of course no one could understand, so it didn't matter what I said). I was also expected to share in the congratulatory toasts of home-brewed palm wine. As the grimy cup was passed around from man to man, I didn't put the unhygienic-looking drinking vessel to my lips but let the rim hit my face somewhere between my lower lip and my chin. I tried not to be obvious as I pretended to take a mouthful and swallow—still, I spent the next two days cramped in spasms of colonic pain and lying prostrate—except when I was dashing off to the loo.

In Ivory Coast near Korhogo we filmed an exciting night sequence called the *Poro*. It was a girl's coming-of-age ceremony attended by about forty costumed dancers. Except for the parade of maidens dressed only in short grass skirts and a few cowrie beads, everyone else seemed to be doing something different. There were stilts, balaphone players, drummers, a man with a long whip cracking like gunshots, flute players, and the leader—a cantankerous old gentleman behind a huge mask with strangely evocative features who had little patience for filmmakers.

It was a long ceremony that ended quite abruptly and unexpectedly when old sorehead went to the fire and extinguished it by throwing a shower of burning logs and coals near and far with his bare hands. "Lights out!" was the clear message. The end.

We were shooting catch-as-catch-can, without the benefit of rehearsal, and I'd had no idea what was coming next. I hadn't expected this sudden conclusion and had my camera focused on the bare-breasted maidens when it happened. To complete the sequence and show the spectacular conclusion, I needed a second take.

After much discussion and promise of reward, the cast was reassembled and proceeded to recreate the final moment of the last act.

To achieve the best filmic effect and share with the audience the surprise of the bare-handed dousing of the fire, I got on my hands and knees and looked at the flames with my camera only a few inches above the ground. I assumed old crosspatch would have some sense of compassion, but he seemed interested only in high drama. At the critical moment he rushed to the blazing fire, reached his bare hands into the flames and glowing coals—and threw the whole lot on top of me and the camera.

Again he'd caught me off-guard, and I'm sure it gave him immense satisfaction and the whole troop a wonderful laugh. But it also gave me a great ending—easily worth the few blisters and burns.

27 The Hippo's Deceitful Smile

When Sieuwke and I arrived back at our home at Bushy Island after our trek across Africa, we were pleasantly surprised that there had been heavy rains. The lake level was high and our hill was an island again, if only by a few inches. Our road was hubcap-deep in water, and as we drove in, a couple of hippos went splashing away.

The habits of the hippopotamus are as varied as their habitats. The postcard photos of hippos lying around like a busload of sumo wrestlers out for a Sunday sunburn is a rare sight at Lake Naivasha, for ours were nocturnal foragers and seldom came ashore in daylight. By way of their low-domed tunnels through the papyrus they emerged from the lake after sunset and grazed the grassy parts of Bushy Island all night long, maintaining the cut of our naturally seeded lawn as evenly as the stubble left by any power mower. During the day our hippos kept to the water, assembling in groups noisy with grunts and bellows, one herd on each side of the island.

Human injuries—and often deaths—due to hippo attacks were frequent around our lake. A Fisheries Department scout was killed last year as he chased poachers through the papyrus and came unexpectedly upon a hippo instead. More recently a poacher was grabbed by a mother hippo when he got too close to her baby. She carried him into deep water and then submerged. The poacher's mangled body floated to shore a few days later.

Our neighbors, filmmakers Allan and Joan Root, were attacked while filming hippos underwater. A nimbus of sediment, churned up by the hippos' feet, rose in the clear spring where Allan and Joan, outfitted with SCUBA, were working. Suddenly out of the cloud a hippo charged. One tusk grazed Joan's cheek. The sharp, wrist-thick tooth missed her eye by only a few millimeters, ripped off her face mask and tossed it away. Then the hippo went for Allan. A tusk poked a hole through his thigh that, as Allan put it, "you could stuff a Coke bottle through."

By great good fortune a physician tourist was on the scene and applied immediate first aid, saving Allan's life.

The hippo is Africa's most dangerous animal, and deaths from hippo attacks number greater than those from buffalo, elephant, lion, rhino, crocodile, or leopard, other species with reputations for causing human fatalities.

It was with Allan's injury in mind, but hardly at the forefront of my mind, that I faced my own dangerous encounter with a hippo. It was an incident that by its oddity proved the point that one can never depend upon the usual when dealing with wild animals—one must always expect the unexpected.

I had just completed setting up a tent for visitors near the lakeshore some fifty yards down the slope from our house. The job done, my helper returned to the house and I stayed behind tightening ropes and tinkering with poles. The cleared area where our visitors enjoyed their canvas guest rooms lay beneath spreading fever trees and was surrounded by a thick undergrowth some four feet high. Two trails ran through the bush from the house to the tent. The foraging of hippos extended the trails down to the lake.

The first sign of trouble was the barking of our dogs. Their excited yapping told me that they were chasing something, not just sounding a dutiful warning to someone walking on the road.

I shouted, "No buck!"—the command that meant not to chase—and the barking stopped. Then I heard the clumping sound of heavy running feet. Almost immediately I saw the backs of two hippos above the brush, one chasing the other. They were moving rapidly toward the lake on the trail parallel to mine.

The hippos would pass me forty feet away. They hadn't seen me and I felt no fear, only curiosity. The time was noon; I'd never before seen hippos running around Bushy Island at midday. This was only the first of the improbable things that would soon become a series of astonishing events.

Although the hippos were going to pass me by a safe margin, I broadened the distance between us anyway. I moved up my path while they went down theirs. This proved to be a mistake—a nearly fatal one.

If I'd remained where I was, unmoving and unnoticed, they would have gone on by. But my movement caught the attention of the lead hippo. He changed direction so sharply that he nearly fell in the turn. Then without pausing he charged straight for me.

He came plowing through the undergrowth like an attacking tank. As I started to run I heard the snap and crash of breaking branches and the thunder of heavy feet behind me.

My next mistake was to think I could beat him in a run. It wasn't far to the house—only forty yards across open ground—and it seemed to be my safest bet. A better choice would have been to make for the closest tree—not to climb it, as there were no low branches to grasp, but to get behind and use it as a shield.

I looked back over my shoulder as I ran and realized that the gap between us was closing too fast. I'd never make it. Strangely, my thoughts at that moment were less about the mechanics of escape than the incongruity of my situation—that this outrageous thing was really happening, that I was being chased by two hippos, at high noon, in my own front yard.

When I realized that I couldn't reach the house in time, I swerved toward the closest patch of bush. At that moment, when the first of the charging hippos was only fifteen feet behind me, the toe of my sandal caught in a loop of grass and I tripped. I hit the ground on my hands and knees, bounced, and flung myself forward in a sort of four-footed scrabbling crawl, ending with a headfirst launch into the thicket.

I crashed into a thorny bush, landed in a mass of prickles, and froze. I looked back as the first hippo thundered past. He was followed immediately by the second, only a yard behind.

Then I took a deep breath. The danger had passed. I lay gasping. I looked at the hippos' footprints gouged in the earth, deep impressions a scant six inches from my toes. I pushed myself up and crawled from the bush, pulling thorns from my fingers and arms, and realized that I was shaking.

I looked up and saw Sieuwke and all the painters, masons, and carpenters who'd been working on the house and had rushed onto the veranda when they'd heard the noise. They were standing in a row at the top of the steps, staring down the slope toward me, mouths agape. When they realized that I was unhurt, grins spread across their faces. They laughed and clapped their hands as if it all had been a grand theatrical show performed just for them.

I shook my head and laughed with them, but ten minutes later my hands were still shaking and my heart still thumping at many times its normal rate.

Ever since then, whenever I lay in bed and heard those heavy footsteps outside the windows, I felt a chill. It's a sound that carried far on a still night, quaking the earth with its intensity. Often when the trembling ground awakened me I would leap from bed and go to the window to watch from behind the safety of thick stone walls as a huge beast passed close by. Its great damp bulk shone in the moonlight—a mysterious, dangerous, prehistoric behemoth, a beast whose title to this land was far more legitimate than mine.

* * * * *

My other brush with death from a wild animal was also due to an imprudent action on my part. Animals don't usually hurt people—unless the people do something dumb.

I was doing my best to shoot a scene in the *Heartbeat of Africa* script. The shot was the point of view of a running man looking back over his shoulder at a chasing elephant. My one-on-one experience with a hippo had taught me the basic elements of the shot. All I needed to do was substitute one large, deadly animal for another.

It wasn't an easy assignment, and it would require considerable preparation, time, and luck. I consulted with my friend, hunting guide and bushwise professional Barry Gaymer. We'd worked together before on other off-the-wall elephant scenes imagined by creative scriptwriters.

Barry and I knew of a place where elephants were plentiful and we wouldn't be restricted by the rules of the National Parks that forbade imprudent human approach. The area had been poached heavily, and as a result the remaining jumbos didn't like people.

My plan was to mount my Arri on a heavy plank clamped to the back of Barry's 4X4 pickup. We'd find an elephant who wanted to charge—you could determine the attitude of these jumbos at quite a distance. Having been shot at with guns, most of these animals were shy; they'd put up their tails and run away at the first sight of a vehicle. But those few who stood their ground and made menacing advances were very likely to charge. These were the elephants we were looking for—the *kali* ones in the African vernacular, the fierce ones.

Once we found a beast with such a temperament, Barry would back us slowly toward the pugnacious elephant, teasing him. In the past, we'd found that we could extend a chase for as much as fifty yards by allowing a charging elephant to get close. Then as the elephant gave chase we adjusted the vehicle's speed to keep him at just that borderline distance where he thought he was going to catch us—and we thought we were safe. Usually that distance put the charging elephant at about fifteen feet behind the rear bumper.

It was hair-raising stuff with the possibility of grave consequences if anything went wrong. But at the same time it was great fun, and Barry and I had done it before with both elephants and rhinos without mishap. In fact, we had done it enough times that we fancied ourselves masters of the craft.

But in our quest for this shot things didn't go as as we'd hoped. The first complication was that only one jumbo in about thirty was interested in playing our game. Most of them ran away at the first sight of us.

When we did find an eager candidate, it had to be in an area where we could drive at the rapid pace of a charging elephant. If there were too many bushes, too many boulders or ravines, or too little flat ground without obstructions, the whole plan would be impossible. And we had to assess the lay of the land on the spot, as we found it. There was no opportunity for a rehearsal.

As with all photography, there was the question of lighting the scene properly. Since we were using natural light, it had to be of the right intensity and direction. And the specimen elephant had to have respectable tusks. It wouldn't do to have toothpicks or no teeth at all, as this was to be a shot in which the elephant was supposed to express extreme menace.

We set up our safari camp in the shade of tamarind trees along the banks of a dry riverbed in elephant country. Two 4X4 vehicles with radio communication between them provided camera platform and support, and Barry brought his plane for spotting elephants. A brief early morning aerial scouting flight would save us a lot of time and cut down on long drives. I hoped to get the shot in a week. It was a big, expensive deal.

By the third day of the shoot, our forays into elephant territory had produced nothing. Conditions hadn't been right for one reason or another, and I hadn't even rolled my camera. On the fourth day, we had found two willing elephants and I'd made two shots, but they weren't up to expectations. The ground had been too rough and the camera too bouncy. I'd already decided to get Steve St. John into the act with his Steadicam, which would smooth out the bumps when filming.

That day, on our way back to camp, what seemed like a perfect opportunity presented itself. We came upon a group of eight elephant cows with three calves. They stood in a tight group a hundred yards away. Even at that distance, the matriarch, with angular sunlight gleaming on a fine set of ivory, displayed an attitude that told us she was definitely *kali*.

I surveyed the scene. The light was perfect. Then I asked Barry what he thought about the roughness of the terrain.

"Seems okay," he said. "We can tell better from a little closer in. We can always abort if it's too rough."

"Let's have a go," I said.

At fifty yards out, Barry stopped. I climbed into the back, lifted the heavy Arri with its attached accessories out of its padded box, and locked it onto the fluid head. I checked to see that all of my gear was bolted down. As Barry turned the car around, I settled myself onto my knees behind the camera, and we began to back in—very slowly—toward the elephants.

Mama already had her ears out and her trunk up, telling us, "Don't come any closer! I dare you." We heard her, but we didn't listen.

When we closed the distance to thirty yards, she let us know she wasn't kidding by charging our vehicle. It could have been a bluffing charge, one that pulled up short of contact. But at the critical point—about twenty feet—the car that she was threatening began to pull away from her.

The elephant believed that she was winning. This big dark menace to her calf or her territory—or whatever she was protecting—reacted to her aggression by running away. So she kept coming. Victorious, she trumpeted her accomplishment and thundered on.

My camera was running; it had been from the start. It was bouncing too much for me to keep my eye to the viewfinder. I knew this would happen and had already closed off the eyepiece. I pushed my knees under the four-by-six inch plank that held the camera and tried to cushion the jiggle by pressing my other hand on the camera's top. The high-hat support was locked off, but with a wide-angle lens there was no fear of losing the elephant in the frame.

Barry was driving skillfully, eyes on the terrain ahead, dodging the stones and bushes as they came. New things were appearing from ahead at every second; he couldn't take a moment to glance back. Instead, Jamie McCloud served as his eyes to the rear. McCloud sat beside Barry in the passenger seat, telling him "faster" and "slower," trying keep the charging jumbo at the critical distance—close enough not to lose interest, but far enough away not to catch us. At this point I was only along for the ride. But what a ride!

Then we hit a brick wall—or so it seemed. One second I was looking into the face of an angry elephant running at twenty miles per hour behind me; the next second, the car abruptly stopped. BAM! I flew backward and crashed against the back of the cab. My head hit something sharp and hard—the gun rack from the car's hunting days. Blood gushed into my eyes. I was dazed but conscious; I could still see.

The elephant, running flat-out, couldn't have stopped if she'd wanted to. Momentum carried her on, and she crashed against the tailgate of the pickup. A bit of flimsy metal didn't slow the tremendous force of three and a half tons of charging elephant. Her head hit the heavy cross plank holding the mounted camera, tearing it loose. The whole assembly flew toward me and crashed across my chest.

The closed camera case, a sturdy box the size of a small steamer trunk, had been sitting beside me at the rear of the pickup bed. The elephant's left tusk went clear through it—in one side, out the other. She wore it like a trophy on her tooth. Three feet of sharp tusk was sticking out of the camera case in my face. Her head and shoulders were right in the truck with me.

I lay on my back with my head and shoulders wedged in the corner between the bed and the cab, my legs in the air. I was pinned to the floor by the heavy plank and camera across my chest, and my feet were shoved against the elephant's head. The tusk wearing the camera box was off to my right; the other tusk was immediately between my knees. My left foot was close to her right eye. She began gouging at me, trying to get me with her tusk, but she was too close. At one moment the tip of her tusk was alongside my cheek. The next moment, as she pulled it back and gouged again, the tusk missed my crotch by an inch.

I tried to think of some way to drive her off—anything to get her away from me. I began to kick her head and ear with my heel, furiously, again and again.

Three times her tusk went up and down, up and down, between my legs. It was there in my face, that massive tooth of shining ivory, an inch from killing me. Up and down, up and down—an inch from my balls.

I had no idea what had happened up ahead. As I continued to kick the elephant, desperately trying to drive her away, I yelled to Barry, "Go! Go! Go!"

But of course we couldn't go anywhere. Barry had cornered a dense bush and the truck's front wheels had dropped into a warthog hole. What had felt like a brick wall, stopping the car in an instant, was the edge of a deep crater in the earth.

I was still kicking the elephant in the ear. She bucked back and her shoulders slid off the pickup bed. With her front feet on the ground again, she got her legs under her and backed away a couple of paces. She stood there, shook her head mightily and trumpeted. The camera box slid off her tusk and soared away. She was as shaken as any of us.

I was completely dazed. Then at this most critical moment when anything could happen—while the elephant was asking herself if she should charge again—I rolled out from under the plank and over the edge of the pickup bed. I began to stumble away on wobbly legs. Going where? Who knows? I was out of my head.

Barry quickly slid from the cab and grabbed me. "Freeze!" he whispered, and I had the sense to do it. We stood there like tree stumps, holding our breath, as the elephant trumpeted, deciding what to do about it all.

Finally, after what seemed like forever, she turned around and walked away. At last we could breathe again.

Our co-pilot pulled himself up from the floor of the cab where he'd been hiding. When Jamie McCloud saw us standing together, he couldn't believe it. From where he sat, in the moment before he'd ducked, he was sure he'd seen the elephant kill me.

* * * * *

I've mentioned that we were using two vehicles during these shoots, so where had our outrider car been during the excitement? Eustache and my son Mike had been in radio communication with us. When the elephant started to chase, Barry had tossed his walkie-talkie onto the seat and put both hands on the wheel as he floored the accelerator. At the same moment, Eustache and Mike had a tire blow out. Their car was out of the action.

When the commotion was over, Barry picked up his radio, clicked the transmit button, and said, "Stash, we've had an accident. We need you."

The walkie-talkie crackled with static. Then came Eustache's reply: "Be there as soon as we get the spare fitted. Just now tightening the lugs."

When they drove up a few minutes later, Mike was shocked. There was his dad sitting on a stone, with Barry wiping away a lot of blood—far more gore than my minor wounds warranted.

Two days later, Steve St. John and Larry Prinz joined me in the truck. We bolted the Steadicam mount to the back of the pickup bed, and went back to work. One shot we filmed showed a charging elephant's trunk reaching out and nearly touching the matte box next to the lens. The tip of the elephant's trunk almost filled the entire frame. It looked like a pink rose blossom. I believe these shots were the most exciting and technically perfect shots of a charging elephant ever filmed.

And we didn't fall into any more pig holes.

28 Maneaters

Good film development projects, like good lovers, are sometimes forsaken. In either case it can be a costly risk both in money and in heart. Movie ventures have been jilted after a courtship costing millions of dollars; and once left in the lurch, it's rare to renew an old love. A few scripts, on the other hand, have been banished to the shelf to sit for years, then rediscovered, dusted off, and made into good movies.

I might not hold the record for incubating a film for the longest time, but I must be a runner-up. A couple of movies for which I planted seeds took more than twenty years to sprout.

I include this tale of a potentially good film gone awry only as an example of Hollywood's strangeness—not that this film's genesis and realization are much different from many even more snakey deals that have slithered through the dank holes of Tinseltown.

In 1973, Carl Foreman, Paul Radin and I were in Africa when we were introduced to a book called *The Man-eaters of Tsavo.* Originally published in 1907, it was the true story of the efforts of construction engineer J. H. Patterson to stop a pair of maneating lions that were holding up the building of an important railway bridge.

One sentence from the book summarizes the drama: "At the crossing of the Tsavo River in Kenya, two maneating lions killed twenty-eight imported Indian workers who had been brought in as skilled labor, in addition to scores of unfortunate African natives of whom no official record was kept." The lions' repeated escapes from certain-death ambushes and traps gave them a mystic aura, and the panic that resulted from nightly lion attacks brought construction of the Mombasa-to-Uganda railway to a complete stop.

As the project supervisor, Patterson considered himself personally responsible for solving the situation and began a single-handed campaign to eliminate his nemesis. It took cunning, brawn, and nerves of steel. Finally, nine months after the killing began, Patterson shot the last of the lions and work on the bridge resumed.

With all of the adventure packed into this story, we thought it would be a cinch to set up a film deal. Carl Foreman knocked out a treatment which he called *Bannister's Bridge*. It was a far cry from the book, which was in the public domain. Carl could have used any of the material within its pages. Why he chose to stray so far from the facts and the title was a puzzle to me, but the yarn he invented had little of the excitement and none of the fascinating truth of the original story.

Carl lost interest after his treatment failed to open the purse strings of a studio, but Radin and I kept the idea alive. We spent a lot of time working on the story and discussed many ideas about how to get the project going, but nothing jelled. *Maneaters* lay as dead on the shelf as the lions and their victims that had inspired the book nearly a hundred years before.

Then—fifteen years later—Radin got reinspired and took off on a wild selling binge. All at once three studios were interested in *Maneaters*. Disney wanted to make it, Paramount was interested, and producers Jon Peters and Peter Guber, who had a production deal at Warners, were sure it would be their next *Batman*.

Radin decided to go with Guber-Peters, who had produced a few hits including *Rain Man* and *The Witches of Eastwick*. They were puffing hard in their ascent toward the peak of their remunerative climb, a record-breaking rip-off that netted them millions before they tumbled back down the mountain.

They talked to Frank Pierson (*Dog Day Afternoon, Cool Hand Luke*) about writing the script. But Radin had stalled just long enough to fall into the hole that Peters and Guber had dug for themselves at Warners. The partners made their big move to Sony, leaving Radin in an awkward situation. Since Guber-Peters had made their offer for *Maneaters* while they were at Warners, did Warners, Guber-Peters, or Sony have the rights to the film? Radin agonized over being caught in the middle of this complicated business. Warners was threatening to sue Guber-Peters for breaking their contract (a case that was eventually settled when Sony paid off more than half a billion dollars to win the services of Guber and Peters). Meanwhile, Radin decided to keep his mouth shut about the Guber-Peters offer and take his chances elsewhere.

Disney wanted in, but they were too cheap. Finally in early 1989 Radin set up a deal with Paramount and eventually brokered a contract for star writer William Goldman (*Butch Cassidy and the Sundance Kid, A Bridge Too Far, All The President's Men) to* write the script. Goldman was to get $600,000 for the first draft, another $400,000 on the start of photography, $1.5 million of the gross, plus 5% of the profits.

It had been fifteen years since I'd been a partner with Paul Radin and Carl Foreman on the project they were going to produce and I was going to direct. Now, except for the mutual support Radin and I had given each other—and a few studio consultations on such practicalities as, "Can you really get the lions to do the things they'll have to do?"—I was just along for the ride. As the producer, Radin was in the driver's seat; it was his job to make the deal.

By the time the studios finally showed interest in *Maneaters* it had been six years since I'd directed a feature. I was now a second unit director-cameraman, so I didn't agonize over any hopes that I'd get the directing assignment. But I was still a partner with a proprietary interest in the project's rights. If a movie ever materialized out of Goldman's script, I'd not only share a piece of the profits Radin had negotiated as the property's landlord, but I also expected to be an associate producer, make executive decisions about the animal section, and shoot the second unit.

Paramount brought in Robert Watts, who had worked for Steven Spielberg and George Lucas as a line producer on films like *Indiana Jones and the Last Crusade, Star Wars,* and *Who Framed Roger Rabbit?.* Radin and I took Watts on a location scouting trip to Kenya.

Then Bill Goldman came out to Africa and we did the same luxury tour with him. We booked our trip with Tor Allan Safaris and dined on quail eggs cooked over charcoal in the wilderness—honest, we really did. It seemed as if everything was going smoothly: luxuriously smoothly.

Back in Tinseltown, lists of actors and directors were being shuffled among the studio executives. Radin was in the loop and kept me posted. Kevin Costner, Tom Cruise, Mel Gibson, Harrison Ford, and Robert Redford topped the list of possible stars. Directors John McTiernan, Peter Weir, Milos Forman, Lawrence Kasdan, Stephen Frears, James

Cameron, John Badham, Walter Hill, Bernardo Bertolucci, and Brian De Palma were listed. Peter Yates got so far as an "interview" with Hubert's lions, and Frank Marshall was said to be "definitely set to direct immediately after wrapping *Alive.*"

Then Paramount went into a tailspin with top executive shuffles. Goldman's first draft of the script, which he called *The Ghost and the Darkness* (and for which Paramount paid $600,000), failed to inspire the new studio brass. Everything went back into limbo.

Yet another shuffle happened at the top, another year passed, and new people were running Paramount. *Maneaters* would have gone back into what's charitably called "development hell"—but with an expensive script written by exalted William Goldman lying around, and with the indefatigable Paul Radin jiggling elbows, the new suits had another look. The script was pulled out of mothballs and handed over to Gale Anne Hurd (former head of production, later an independent producer with a Paramount production deal). Hurd persuaded Goldman to write a new draft—to the tune of another $700,000.

The lists of actors and directors were dusted off. With the recent critical success of *Much Ado About Nothing*, Kenneth Branagh was offered the directing plum of *The Ghost and the Darkness.* He agreed to take it but only on the condition that he'd play the starring role as well. That didn't sit well with the Paramount brass, and he was dropped. Sid Ganis, president of the studio, wanted Peter Yates to direct. Another Paramount executive of the day, Lance Young, favored Brian De Palma. The fight got so hot that Young quit over the argument (he later returned to the fold).

At one point, in reply to Paul Radin's query as to what was happening, Sid Ganis said, "We have the script of the century. Kevin Costner wants to do it, and we don't want to make any mistakes. So we're moving slowly."

Still thinking it might be fun to direct the second unit on this project, which could be the most complicated (and thus for me, the most interesting) lion film ever, I tried to keep my name alive with each new set of executives as they came and went. Although she'd never heard of me, I let Gale Anne Hurd know that I'd been instrumental in the genesis of her project. As a charter member of the venture I felt that I was still entitled to be considered for at least a minor role on the production team. This resulted in a meeting with Mike Joyce, Hurd's production manager. We hit it off well, and I told him how I wanted to handle the lion work.

It seemed to me that for this film, which could be a winner in its genre, we needed to look at the movie *Jaws* as the ultimate model for beastly attacks on humans. In *Jaws*, after the monster had killed so many people, the only appropriate retribution was the execution of the beast. A shark, with its fixed expression of malevolence, is as easy to want to kill as a rattlesnake. A shark is easy to hate.

Lions, on the other hand—warm-blooded, the pussycats of *Born Free* and *Living Free*—were something else entirely. In spite of its predatory nature, a lion is expressive and appealing. People might fear lions but they like them—a cub is cute. By contrast, a baby shark is just a small effigy of its malevolent-looking parent. To create an atmosphere in which an audience would want Patterson to succeed in killing the lions, we had to change the perception of the cats to be more like sharks. To justify the hunting down and shooting of lions, you had to loathe them. And the way to do this was to show some really scary, horrible, and—most of all—realistic lion attacks on humans.

In my opinion, no one had ever staged a truly realistic lion attack on a person. It had been tried dozens of times beginning from the days when circus performers doubled as movie trainers. I'd probably filmed half a dozen big cat attacks on humans for different movies. It was done with a trained lion (or tiger, or cougar) jumping on a trainer in play, and then cutting to closeups of jaws and claws. In the most ignoble cases, fake lion heads and stuffed paws with claws were then brought into play, with the actor rolling around in the dust trying his best to fend off the attacking stuntman in a lion suit. Then the lion would run off dragging a floppy rubber dummy in its jaws.

There had been incidents when the attacking big cat got carried away with the fun of it all, the trainer got roughed up, and the camera recorded a few seconds of convincing film before the standby trainers ran into the shot to chase off the cat. These "accident" shots often looked better than the others, but a director couldn't take risks with a trainer's neck. You don't invite a real attack with an animal as potentially deadly as a lion, no matter how well-trained it might be.

In years past, a great still photographer and would-be filmmaker, notable for off-the-wall ideas, had visions of making a *Maneaters of Tsavo* movie. He, too, had recognized the importance of making horrendous beasts of the lions. His interest in the story happened during the years of Idi Amin's bloodletting in Uganda, the country next door to Kenya, where the story took place. His solution for monsterizing the lions, as it was quoted to me, was, "We can easily get human corpses from Uganda. Can you imagine the impact of seeing lions tearing apart real humans? Pulling off arms and legs to the sounds of crunching bones?"

One must remember that this was in the days before CGI and perfected special effects such as those in *Jurassic Park* and *Avatar*. This was in a time when real animals were performers.

I believed that my idea would have more impact, if a bit less authenticity. The gag I yearned to shoot because I knew it would look wonderfully real and terribly hideous, was not to dismember a real carcass or use a dummy lion's head and claws to clobber an actor, but to reverse the situation and use a real lion and a state-of-the-art animatronic human figure. These realistic characters had been pioneered by Roger Brogie in the Disney machine shop (Abe Lincoln orating the Gettysburg Address at Disneyland was the first). With their articulated limbs, molded plastic faces, and electronically controlled movements, the animatronic figures were nearly indistinguishable from the real thing.

It would be fairly simple—albeit expensive due to the costly animatronics—to train a lion to maul one of these figures as it thrashed around in realistic agony. Kill a few adults in this horrible and convincing way and throw in a child or two (à la *Jaws*), and even the most pro-lion *Born Free* junkie would be crying for cat blood. And the main story problem—how to make an audience cheer when the hero is shooting lions—would be solved.

As one producer and production manager after another came and went during the long development of *Maneaters*, I sang my dream song of filming this gimmick to every one of them.

When Paul Radin called to tell me that Paramount had put *The Ghost and the Darkness* onto their "go list," he read off the names of the actors and directors who were now being considered. To play the part of Patterson: First choice, Kevin Costner. Then, not necessarily in order of preference: Robert Redford, Daniel Day-Lewis, Hugh Grant, Mel Gibson, Tom Cruise, and Brad Pitt. To play Patterson's sidekick, Redbeard, there was only one contender: Goldman had written the part for Sean Connery.

In June 1995, Radin read me a letter he'd just received from Gale Anne Hurd saying the picture was a definite "go." Michael Douglas's company, Douglas/Reuther Productions, had taken over the production with Paramount still retaining overall responsibility. Val Kilmer was to play the part of Patterson, and Michael Douglas would play Redbeard. With the Douglas/Reuther company now running things, Radin's role was over. Even Gale Anne Hurd, who still had an interest, would be riding in the back seat from then on.

Stephen Hopkins, who had directed *Predator 2* and the fifth installment of *Nightmare on Elm Street* and was therefore categorized as a spooky, special effects-oriented director, was signed for the project. I wondered why they wanted a special effects man to direct. When I saw the finished movie I realized the reasoning behind it, however wrong it had been. The studio powers thought that creating animal effects—changing an animal's facial expressions, giving animals mannerisms through digital animation, all of that state-of-the-art electronic wizardry like CGI—computer generated imagery—that had worked so well in the pig movie *Babe*, was just what was needed to make the lions in this piece look awesome.

CGI was still in its developmental infancy and a bad choice for *The Ghost and the Darkness*. The furry face of a lion was more difficult to alter convincingly with the limited technology of the time, and sloppy effects spoiled the illusion. The digitally-manipulated lions didn't look real; therefore everything had to take place in big closeups and quick cuts. A lot of the menace that would have been implicit in master shots flew out the window. The effect failed miserably and was just the opposite of what I'd hoped to achieve with my real lion and animatronic man.

Hubert Wells was put on salary to begin training the lions which would be digitally "treated" with CGI, but like everything else with this movie, the situation was turned upside down. Hubert's old friend and partner, Sled Reynolds, who had been Hubert's assistant on *Sheena,* was now head trainer and Hubert was the assistant.

Paul Radin told me that "the script has gone out to some Russian they want as cameraman." I thought he probably meant Janusz Kaminski, who had just come to prominence with his Academy Award for *Schindler's List.* But the reference actually was to Hungarian Vilmos Zsigmond. Maybe all the "V"s and the "Z"s sounded Russian to Radin.

Radin said he'd talked to Stephen Hopkins and had mentioned my name. When I called Hopkins about doing the second unit, he asked me to come by. We got along fine, but after my employment agreement was set, I received a call from the producer.

"We've got a little problem with your deal," she said.

"Oh?"

"We've just signed Vilmos Zsigmond as director of photography, and it's in his contract that he has approval of the second unit cameraman. He's never heard of you."

I phoned Conrad Hall, who knew Vilmos, and told him the story.

"I'll call you right back," Con said.

He was on the line again in twenty minutes. "Don't worry," Con said. "Vilmos is happy to have you. But you know what he said? 'Hey, Con, this guy may have been great in his time. But do you know how old he is?'"

"Yeah," Con had said. "Of course I do. And do you know how old I am? And how old are you? I'll make you a bet, Vilmos. You pick a mountain and start climbing. Jack will start half an hour later, and if he doesn't beat you to the top, don't hire him."

Vilmos—who was 66 years old, just six years my junior—and I worked at opposite ends of Africa. I shot atmosphere shots, wildlife, and background plates in Kenya. A *second* second unit worked with Sled and Hubert and the lions in South Africa, where the main part of the film was made. As rumors of problems came to me on the jungle drums, I was happy to be a thousand miles away.

Originally, Paul Radin had wanted to go to Africa as one of the three co-producers on the film. In the end Radin lost interest even in visiting the set. He'd served his function, keeping the project alive all those years and helping to set Goldman as writer.

On this film which had spent so long in gestation, I ended up working with people who didn't even know of my role in creating the project. Over the years I'd told everybody connected with the production about my dream sequence—the attack of a real lion on an animatronic man—but the shot was never made. The attacks in the finished picture looked no better than lion-attacking-human shots have looked since Charlton Heston wrestled a fake lion in *Ben Hur* back in 1959.

Twenty years after Carl Foreman, Paul Radin, and I had put this project into play, I was the only one of our trio who saw it to completion. Carl Foreman was dead. Paul Radin was bought out and sat out the production at his home in Santa Barbara. My son, Mike, was my camera assistant and we had a joyful month of safari together. We were filming in the Maasai Mara during the time of the massive wildebeest migration from the Serengeti—one of the greatest natural history spectacles in the world. The weather favored us with gorgeous cloud-filled skies. You couldn't point a camera and not see a prize-winning picture. I considered myself well-paid, even though it took two score years to collect the bounty.

Back in Hollywood where the real maneaters prowl, they called my team "The Kenya Beauty Unit."

29

Out of Africa

I've always been thought of as easygoing on a movie set. Most producers liked me. At Disney I was appreciated for my ability to take a script and a pocketful of small change, disappear for a few months without bothering anyone, and return with a good film in the can.

I respected most of the actors, adored some of them, always fell in love with the kids, and my connections with technicians were agreeable. Many crew members became lifelong friends.

After a few false starts and aborted scripts, in 1984 when Sydney Pollack at last announced a shooting date for *Out of Africa*, my creative juices began to flow. It seemed like a job made for me in heaven; I was a natural for it. Although essentially a character-driven love story, there were a few exciting action sequences and they all involved animals. I was doubly intrigued because the action was far from ordinary. A few script sequences described animal performances that at first look I didn't have a clue how to shoot. They involved principal actors interacting with dangerous animals in ways that had never been done before—or had never been done well before. These were challenges that would take careful planning and execution.

My agent, Ben Benjamin, arranged for me to meet with Pollack at his office. With his reputation as an exacting filmmaker, and his long list of successful movies (*Tootsie, Jeremiah Johnson, The Electric Horseman*), Sydney's was a Hollywood name that intimidated all lesser beings. In spite of this, I arrived on time and full of self-confidence.

In most movies about Africa that I'd seen, the Africans looked and spoke like cartoon caricatures. As a schoolboy, I'd laughed with my friends at meaningless phrases of dialogue that even as kids we realized lacked resemblance to any known African language or dialect.

I'd read the *Out of Africa* script, which was based on one of my favorite books, and I loved it. Kurt Luedtke, the scriptwriter, had caught the ambiance of the time and place in a way that was just right. It was the first script about Africa I'd ever read where the Africans really talked like Africans. It took a special writer to produce words with such an authentic ring.

When I came to the meeting with Sydney Pollack I had already broken the script down into the sections I thought Sydney might want done by a second unit, and I'd already discussed the animal sequences with Hubert Wells, who had been signed on as head trainer. I'd met Sydney's Line Producer, Terry Clegg, when he was on a scouting trip in Kenya. I was working on *Sheena* at the time and *Sheena's* line producer recommended me to Clegg, but during our brief meeting in Nairobi I couldn't read Terry Clegg at all. He seemed to be as boxed up within himself as a tortoise. He had the cool eyes of a reptile on a winter day. When he spoke, which was rarely, the words came through tight lips that hardly moved.

Terry had hit it off with a Nairobi film logistics veteran whom we'll call Dorian Boyle. To use his real name and those of his close associates might invite, well, trouble, so we'll play it safe.

Terry Clegg would be using Dorian to liaise between the film company and local businesses and government officials. Dorian would also be in charge of obtaining filming permits and generally serving as the local expediter.

Dorian was an old friend who'd done the same services for me on my first outings to Kenya. In fact, he'd performed the job on nearly all the feature films shot here for the past twenty years. *King Solomon's Mines, The Lion, Born Free, Living Free, The Snows of Kilimanjaro, Mogambo*—Dorian had done them all. He knew the ins and outs of Nairobi business and government as well as anyone. He understood the subtleties of when and how to go *chini-chini* (under the table) and when to deal out in the open—an important aspect of business in Africa. He had also carefully spun a web of mystique around himself.

At the end of a first-time meeting with Dorian one went away with the feeling that he was the only man in town who could guide a neophyte outsider through the complexities of business in Africa without having the shirt stolen off his back. Dorian played off the fact that things were done differently there than in Europe or America—an abstraction which was only partly true.

Dorian had started out on *Sheena* in his usual role of "Local Expediter" where he remained until things got out of hand with budget overruns, questionable executive decisions, and director John Guillermin's imperious and expensive edicts.

Then the *Sheena* suits in Burbank had sent out a sharp line producer named Yoram Ben-Ami and his assistant, Udi Nedivi. They spoke Hebrew when they talked of confidential things and didn't want to be understood—thus their arrival had meant that yet another alien language had joined the polyglot circus of tongues already being heard on the multinational set of *Sheena*. Yoram had never been to Africa before, but he figured it wasn't that much different from the other exotic places where he'd done film business. He soon found out that it was easy to do for himself all of the things that Dorian had made seem so difficult. Yoram's synopsis of Dorian's business style went like this:

"Dorian trots off to a government licensing meeting full of smiles, then he comes back to the production office wearing his sad face. He's full of tales of one stumbling block after another. If we're lucky enough to be allowed to get a production license at all, it's going to cost us the moon in kick-backs, under the table pay-offs, and all sorts of shady deals. The hand-wringing goes on for a week. Then, just when everyone's thinking of packing-up to move to Timbuktu, he solves the problem. Presto! Dorian has been back to the film licensing department, waved his magic wand, and everything we wanted is handed to us on a silver platter. Suddenly Dorian's become a hero.

"His secret? Dorian creates an insurmountable problem—then he's a master negotiator when he solves it."

I went into my meeting with Sydney Pollack knowing that Dorian had been pushing hard for his partner to do the job I wanted, and because of Dorian's friendship with Terry Clegg I figured my odds were iffy at best. Perhaps the strongest point in my favor was that I'd had experience working with trained animals performing scripted actions, whereas my competitor's background was in the field of the pure documentary—shooting wild animals as he found them in the bush. I'd done that too, but Sydney Pollack's job required different skills than the catch-as-catch-can approach of a nature photographer. Each mode of shooting has its place in the world of filmmaking. One isn't better than the other, but they serve different masters. I hoped that Pollack was aware of the distinction.

Sydney didn't keep me waiting. When I came into his office and introduced myself, Pollack's first question after looking me over set me back on my heels.

"Why does an old duffer like you want to take this job away from younger guys who are trying to come into the field? Why not give them a chance?"

The question was off-the-wall—unexpected first words that I wasn't prepared to answer and put me at an immediate disadvantage. For Sydney Pollack, the socially conscious champion of filmmakers' rights, asking such a question didn't seem right—and at just the period when the sinister concept of "ageism" in Hollywood hiring was getting so much air time. Probably the subject's topicality was the very reason he'd mentioned it.

I got hold of my wits and told him that *Out of Africa* had always been one of my favorite books. "I think this is going to be a wonderful movie," I said. "Yes, I've been in the business a long time. That doesn't mean I'm ready to hang my hat on the wall. Film is my life. If I stop filmmaking, my life is over." I told him that I'd never wanted to work on a film more than I wanted to work on this one. That I'd thought about the animal action problems. They were difficult, but I knew how to do them.

"My years of experience make me the man for the job," I said. "It's precisely because I'm an old duffer that I'm the best person you can find to shoot these things."

I heard later that based on the new close relationship Dorian had cultivated with Terry Clegg, Dorian had already gone out on a limb and promised the job to his friend and partner Tom Nolan. But Dorian had no authority to make such a commitment.

So when Ben Benjamin set up my deal with Universal, those earthshaking rumbles I felt in California could have come all the way from Tom's and Dorian's exploding tempers in Africa.

I didn't know it then, but Dorian Boyle hadn't given up—and he still had some sinister tricks up his sleeve.

* * * * *

I went to Kenya with Hubert and his lions and training staff a few weeks ahead of the scheduled first day of shooting. There were several second unit scenes that I could do without a support crew. Hubert had asked for prep time on location, and I was happy to work with him from the start.

Hubert and I pinned up cards on a tackboard in the feed shed at the animal compound. We arranged the cards like chapter headings for each of the important animal action sequences, then discussed the problems and arranged the cards beginning with the actions which would require the longest training time.

One scene described in the script would be impossible to film as it might happen in nature. But this was one I knew how to do—for I'd done it before. The scene was this: On a romantic outing, Karen Blixen (Meryl Streep) and Denys Finch-Hatton (Robert Redford) fly over the African bush in his open two-seater Gypsy Moth biplane. High in the clouds they encounter a soaring eagle, and Finch-Hatton slides his plane over until they are flying wingtip-to-wingtip and eye-to-eye with the great bird. In a magical moment, with all of Africa below, Karen looks into the eagle's eyes and feels that the eagle is *her* winging through the clouds. At least that's the way I read the script.

This was a concept too specific to capture as it might happen by chance in the sky. A camera plane could fly around for months alongside the Gypsy Moth looking for an eagle and hoping for the right combination of factors to put this scene on film and never have it happen. It was a writer's fancy that most directors would automatically scratch off their list and go for the next best thing. I think Sydney had already done just that.

When I told Pollack that I could shoot this apparently impossible sequence—and do it rather simply—I didn't know if he really took in what I was saying. His response was vague, even disinterested. In retrospect I think his lack of attention was my own fault. Unlike many directors, Pollack was a meticulous craftsman who knew a great deal about the technical aspects of shooting. I knew exactly what I could shoot, and I didn't paint a clear enough picture of the method I would use and the spectacular effect I could guarantee would result.

There are no secrets or copyrights on technique in the Hollywood animal training business. If there are any new developments, word is soon all over town. Hubert wasn't shy about adapting one of the methods of bird training Gary Gero had developed on *Jonathan Livingston Seagull,* a trick I had already filmed. Taking Gary's method, we'd train an eagle to hover in the steady blast of a wind machine—an engine on wheels with an airplane propeller in a safety cage. It was a standard, everyday piece of moviemaking equipment.

Once trained to hover in the wind machine's air flow, the big bird could effortlessly hold a steady position as long as the wind blew. With a mockup cockpit section of the plane set up against the sky, and the eagle's flight zone limited to the area next to the cockpit, Redford and Streep, with their hair blowing in the wind, could sit there all day while we shot any variety of cross-angles. The setup, including the sky, the airplane, the eagle in flight, and the two actors, would be utterly convincing imagery which would tell the story perfectly.

For the complimentary establishing long shot of the plane and eagle flying side-by-side over Africa, we'd use a life-sized radio-controlled glider shaped and painted like an eagle, similar to the model of Jonathan Livingston that we'd used in the seagull film. It would be a piece of cake.

The first thing I did when arriving in Kenya was to contract with the California glider expert who had built our loop-the-looping seagulls to begin building a mechanical eagle-glider. At the same time I requested a wind machine to be shipped to Nairobi from our London equipment supplier.

* * * * *

As Hubert and I arranged our training schedule cards on the feedhouse wall, we immediately realized that the most difficult and potentially most dangerous sequence—the Meryl Streep character whipping a hungry lion off a downed ox—could not be trained at all. The excitement and realism of the scene would rely on a natural, spontaneous performance. Set it up right, and the lions would do the right thing through natural inborn behavior.

Of the four lion sequences in the script, this most difficult scene to shoot would be too dangerous for the principal actors to take part in. Instead I would use lion trainers as doubles, and Sydney would later shoot Meryl Streep's closeups matched to intercut with my material.

This was the action highlight of the film, the climax of Karen's trek with a wagonload of supplies drawn by a team of oxen and destined for her husband's military camp in the wilderness. Karen Blixen/Streep and her African helpers bed down for the night around a campfire. Nearby, the oxen are corralled inside an overnight holding fence made of stacked thorn bushes.

Streep awakens to the sounds of lions attacking the oxen. She grabs an ox-driver's whip and bursts through the thorn enclosure to face a wild stampede of panicked oxen and chasing lions. It's a scene of pandemonium. Dust rises from thundering hooves, lions dart in and out between the crazed oxen. The air is full of dust and sounds of snorting, growling, bawling.

Karen sees a lion drag down an ox and crouch over it. Swinging her whip, she runs through the chaos toward the victim. As she nears the lion, it snarls and charges. Only a whip's length from the fangs, she beats the snarling lion off the downed ox and out of the enclosure.

Hubert had a basic idea for creating this dangerous animal action without getting anyone hurt. He worked from a natural behavior he'd seen hundreds of times: when a hungry lion was given a chunk of raw meat, it would defend it from all comers. Even the most docile trained lions in their enclosures, when feeding time came, often charged out toward a keeper or another lion, snarling a fierce warning. But it was a bluff—the hungry lion always stopped short of contact.

This instinctive behavior comes from the animals' history in the wild. When a defending lion leaves its prey, other hungry cats quickly rush in and grab the unguarded food. Thus, after feigning an attack, a lion must break off its threat quickly and get back to protect the meat. The purpose of the false charge is only to make a forceful statement. With such a ferocious display of teeth and savage snarls the lion defending his food says very definitely: "Danger! This meat is mine! Don't mess with it!"

If we were to give a lion a whole dead ox, he'd defend the carcass until he was surfeited. He'd eat until he was stuffed. Then he'd only want to lie down and sleep. Thus a dead ox wouldn't do for our film sequence. It would be too much; we'd lose control of the lion. A fully-fed lion wouldn't work again for a week.

The answer was to offer a chunk of meat just large enough that the hungry lion couldn't gorge it down in one gulp—a bucket-sized chunk that it would have to defend if someone threatened to take it away. When filming, we'd push the lion to the edge, shoot three or four of those intimidating charges, and then stop the session short of the charge that really meant business, the one where the lion was saying: "Okay, enough of this crap! This is it!"

The trick, of course, was to hear the lion speak. For that, I depended upon Hubert, who speaks their language. Hubert knew when to back off and let the lion have his way, and when we were on the verge of pushing the big cat too far.

For this sequence we'd need a totally unpalatable dummy ox, a stuffed prop as tasteless as a log of wood, to which we would attach a hidden chunk of real meat. A few wires tied to articulated legs and head, when pulled at the right moments, would give some life to Karen's "dying" ox.

* * * * *

O*ut of Africa* was the biggest production I'd ever participated in. Several hundred people were involved, and it seemed that most of them had separate agendas in addition to the goal of getting the movie made. Personal plots and subplots were often as interesting as the ones on the screen. Political parties were formed, reshaped, dissolved; alliances were made and dumped on a daily basis. We in the second unit thought we were beyond all of that. We were our own clique which we believed we could keep pure.

My philosophy, which I expressed to my crew when I was told of attempts to engage us in someone else's feud, was, "If we do our job well and mind our own business, we will get the respect we deserve." But what I didn't know was that there was a mole burrowing around deep under our turf.

* * * * *

At the beginning of pre-production, while sets were being built and the dummy ox was being made, I'd given our expediter, Dorian Boyle, the responsibility of acquiring that everyday bit of moviemaker's equipment—a wind machine—with which to train the eagle. A phone call to our equipment supplier in London would have the machine on its way in a day. But weeks went by and there was no wind machine. Without it, Hubert couldn't begin training the eagle. We were falling behind schedule.

Was this the old Dorian, making things seem difficult so he could solve the impossible at the last minute and become a hero? My crew, who had better inside access to the office rumor mill than I did, suspected that Dorian was taking on a new role: trying to mess up my program so he could slip his pal Tom Nolan into my shoes.

As a backup manuever, I finally sent my assistant to a machine shop in Nairobi where it took only an hour's planning to come up with a jerry-rigged wind machine. With typical African ingenuity, the builders used the power takeoff from a farm tractor to turn an airplane propeller. They welded up some iron and wire into a propeller safety screen, piled the parts onto a trailer, and drove the tractor to the animal compound. Hubert started training the next day.

Although we were already three weeks behind schedule, the eagle was a quick learner. She seemed to love the effortless flight created by the artificial wind. All we needed was an airplane or cockpit mockup—and Redford and Streep.

* * * * *

The scope of the production for *Out of Africa* was staggering. A crew of art directors, carpenters, painters, landscapers, and road builders were creating a replica of old-time Nairobi on the outskirts of the modern highrise city, while a house at the foot of the Ngong Hills was being remodeled to resemble Karen Blixen's home and coffee farm. More craftsmen from London and Hollywood arrived: a crew to remodel a modern diesel locomotive into a faux steam engine, propmakers to build ox wagons, costumers, makeup people who would turn modern Africans into old-time-looking tribespeople with long earloops (made of rubber and glued to the ears). The production crew swelled into the largest ever assembled in Africa.

As the unit grew to army size, a fleet of hired cars and trucks with "OUT OF AFRICA" placards stuck on their windshields were racing on different errands all over the country. I was kept busy shooting atmospheric backgrounds that would set the scene for dramatic sequences, wildlife shots that didn't require a crew, and scenes with doubles. I also scouted and photographed locations for Sydney's approval.

* * * * *

When the first day of production was just 24 hours away, construction people went home and production crews arrived. Ordinarily for movies we shoot sequences with no thought as to their place in the story continuity; but as it happened, the first sequence with lions in the script was the first one we in the seond unit put before the camera. Our portion of the lion-stalking-Meryl-Streep, Robert-Redford-to-the-rescue sequence was in the can in a couple of days.

We joined the main unit and did a variety of second camera shots: citizens amassing for Kenya's role in World War I, an assortment of doubles "comin's and goin's" as Irving Lerner used to call them, Karen's ox wagon trek through the bush, pictorial shots and plates for the introductory scene of an old train puffing through the wild African countryside.

It was all rather ordinary second unit work, and Hubert and I were eager for the time when we could tackle the most difficult sequence on our list: the night shoot of the lions attacking the oxen and Karen whipping one big cat off an ox.

The scene was to be lit with a location-made version of a Muscolite, the simplest of lighting sources (this was before the Muscolite had been invented). To achieve the effect, a powerful bank of lights attached to a ten-by-ten-foot frame was hoisted into the air by a crane. Suspended high in the sky, it created a realistic effect of wide-spreading moonlight. With a Muscolite or its homemade equivalent a cameraman could bathe half a football field in realistic-looking moonlight.

For this shoot I'd need more production resources than were usual for a second unit. I'd be tying up a part of the main unit's electrical crew, a couple of prop men to pull the strings to the fake dying ox and make it wiggle at the right times, a generator, crane, lights, and their operators. And because we would be working from dusk until dawn, we'd need midnight meals delivered by a catering service. For the second unit to have the use of all of this backup was a major concession from the main unit, but the extra crew and equipment I required were slipped into the schedule.

Then our night arrived, the Big One for which we'd been preparing for the past weeks. We'd been looking forward to it with the greatest anticipation. Our team arrived in three minibuses at the location in the flats at the bottom of the Rift Valley. A windstorm was skidding down the slopes of the Ngong Hills, and the brush around the thorn *boma* set was straining against its tie-down wires. Our crane operator surveyed the scene and shook his head dubiously. As dusk turned into night, he raised the light to about half-height and said that if he went any higher the wind would topple his crane. So we switched on the light at that less-than-perfect height. The "moon" swung in the wind like a pendulum, and the light turned the dust blowing across the sky into a background of silver rather than the required black.

Not only did we have a moon that cast unrealistic moving shadows and a night sky that glowed like the smog over Los Angeles on a Saturday night, but the wind was also creating animal problems. The oxen bawled with unease and the lions paced nervously in their traveling cages. Wind is always a distraction to animals, and even if we'd been able to light the scene properly, the lions and cattle wouldn't have performed.

Unable to shoot, we sat dozing in our cars as the window panes shook and dust swirled through the cracks. At two in the morning I called a wrap. There was no point in wearing ourselves out by doing nothing, and it was obvious that the wind wasn't going to go away. Better to save our energy and try again tomorrow.

The first night of our big shoot had passed and we hadn't even taken a camera out of a case. Because of the drain on main unit crew and equipment, I'd asked for only three nights to shoot this complicated sequence. A full week would have been preferable. Now only two nights remained.

I was awakened the next morning by a call to report to Terry Clegg's office. He was fuming. Our activity report stated that the previous evening had been wasted. The second unit continuity girl was Louise Boyle—Dorian's daughter—whom I'd accepted in my crew at Clegg's request. It was her job to write the night's report—and she hadn't mentioned the windstorm. From her report, it seemed that we'd made a lark of the evening, goofed off, and quit early.

Louise's motive for filing such a deliberately misleading report was so transparent that I took it lightly—an irritating but obviously inept attempt at sabotage. Surely anyone could see through the deception. It was a joke.

Louise and her father had put their heads together in a scheme to make us look inept and have us replaced with Dorian's present partner and his daughter's future husband (Tom and Louise intended to be married).

I had to laugh. "Don't worry," I told my irate crew. "Sydney Pollack's no dummy; our work speaks for itself. When we get this sequence in the can, it's going to blow him away."

* * * * *

On the next night, the sky over the set was calm. No wind rustled the bush or stirred the dust, and the shoot went without a hitch. The footage of lions seemingly attacking oxen exceeded even my expectations. The pandemonium of charging lions, kicking, bellowing oxen, tossing horns—

shot through the dust of the trampled ground—was very exciting. I didn't have to see it on the screen; I'd seen it all through the viewfinder, and I knew this was some of the most thrilling footage I'd ever shot.

And that was only the beginning. The footage of the lion defending its prey against Karen Blixen as she tried to whip it off the ox played out just as we'd planned. The lion grabbed the ox, and as Streep's double (Doree Sitterly, one of the female trainers) moved in, the lion charged out just as it was supposed to do, snarling in fury and making raging swipes with its claws. Doree cracked the long cattle whip beside its ears. The lion held its ground, lashing out and snarling fiercely. Doree advanced, popping the whip. The shots couldn't have been more dangerous-looking and convincing.

We worked flat-out until three in the morning. Then after a warm meal on the set, Hubert announced that the cats were through acting for the night. They'd been rewarded with enough baits and weren't hungry anymore. That meant the end of their working hours. If we fed them more tonight, they'd be "off" tomorrow.

The next night we completed more lion shots and then turned to the more manageable oxen. It was around midnight when Sled was running around with his lariat and the rest of us were chasing and herding oxen to help him nab the right one. We were all playing cowboy, yelling "Yahoo!" and waving our arms, having a hell of a lot of fun doing our job, when production manager Terry Clegg drove out to the location with Dorian Boyle beside him. Although they found us hard at work, it was work of an unexpected kind. Clegg made it clear that, in his estimation, laughter and fun didn't go together with toil. I'd always taken the opposite point of view, but we didn't get into a philosophical discussion that night.

Sled pulled off some clever roping and bulldogging to get the live ox that matched our fake one spreadeagled on the ground. With the animal prone and hogtied, I shot closeups of the ox's wild eyes and bellowing gape as the offscreen lion was supposedly killing it, while an unseen Karen Blixen swung her whip.

The next day I received notice that I was being replaced by Louise's fiancé, Dorian's son-in-law-to-be.

I received my pink slip before anyone had been able to see what I thought was some of the best work I'd ever done. Clearly, I'd had been hit below the belt by the script girl and her father so her boyfriend could replace me.

All of my crew quit in my support except Louise Boyle, who was reassigned to the new second unit. I asked Clegg to hold off until Sydney had seen the result of my latest work. I knew that when Pollack saw what I'd made out of the lion-oxen-Karen sequence, he'd be delighted, and it would be impossible for Clegg to justify sacking me.

But Terry Clegg knew it too. If he was going to "git me outa there," it was now or never. Dejected, I returned to my home on Bushy Island.

* * * * *

We had a five-day turnaround time for dailies—exposed film had to be flown to London, developed and printed, returned to Nairobi, and cleared through customs. Then another day passed while it was assembled in the editing room and prepared for viewing that evening.

Contrary to the style of many directors, Sydney Pollack had a liberal attitude about his crew viewing the rushes, and all heads of departments—and many others—attended. The night my latest sequence appeared in the Nairobi screening room I was back at Bushy Island feeling bad.

In Nairobi, my footage received enthusiastic applause—a rare event for a showing of dailies. Sydney was excited and complimentary and looked around the screening room to express his pleasure to me. Later I was told that he seemed confused when he discovered that I wasn't present—as if he wasn't sure, or couldn't understand, why I'd been fired.

To me it didn't seem possible—that somehow, in spite of superior work, my coveted job had been snatched away by the conniving of the "low man" on my crew—my continuity girl and her scheming father.

After a number of years in this business one becomes somewhat inured to disappointment. There are so many frustrations, so many setbacks. One has such high hopes for every film—and so many of them turn out unhappily. Maybe the movie is bad, or maybe it's good but no one goes to see it. So I've developed a hard shell for disappointment. But this was different—an affair of pride and the heart. I was furious and emotionally in the pits.

Sydney Pollack wasn't one of the conspirators, nor was he the main villain in my drama. But as the boss, all of my anger and anguish fell on him. He was the one who had hired me. He was the only person among the executive contingent whom I respected. I'd thought he was artistically my ally and supporter. I'd thought I was helping him and that my work was appreciated.

Now, with Sydney dead, I find it dfficult to speak negatively of this distinguished icon of the film world. I admired his work, and had been greatful for his trust in me.

Most of the important second unit work had been completed by the time this unexpected hitch occurred. There were only a few shots remaining to be done. My replacement's contribution was more or less to push the camera buttons on the methods and setups I had formulated with Hubert. The main sequence yet to be done was the eagle and the plane. My substitute didn't know what to do with the trained eagle and its flying model counterpart—and Hubert was in no frame of mind to enlighten him. All the bits and pieces were in place, but the sequence was never shot. The airplane flying sequence into which the eagle scenes would have been inserted was filmed by aerial cameraman Peter Allwork. His work was beautiful without the eagle, but what a magic moment it would have been with it. I'm sure that Sydney hadn't a clue as to what he missed.

At the Academy Awards ceremony in March 1986, *Out of Africa* won five Oscars. The event was held at the Dorothy Chandler Pavilion in Los Angeles. When he accepted his Academy Award for best cinematography, the director of photography graciously paid tribute to the second unit cameramen who helped make his work look so good and thus were entitled to share his honor. There had been three of us, including Peter Allwork with his inspiring aerial sequence. But the speaker stepped into the bootlicking mode of toadyism. My work made up by far the largest share of the second-unit work in *Out of Africa*, yet there in the bright lights in front of the Academy and TV audience ol' whatsizname mentioned my collaborators one and two, but couldn't seem to find my name in his crib notes.

Probably just a case of stage jitters, I figured.

Oh well. I often suffer the same lame-brained decrepitude.

30 Milagro (Magic)

After the shock and disappointment of having been fired from my job on *Out of Africa*, it was more than a year until I wanted to work on a film again. I'd been so crushed and felt so wronged, that the seduction of films lay like a run-over dog in the road. Even the flies weren't interested. I didn't go into a sulk and withdraw from life, but turned to other things—writing and planting a few cabbages in the garden at Bushy Island, keeping mind and body busy.

But my head must have been somewhere else, for I often dreamed in my sleep about filmmaking experiences. I'd been making movies all of my professional life, and it was in my blood.

Then, in 1987, nearly two years later, I got a phone call from a production manager in New Mexico. Robert Redford was directing a movie in Santa Fe and asked for me to shoot some atmospheric shots. If I wanted the job it was urgent that I move quickly as it was August, the monsoon season, when every afternoon dark thunderstorms with towering piles of cumulus rumble over the Sangre de Cristo Mountains. The main unit was occupied with shooting story material. Redford wanted some of the color and character of this wild countryside to which he was so attracted, and he wanted it now, when it was at its most beautiful.

The film *was The Milagro Beanfield War*, and the camera crew were top of the line. The son of my old pal Conrad Hall—Conrad Jr., Winnie as we call him, now a DP—was assistant cameraman; Robby Greenburg was the director of photography; and John Toll, now an Academy Award-winning DP himself (*Legends of the Fall, Braveheart*), was the camera operator.

I packed a bag and reported to Santa Fe, expecting to stay a week. Two and a half months later, as the snow fell, the picture wrapped and we all went home.

You could say that Robert Redford saved my life; he was the best tonic I could have had. I had no idea how much he knew about my problem on *Out of Africa*. Whether or not Redford talked to his old friend Sydney Pollack before he hired me, or what Pollack said if he had, I never asked. But he knew about my work. And he knew that I'd made a significant contribution to *Out of Africa*. In New Mexico we had other things on our minds and talked little about that time.

Good luck was with me in Santa Fe. The weather was perfect for the kind of dramatic scenic shots Redford wanted, and when my first material was screened at dailies everyone was pleased.

Then Bob sent me out with a couple of trainers and a huge white pig. The animal was the movie companion of the elderly Latino character played by Carlos Riquelme, a charming gentleman and a wonderful actor. Riquelme's pig, the village troublemaker and the catalyst for the story's turning point, was forever digging up someone's vegetable garden or knocking down a clothesline full of clean wash. I filmed some of the pig's amusing escapades and they went over big at rushes.

Ordinarily a second unit guy doesn't work with the show's main actors, only with doubles. I knew I'd won Bob's trust when he sent me out to shoot some material with Riquelme driving a tractor over a cliff. Then my assistant, Michael Thomas, and I became a two-man band, making pickup shots and shooting action sequences with most of the show's main characters.

Redford was like a magnet drawing stars and important people to Santa Fe that summer. He asked his friend Twyla Tharp to help him choreograph a dance sequence. She was interested in camerawork, and to my great pleasure she spent a week traveling with the second unit, forever asking technical questions that I struggled to answer.

My second unit did more with the main players in the film than I'd ever been privileged to do before. We did shots or whole sequences with most of the stars. They were wonderful, not in the least disinclined to work with the lesser beings of a second unit. There were none of those self-important types who were too insecure to trust themselves into the hands of a second unit cameraman.

Redford's trust cured my funk, renewed my interest, and restored my confidence. I was back in the movie business again.

Epilogue

A visitor to Naivasha today will not find the same place I have described in these pages. When one turns off the main road that circles the lake onto a track through the forest and passes a boundary stone that says BUSHY ISLAND, PRIVATE, it seems as if a drawbridge has been pulled up. The island has been closed off from the real world.

Sieuwke's and my adventure in Africa began in the year 1972. Since those bygone days a whole new industry has brought thousands of workers and their families into a region that at the time of our arrival was occupied only by a few widely scattered settlers.

The high-tech flower farms that created this influx have changed the landscape by erecting many acres of huge plastic greenhouses. Clusters of shack villages have turned the wild landscape into a depressing scene. It's ironic that the fastest-growing agricultural sector in the country is the cultivation of roses for export to Europe, while at the same time international aid organizations struggle to import edible grains to feed the starving. People seem to be blown around Naivasha as carelessly as the fields of plastic bags that flutter like dirty white flowers on the trees and bushes at our borders.

The wild animals still surround our house—more than ever because encroaching development has crowded them in. And the birds still sing, although fewer than before. The lake's clear shallows had been covered with blue flowering water lilies when we arrived, home to immense flocks of coots, ducks, geese, lily trotters, gallinules, and waders. Now foreign species have invaded. Louisiana crayfish proliferated and ate the lily roots, Chinese carp dredged the bottom, flower farm runoff seeped in. Now the water is turbid and stinks of rot. Not a lily blossom remains; the water birds have gone.

In the year 2002 Sieuwke began to lose her memory and cognizance. Alzheimer's eroded her body and brain. Like a mortally wounded great cat, Sieuwke—formerly known as *Mama Simba* (Lion Lady)—was helpless. She became bedridden and had to be moved frequently. In her last months Sieuwke was gently attended to by caring Kikuyu nurses. But her painful bedsores worsened. Every time she was moved her cries filled the house—and my heart.

At last Sieuwke died peacefully in her sleep beside me. It was a blessing for her and for me.

* * * * *

Of the thirty-three years I lived in Africa I made at least one trip a year to California and my son Mike made one annually to Kenya. Mike's interest in natural history blossomed and he studied zoology and journalism in university. Our years of sharing experiences that began with digging fossils, catching snakes and bugs, dragging shell-collecting nets through the depths of the Pacific, and spending summers together in the California salt marshes, Arizona Canyons, the Galápagos Islands, and Africa sowed a logical conclusion.

Mike is now a professional biological consultant who searches out rare, threatened and endangered species in California. The data he collects is written into environmental impact reports used by land developers, utility companies and wildlife agencies. There is no one happier in his work than Mike.

* * * * *

Now we go back forty years. Remember Jean Allison, the high-spirited young actress in her and my first feature movie, *Edge of Fury?*

Shortly after our liaison, Jean divorced from her husband, actor-director Lee Philips. It was an amicable separation. She got a few parts in New York TV shows, did a stint in the chorus with the June Taylor Dancers, a gig as a dancer in Vegas. But dancing was only to pay bills. She also acted in theater and touring company shows, one with Shirley Booth called *Time of the Cuckoo.*

Lee introduced Jean to New York acting teacher—Sanford Meisner at The Neighborhood Playhouse and to actors they met and palled around with at the Playhouse and while doing rounds—Steve McQueen, Rod Steiger, Marlon Brando, Mark "Morty" Rydell, and director Elia Kazan, who gave Jean a tiny part in *On the Waterfront* to qualify her for membership in the Screen Actors Guild.

She met and connected with an aspiring actor named Jerry Boyd. But Jerry also had another driving ambition. He wanted to be a bull fighter. They moved to Mexico City, married, and their child, Erin Boyd, was born.

After two gorings in Mexican rings, with Jean carrying two-month-old Erin in a basket the family headed for California. Jean was uncomfortable in her marriage with Jerry and they split. As a newcomer in Hollywood, Jean had no connections, but unlike the everyday stories we hear of girls aspiring to be movie stars who flock to Hollywood and battle the system for years and never achieve their goal, Jean's ascent in show business came quick and easy.

She landed a starring part in a play, *Teach Me How to Cry,* by Patricia Joudrey, at the Player's Ring Gallery in Hollywood. There, she was seen by agent Doovid Barskin who signed her. Jean had been broke when she arrived in tinsel town. Her wardrobe consisted of a peacoat, jeans, and a couple of blouses. For the first few casting interviews arranged by her new agent, Jean wore clothes loaned to her by Doovid's wife.

But parts in leading TV shows came quickly. She was the guest star on most of the big series of those years—*Bonanza, Starsky and Hutch, Charlie's Angels, 77 Sunset Strip, Gunsmoke,* and others.

What of Jerry Boyd? Following his disenchantment with bull fighting, he turned his idiosyncratic energy to the field of prize fighting where he became a ringside cut man. Throughout his life Jerry wrote stories. But no publisher recognized his talent and published him. Then three years before his death at the age of 72, writing under the pseudonym F. X. Toole, he made his first sale, a collection of short stories called *Rope Burns.* One story was turned into an Oscar-winning Clint Eastwood film called *Million Dollar Baby.* He didn't live to see the movie.

Jean had no aspiration to become a contract player. The idea of stardom and the hype and public adoration that went with it is repulsive to her. She was a very private person, and when her name appeared as the answer in an *L.A. Times* crossword, and friends called to say they'd noticed, she was embarrassed. That was a mile further down the road to stardom than she wanted to travel.

But she was proud when as a single mother she was able to buy her own house in the San Fernando Valley.

The experience of bearing and raising her first child had infected Jean with a new passion. In 1960 she found the perfect man, Stanford University football player and electrical engineering student, Phil Toorvald. They married, and having discovered motherhood to be the most rewarding time of her life, Jean quit being an actress while at the peak of a booming career. She mothered another daughter, a son, adopted another girl, and raised two more.

Throughout most of those years, Jean and I had kept tenuously in touch—an occasional phone call or postcard with years of silence in between.

Phil Toorvald died ten years before Sieuwke; Jean's kids were grown. Yearning for adventure, she answered an ad and joined a small circus. She traveled in her little motor home with the circus, Texas to Canada and back, for a couple of years, doing menial jobs like working a ticket booth, and enjoying the protective family-like atmosphere, then she lived alone.

I realized that my love for Africa had been less for the place than for the woman. However smitten I was with the country and the woman, both Africa as it was before and Sieuwke were now gone.

I hadn't seen or talked to Jean in years. I called her and we had dinner. We found again the joy of the same warm companionship we had enjoyed in our youth.

Jean and I have begun a new life, happy together, in the country of our birth.

* * * * *

I had to return to Kenya one more time to tie-off thirty-three years of investment in property, soul, and friends. I had the notion that Jean should see something of the world and life I'd lived in Africa and she acompanied me.

Bushy Island had Sieuwke's ashes scattered widely and my heart deeply buried in its soil.

I felt responsible for Sieuwke's commitment to the old settler, Dulcey Wills Pittaway, who had loved the land for its wildness and wildlife and had given it to Sieuwke on the condition that she would do everything she could to maintain it as a sanctuary for the birds and animals that they both felt truly "owned" it.

In the same motivation as Mrs. Pittaway's, I gave the island to the only family I knew who I could be sure would carry on the tradition, third generation Kenyans with the same loves as Mrs. Pittaway, Sieuwke, and me. I left Bushy Island and its wildlife as safe as it can be.

Then Jean and I flew to the house in Lamu for my last goodbye.

It was one of those grand evenings on the Indian Ocean coast. The sky was resplendent with God's grandeur and heaven's orchestra was playing a fugue. I could hear a muted tympani from up there along the Kiwayu hills where lightning was rimming the high thunderheads. Cicadas shrilled in the neem tree, bats chink-chinked with their radars turned on as they flew about, and ocean waves made a steady rumble as they broke on the shore out beyond the dunes.

Jean and I sat on the rooftop terrace, watching the sunset as coco palms rustled in the wind and the swifts and swallows swooped between the fronds looking for places to roost. I wondered if some of Sieuwke's restless ashes were swirling in the wind eddies in the corner of our garden. Mountains of clouds rolled in from across the Indian Ocean and black rain squalls slanted down to the sea. The raging surf carried the fine clean smell of the sea wind.

The muezzin on the roof of the nearby mosque was silhouetted against the water with the strong tide running, rippling past the mid-channel rocks where I'd dove so often for lobsters. He began to chant his evening song, melodious and always a bit strange to our ears. He finished, smiled and waved to us, and disappeared into the shadows. Then there was only the distant sound of thunder as the clouds spread over the dry coastal forest where the elephants and the topi and the lions and the whole menagerie that is the African bush wanted the rain so badly.

"I wonder if it's raining on Bushy Island?" Jean asked.

The question of rain—or lack of it—is an age-old subject of great importance to people who are close to the land.

"No," I said. "But tonight it will begin here and then in two weeks it will rain upcountry."

"Is it always that way?" she asked.

"Always has been."

We sat in silence.

"Life is wonderful, isn't it?" I said.

Index

CPSIA information can be obtained
at www.ICGtesting.com
Printed in the USA
BVOW09s1326231017
498409BV00032B/1571/P